HELLBOY™
THE ART OF THE MOVIE

Including the final shooting script

Screenplay by
GUILLERMO DEL TORO

Screen Story by
GUILLERMO DEL TORO *and* PETER BRIGGS

Based upon the Dark Horse comic created by
MIKE MIGNOLA

Illustrations by

MIKE MIGNOLA ✠ WAYNE BARLOWE

TYRUBEN ELLINGSON ✠ SIMEON WILKINS

STEVEN SCOTT ✠ YASUSHI NIRAZAWA ✠ KATSUYA TERADA ✠ DEAK FERRAND
JOSE FORS ✠ JEFF REBNER ✠ ART LEE ✠ LEO DURAÑONA ✠ WENDY PARTRIDGE
DDT SPECIAL EFFECTS ✠ SPECTRAL MOTION ✠ RICK GEARY

Introduction by
GUILLERMO DEL TORO

Publisher
MIKE RICHARDSON

Editor SCOTT ALLIE

Assistant editors MATT DRYER and SHAWNA ERVIN-GORE

Book Design CARY GRAZZINI

Guillermo del Toro would like to thank Lorenza, Marisa, and Mariana ... for their patience.

Dark Horse Books is grateful for the input of
Guillermo del Toro, Mike Mignola, TyRuben Ellingson, Wayne Barlowe, and Simeon Wilkins.

For their help in the creation of this book, we thank
Holly Wyant, Jason Geffen, Rick Williams, Wendy Partridge, Javier Soto, Eric Moro,
Esther Margolis and Tara Hoffman at Newmarket Press, Scott Bernstein and Revolution Studios,
Paul Alvarado-Dykstra, Jonell Napper at hellboy.com, Chad Waters and Matt Rose at Cinovation,
and Mike Elizalde and Brian Walsh at Spectral Motion.

Thanks also to the many artists involved in the creation of the film:
Rick Baker, whose Cinovation effects shop created the Hellboy makeup, Steven Scott, Deak Ferrand, Jose Fors,
Yasushi Nirazawa, Katsuya Terada, Art Lee, Leo Durañona, Jeff Rebner, Ed Irastorza, David Van Dyke, Rebecca Ramsey,
Sandoval and DDT Efectos Especiales, The Orphanage, Jose Fernandez, Dave Stewart, Blair Clark and Tippett Studio, and Steve Wang
and everyone at Spectral Motion—Carlos Huante, Jordu Schell, Norman Cabrera, Mark Setrakian, Jose Fernandez, Moto Hata,
Thom Floutz, Simon Webber, Nigel Booth, Don Lanning, Russ Lukich, Tim Gore, and Hiroshi Katagiri.

Special thanks to Chris Horn, Dan Jackson, and David Scroggy.

The character biographies presented in this volume were created by Rick Geary,
adapted from Guillermo del Toro's notes.

www.hellboy.com
www.hellsite.com
www.darkhorse.com

Published by Dark Horse Books
A division of Dark Horse Comics, Inc.
10956 SE Main Street
Milwaukie, OR 97222

February 2004
First edition
ISBN: 1-84023-881-X

3 5 7 9 10 8 6 4 2

PRINTED IN CHINA

WELCOME

INTRODUCTION
GUILLERMO DEL TORO

The book you hold in your hands documents—quite accurately—what may be the most joyful experience of my professional life. *Hellboy* became a movie after about half a decade of struggle, and this volume presents the unabridged script (changes were made in editing and post) and a delightful sampler of the design work done in the conceptual stage of the film. As I write these lines, comic-book-based movies are a common occurrence, an accepted sub-genre in

a Geekified Hollywood in search of the elusive "mainstream." Five years ago, when this project was coming to life, things were quite different. *The Matrix* or *X-Men* were not yet in the horizon, and the only way a comic-book movie was meant to exist was in the tongue-in-cheek Schumacher style.

The moment I learned that Larry Gordon, Lloyd Levin, and Mike Richardson were attempting to tackle *Hellboy* as a film, I dived in full force

Sometime in 1997 or 1998 I met with director Guillermo del Toro for the first time to discuss the *Hellboy* movie he wanted to make. At that time, he'd made only two films: *Cronos* and *Mimic*. I thought both were great—both beautiful and creepy and very smart. If this guy wanted to make the *Hellboy* film, I was all for it. I assured him that he could do anything he wanted with the characters, and that he could make any changes he wanted, and it would be fine with me.

Well, it turns out Guillermo was the perfect guy to make this movie. He loved the comic and he understood it. He didn't want to change the character at all, and I felt that most of the changes he wanted to make in the story were changes for the better. As for the changes I didn't like, most of them were gone within a couple of hours. Too easy, and of course, way too good to be true, so I promised myself that I wouldn't take it too seriously. I used to say, "When I see Ron Perlman"—both Guillermo and I always knew who should play Hellboy—"painted red with cameras pointed at him, then I'll believe it."

Some years went by. When Guillermo began work on *Blade 2*, he had me come in to do a couple months of pre-production design work, where I met TyRuben Elingson and Wayne Barlowe. It felt a lot like a warm-up for *Hellboy*. I tried not to get my hopes up...

On June 20, 2002, I walked into the Hellboy production office in L.A. for the first time. There, over the next three months, myself, Guillermo, Ty, Wayne, Simeon Wilkins, and others would begin the long and amazingly strange process of making this film a reality. Not only would I be involved to some degree with almost every aspect of design, but I would also help Guillermo polish the script, and assist him in scouting locations in Prague, eventually "complicating the life" of Production Designer Steven Scott. To call it a unique experience doesn't really begin to cover it.

On March 4, 2003, on a freezing Prague morning, sitting next to Guillermo, inside a car, inside a cargo plane, I finally saw Ron in front of the cameras as Hellboy. The "I'll believe it when I see it" moment came and went, and, after all the years of building up to that moment, the whole thing seemed very ... normal. How weird is that?

—Mike Mignola

I felt possessed by a divine madness. Hellboy was already an important part of my life. How? Years ago I had come upon the character in the pages of *Dark Horse Presents* and felt the exact same pleasurable pang that I used to experience as a child when reading about my favorite heroes. At the ripe age of thirty-something, I found myself dreaming of becoming Hellboy when I grew up. But the world around me kept reminding me I was already all grown up. That it was too late.

It was a time of creative dread. Days of bleak, steel-gray skies and cold, cold hearts. I was shooting my second movie, *Mimic*, in Toronto,

Excerpts from Guillermo del Toro's diary.

and every few weeks I would venture in sub-zero temperatures to find the latest issue of *Hellboy* at the Silver Snail Comics shop. There, in those pages, I would find that big-jawed, red guy with a big heart and a short fuse. A blue-collar super-natural worker that spoke in short sentences, half Hemingway, half Sam Spade. His dry wit and working-man complaints made every line work. These were not one-liners meant to make you laugh ... these were the musings of a disgruntled employee who, being seven-feet-tall, bright red, and horned, was, at heart, just a regular guy.

It was amidst Mignola's vast pools of black ink, that the fragile, childlike quality that makes men dream found solace that winter.

O n the first day of *Hellboy* preproduction, del Toro held a meeting with the designers and artisans he'd pulled together for the project and walked us through the script.

As he led us over the pages, Guillermo called out design assignments like a madcap head chef at a five-star restaurant—"Mignola, I need you to create ancient magical relics for the BPRD. Barlowe, you should get started on Sammael right away, he needs to have a mass of tentacles growing from his head and lots of 'nernies' (del Toro's name for large, wart-like appendages). Ty, you must create the most bad-ass mutha of guns imaginable!"

Guillermo possesses the uncanny ability to give out assignments that fully exploit the talents of specific designers, while simultaneously compelling them to stretch and expand their skills for maximum effect.

He has an amazing imagination. He draws well, and is very hands on. But he expects members of the design team to bring their personal voice and perspective to whatever creative task is at hand. He's a person filled with genuine respect for the talents of others.

Mike and I shared an office together on *Blade 2* and had a blast. When things were getting set up at the *Hellboy* office, we took desks near one another. This arrangement proved to be a great benefit to me, as I could ask lots of questions about the origins of elements that appeared in the script and gain a deeper understanding of what things were all about.

Mike knows the world he's created in *Hellboy* inside-out and backward. Whenever I questioned him about elements in the book, he'd typically have something interesting and entertaining to say. He'd tell me how this or that related to some old Japanese fable about a girl who'd been condemned to dwell in the roots of a tree that was later dug from the earth and carved into an urn so her grandmother could hide the severed hand of a notorious one-eyed fisherman—or some-thing strange like that. Other times he would simply tell me, "Oh, that thing, I have no idea what that is, I just made it up—it's crap!"

—TyRuben Ellingson

I met with Mike from the very start of the project. I immediately made it clear that I wanted him involved. Fully involved. Yes, this was a very personal project to me. One that I would pursue for as long as needed. But it was a riff on the world he had created. An "Elseworlds" version of his Cosmology. Since the day I met him, Mike has become one of my very few life-found brothers. We joke sometimes about being the same guy. We are not. Our differences make us richer and, I believe, have enriched the Hellboy Universe with a new, fresh palette of colors *not* found in the comic-book incarnation of the character. We have riffed the same tune at a different key and we have enjoyed it enormously. Prepping and shooting *Hellboy* remains one of the two best experiences of my filmic life (the other one being *The Devil's Backbone*), and represents a newfound peak in my life.

Each of the illustrations accompanying this script means a lot to me and to the film. A group of brilliant artists were forced to be locked for months in the same office space as me—a fate worse than death. Everyday, amidst great lunches, dire moments of soul-searching, and brilliant eruptions of creativity, a multitude of lines made their way to paper. It was Summer Camp for Freaks, and we had a blast at it. You will sample a lot of approved designs that made it to the screen absolutely intact. Many of them on the first try. But you will also have a chance at seeing things transform from one concept to the next—a mercurial Sammael gaining and losing pounds and tentacles in the blink of an eye.

All in all, it is my belief as a geek that this book contains the very things that made me cherish any *Art of ...* books. It will give you a peek at the film in its earliest, purest state before it fought reality, before it faced a schedule, a budget, or the laws of physics. You hold in your hands a dream.

Dream it with us.

GUILLERMO DEL TORO

CALIFORNIA

HELLBOY
FINAL SHOOTING SCRIPT

The opening sequence involving the submarine, storyboarded by Simeon Wilkins, was replaced in the movie by Broom's voiceover through clouds.

Interior, Darkroom—Interview #1. In a photographic darkroom: old optical enlargers, porcelain trays, timers, and stills hanging out to dry. George Matlin, a slightly obese, nearsighted man in his seventies.

OLD MATLIN
Is he real? Oh, yeah—Absolutely.

TITLE
Cpl. George Matlin, combat photographer.

OLD MATLIN
I haven't talked about it for years, you know?

Looks at the camera.

OLD MATLIN
Everyone called me crazy …

Matlin smiles as he paws through a box of old negatives.

OLD MATLIN
But I have the negative.

Someone turns on the darkroom's red safety light for an eerie, dramatic effect.

TECHNICIAN'S VOICE
Get ready, 3-2-1 … Roll tape.

OLD MATLIN
It all started back in '44. I was a Corps photographer aboard an allied submarine …

Cut to:

Interior, Submarine Hallway—Night. Young Matlin's hands again paw through a bunch of negatives, again under a red light. Now, at 21, he's wedged in a submarine corridor, a crowded maze of pipes and gauges. 35mm still cameras dangle from his neck. He shrinks back as a squad of marines hustles past him, loading weapons.

OLD MATLIN'S VOICE
… off the coast of Scotland. Classified mission. I was 21 …

Sgt. Whitman, 44, tough as nails, pushes through, his uniform soaked in sweat.

OLD MATLIN'S VOICE
We had an English civilian on board. Not much older than me but already an advisor to President Roosevelt. "Paranormal" advisor, I kid you not—

Whitman continues down the passage-way until he reaches a small …

Interior, Submarine Stateroom—Night. Within, an incongruously proper young Englishman "reading" an ancient set of Tarot cards.

OLD MATLIN'S VOICE
His name was Trevor. Professor Trevor—

WHITMAN
Broom! Topside, now.

Trevor "Broom" Bruttenholm is a gaunt, olive-skinned man in his late twenties. In his hands, a tarot deck. He turns the cards face up: The Fool, The Moon …

WHITMAN
The sooner we're done, the better.

Broom grabs a worn-down wooden box full of books and amulets. It has a leather strap that allows him to carry it, much like a carpenter's tool box.

BROOM
This is an important mission, Sgt. Whitman. I hope you realize that.

WHITMAN
Oh—you don't wanna know what I think. Topside, now.

BIOGRAPHY: PROFESSOR TREVOR BROOM

HE WAS NAMED AFTER HIS GRANDFATHER: RENOWNED ENGLISH WAR HERO AND ARCTIC EXPLORER: TREVOR BRUTTENHOLM.

HIS FATHER, A WEALTHY IMPORTER FULLY EXPECTED THAT HIS ONLY MALE HEIR WOULD IN TIME ENTER THE FAMILY BUSINESS.

WHEN TREVOR'S TWO YOUNG SISTERS DIED OF PNEUMONIA, HE BECAME THE "TREASURE" OF HIS PROTECTIVE MOTHER.

SHE CONDUCTED SEANCES TO TRY TO REACH HER DEPARTED "ANGELS." TREVOR WAS ENRAPTURED BY SPIRITS AND MAGIC.

OVER TIME, HIS MOTHER AND FATHER GREW DISTANT FROM ONE ANOTHER, EVENTUALLY LIVING IN SEPARATE HOMES.

HIS AGED GRANDFATHER THEN BECAME TREVOR'S KEY EMOTIONAL RELATIONSHIP.

TOGETHER, THEY TRAVELLED THE WORLD.

DURING TREVOR'S TEEN YEARS, ACADEMIC AND SPIRITUAL PURSUITS OUTWEIGHED ANY DESIRE FOR AMOROUS ADVENTURE.

AT AGE 17, WHILE TOURING TUNISIA, HE WATCHED AS AN OLD WOMAN WAS EXORCISED OF SEVERAL UNCLEAN SPIRITS.

SHE THEN PROPHESIED TO TREVOR THAT HE WOULD ALWAYS TRANSIT A LINE BETWEEN LIGHT AND SHADOW, HEAVEN AND HELL.

THROUGHOUT HIS YOUTH, TREVOR CORRESPONDED WITH CHARLES FORT, THE PIONEERING RESEARCHER INTO THE PARANORMAL.

THE TWO SHARED A BELIEF THAT THE FANTASTIC AND THE BIZARRE ARE EVERYDAY OCCURRENCES.

TREVOR MET AN ARISTOCRATIC YOUNG WOMAN WITH A UNIQUELY CURIOUS MIND: LADY ELIZABETH COLTON.

THEY FELL QUIETLY IN LOVE, ALTHOUGH HER FATHER OPPOSED THE UNION.

THEY AGREED TO ENDURE A SEPARATION, AS TREVOR ATTENDED A SERIES OF LECTURES BY NIKOLA TESLA.

INEVITABLY, WHILE HE WAS OVERSEAS, HIS BELOVED DIED.

BACK IN LONDON, HE VISITED ELIZABETH'S GRAVE — AND MADE A PERSONAL VOW...

"IT IS NOT THE FATE OF MY OWN SOUL THAT WILL CONCERN ME NOW, BUT THAT OF THE WHOLE WORLD."

TREVOR SERVED ENGLAND'S NEEDS DURING WORLD WAR II, DEVISING A METHOD FOR DECODING NAZI ENCRYPTION SYSTEMS.

HE BECAME THE FOREMOST AUTHORITY, OUTSIDE GERMANY, ON NAZI OCCULTISM.

AFTER MEETING WITH PRESIDENT ROOSEVELT, HE FOUNDED THE BUREAU OF PARANORMAL RESEARCH AND DEFENSE.

AND THEREAFTER PERFORMED "VALUABLE AND HONORABLE SERVICES" FOR THE GOVERNMENT OF THE UNITED STATES.

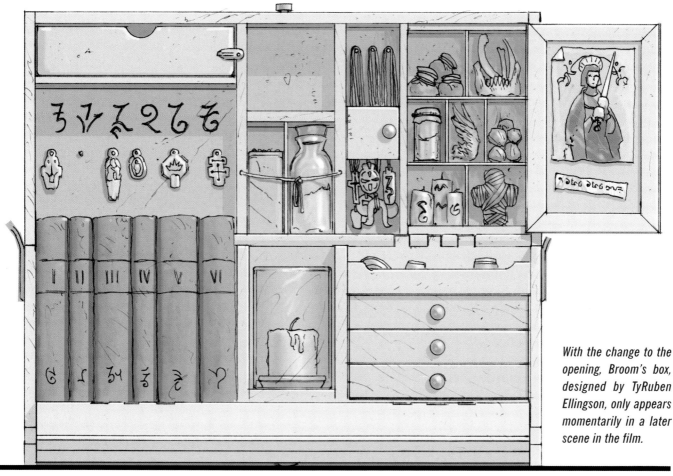

BROOM'S BOX - OPEN
SCALE APPROX - 1" = 2.5"

HELLBOY

T.RUBEN SEPT. 24 02
1 OF 4 DRAWINGS

With the change to the opening, Broom's box, designed by TyRuben Ellingson, only appears momentarily in a later scene in the film.

He moves away. Broom takes a small box and a few amulets. Before exiting, he pauses and tensely turns the last tarot card: The Devil. Cut to:

Interior/Exterior, Scotland—Tunnel—Night.

TITLE
October 9, 1944, Scotland.

It's raining like hell now. Soldiers move through a short tunnel carved into the mountain. Whitman signals his men to spread out, then comes alongside Broom.

BROOM
Sgt. Whitman! Sgt. Whitman! May I have a word?

WHITMAN (*impatient*)
What is it?

BROOM
In private, if you don't mind …

Exterior, Scotland Chapel Remains. They enter the remains of a small chapel. Broom produces the small box. It's full of rosaries.

BROOM
Your men—They'll need these—

Whitman scowls and huffs. A life-sized wooden Christ contemplates the scene from above.

WHITMAN
You are a Catholic?

BROOM
Amongst other things, yes—but that's hardly the point.

Whitman locks and loads an automatic.

WHITMAN
Here. You'll need one of these.

BROOM
I abhor violence.

Whitman moves away.

BROOM
Sergeant Whitman, I hope you don't think me mad—

WHITMAN
Three days too late for that one, "Professor."

CHURCH RUINS

After a couple of days doing my "friendly" creatures (see page 78 to 79), I moved into my first major design job on the film—the abbey ruins.

While I have been inside a lot of churches and I've drawn them several times, I don't really know enough about them to *build* one, but del Toro had a pretty clear idea of what he wanted. He provided me with very rough floor plans and very specific instructions: This area had to be here, that area there; he needed the Hell-Hole Generator there so you could see both it and the altar from this certain angle; this wall had to be up, that wall had to be down; roof here, no roof there; a certain number of arches here, broken columns here, a broken column on the ground there, etc. He knew what he was going to shoot and where he was going to shoot it from, so there wasn't a lot of guess work on my part.

—MM

HELLBOY -
CHURCH RUIN
FRONT WALL

MIGNOLA
7/18/02

HELLBOY
CHURCH RUIN
SET PLAN
#2 (with vegetation)

MIGNOLA -
7/18/02

CROSS

This was originally intended to stand behind the blasted altar. I found an old photo of a cross in a bombed-out church. The arms were broken off the Christ figure, which I thought was a powerful image. Does the broken-off right arm relate in some mixed-up way to Hellboy having that big stone right hand? Who knows. In the final film, the decision was made to put a tree behind the altar instead of a cross—also a very powerful image.

—MM

MIGNOLA
7/18/02

HELLBOY
CHURCH RUINS
Behind Alter
to the right

HELLBOY
CHURCH RUINS
STUDY #5
7/13/02

Inner Wall
with
arches

Left Side
Exterior

Exterior
Wall

MIGNOLA

MIGNOLA
7/17/02

HELLBOY
CHURCH RUINS

He moves away. Broom looks up to the wooden Christ: It has no eyes.

Exterior, Ditch. Matlin hauls his tripod and gear and joins the troops on the move. Broom catches up with Whitman.

WHITMAN
You're wasting our time. There's nothing on this island but sheep and rocks.

BROOM
Ruins. Not rocks. The remains of Trondham Abbey. Built on an intersection of Ley Lines, the boundaries between our world and the other—

WHITMAN (interrupts him)
What a load of crap. Hell, a week ago I hadn't even heard the word parabnormal—

BROOM
"Paranormal."

Whitman moves on.

BROOM
But—you read the transmission.

WHITMAN
Half transmission. Nonsense—German ghost stories!

BROOM
I have seen ghosts, Whitman.

WHITMAN
Oh, I'll bet you have.

Reaching a slope, Matlin sets down his camera. Turning, he sees lights.

MATLIN
Sweet Jesus.

Drenched, Broom and Whitman look down upon an impressive Romanesque ruin. Under worklights, dozens of Nazi soldiers swarm among thick stone walls and archways.

HELLBOY
Church Ruins

BROOM
They must be here for the sheep.

Exterior, Among the Ruins—Night. A dozen German soldiers swiftly assemble a large steel machine. The work is monitored by a spindly Nazi in black leather, his face covered by an odd gas mask: Kroenen.

WHITMAN
The freak in the gas mask—

BROOM
Karl Ruprecht Kroenen, one of the Reich's top scientists. Head of the Thule Occult Society.

Exterior, Nearby—Broom—Night. He lowers a pair of binoculars and passes them to Whitman.

BROOM
If he's here, this is worse than I thought.

WHITMAN (*to the radio man*)
Air and sea backup. What's closest?

The radioman cranks a transmitter to life.

RADIO MAN
Londonderry, sir. Forty minutes away.

BROOM
We don't have forty minutes.

ALTAR

I did have an idea about the altar. I had some vague notion that once upon a time some great (or terrible) thing happened in this place, making it the perfect place for the Nazis to do the Hell-Hole Generator thing. I drew the altar cracked down the middle thinking that perhaps it had been struck by lightning. Then, to show nature reclaiming this long-abandoned place, I had flowers growing out of the ruin. I thought that was kind of nice. Behind the altar I placed a jumble of overgrown statues. Since the beginning, statues have been a big feature in the *Hellboy* comic, and del Toro was sure to feature them prominently in the film.

—MM

Exterior, Abbey Ruins—Altar Area—Night. Kroenen throws a switch: On the machine, dozens of gears respond! Steam pistons thrust copper rails upright, lifting two mighty metal rings, not unlike a gyroscope. Kroenen grunts and signals for more floodlights to be turned on.

Exterior, Behind the Altar—Night. The lights flood an ancient sacristy lined with eroded stone saints. Grigory, tall and gaunt, stands naked, arms fully extended.

GRIGORY
No matter what happens to me, you must carry on with the work.

Ilsa, a severe, ageless Aryan beauty, reverentially drapes an embroidered robe over his bony shoulders.

ILSA
I will not leave you.

GRIGORY
Yes, you will …
Leave me. Deny me.

ILSA
Never—

He hands her a small leather-bound book. It contains hand-drawn notes and illustrations.

GRIGORY
This will guide you back to me.

He pulls her close, the clouds of their breath mingling.

GRIGORY
I grant you everlasting life, youth, and the power to serve me.

He dips his fingers in a wooden bowl full of blood, then wipes her tears away with a crimson thumb, both a consolation and a ritual.

Von Krupt, an acrid German General, wearing dark scarlet glasses and leather gloves, appears. Looks at his pocket watch. On the gold lid: a swastika.

HELLBOY
CHURCH RUINS
STUDY #6
7/13/02

ALTAR

HELL HOLE GENERATOR

TO BABY HELLBOY

SAND BAGS

HELL-HOLE GENERATOR

The Hell-Hole Generator was great fun to design. Guillermo described it as a complex folding device that spins. The Nazis built this machine, so it really needed to have a 1940s look and feel.

Rather than trying to figure out how this thing would ultimately fold up and be stowed, I began the design process by trying to figure out what it should look like in "spin mode," and how to make that cool.

I tried to think back to electrical transformers I'd seen as a kid and use that aesthetic as a starting point. Some early sketches look more like an old washing machine than a device developed to open a door to another dimension. Some of the shapes began to look interesting, so they became part of the next round of studies.

Once the "spin mode" version was looking good and signed off on by GdT, I looked over the design and subtly added in areas where folding and turning mechanisms could be employed to collapse the machine into its base.

—TE

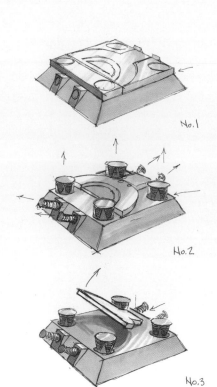

No. 1
No. 2
No. 3

No. 4

No. 5

No. 6

THE UNFOLDING OF THE HELL HOLE GENERATOR
HELLBOY-070802   ELLINGSON

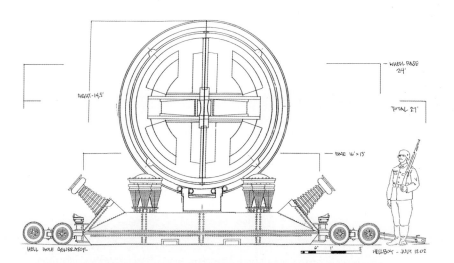

HELL HOLE GENERATOR

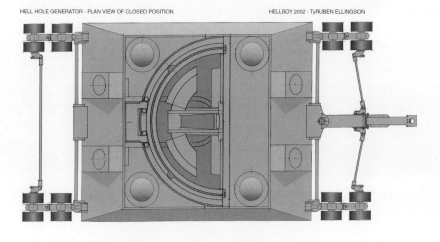

HELL HOLE GENERATOR - PLAN VIEW OF CLOSED POSITION   HELLBOY 2002 - TyRUBEN ELLINGSON

HELL HOLE GENERATOR - CLOSED IN DOWN POSITION   HELLBOY TyRUBEN   07.02.02

THE ART OF THE MOVIE

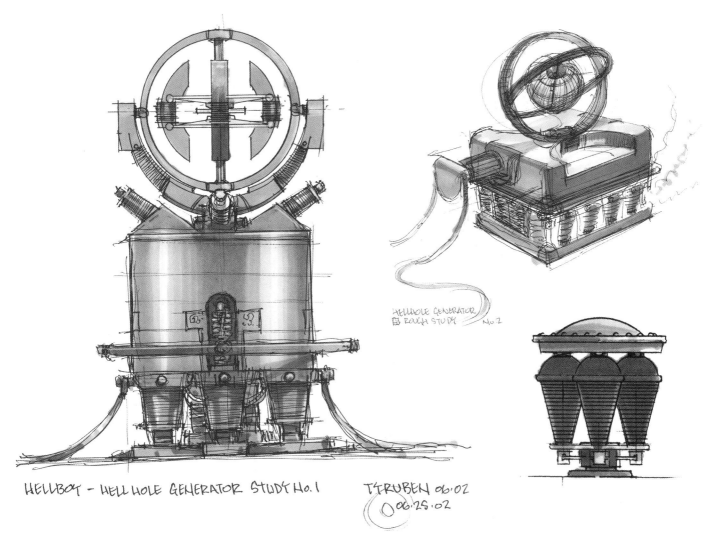

HELLBOY - HELL HOLE GENERATOR STUDY No. 1   T. TRUBEN 06.02
                                                        06.25.02

HELLHOLE GENERATOR
ROUGH STUDY   No 2

THE ORPHANAGE

Digital concept art of the Hell-Hole Generator in operation.

MECHA GLOVE

Like so many drawings I did for this film, this one was much too "quiet" for del Toro. He would often say, "I am a simple creature. I like things that move." Ty, being much more mechanically inclined than I, was able to deliver what del Toro was looking for.

—MM

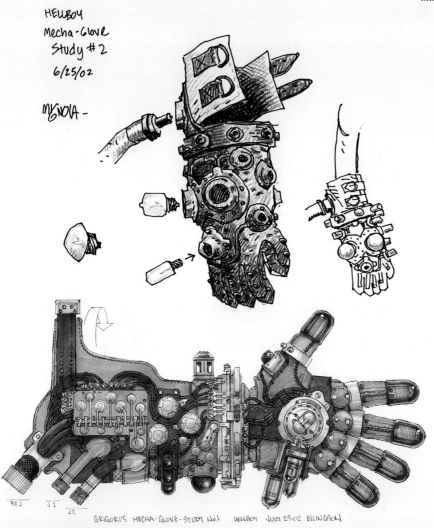

Karel Roden as Gregory Rasputin.

VON KRUPT

It's time.

Exterior, Abbey Ruins—Altar Area— Ceremony—Night. Grigory walks toward the machine, its colossal steel and copper clockworks gleaming in the floodlights.

VON KRUPT

Five years of research and construction, Grigory. Five years!

He strides alongside Grigory and Ilsa, who holds an umbrella to shield her master from the pouring rain.

VON KRUPT

The Führer doesn't look kindly on failure.

GRIGORY

There will be no failure, General. I promised Herr Hitler a miracle. I'll deliver one.

Kroenen mutters excitedly as he opens a polished oak box containing a massive gold and copper Mecha-Glove. Grigory extends his hand so that Kroenen may fit him with the contraption, which is attached to cables and hoses.

Exterior, the Hilltop—Allied Soldiers— Night. The Americans fan out, unseen. Broom and Whitman dive into a ditch barely in time to avoid a German foot patrol. Other GIs take up positions below a machine gun nest.

Exterior, Abbey Ruins—Altar Area— Night. Grigory walks to the top of the altar, cables trailing behind him.

GRIGORY

Tonight, we will open a portal and awaken the Ogdru Jahad—The seven Gods of Chaos. (*Beat.*) Our enemies will be destroyed. In an instant, all impurity in this world will be razed and from the ashes a new Eden will arise.

He looks down at the machine and whispers—

GRIGORY
Ragnarok, Anung Ia Anung.

He flexes his fingers and in response, the two metal rings swing around the machine's central axis. Tchink! Whirrr! Steam escapes from the ducts and pipes. An invisible blast of energy forces the falling rain to swerve momentarily away from Grigory's body. Ilsa signals two Nazi scientists standing at a control panel.

ILSA
More power! Don't let the level drop!

One of them inserts a 20-inch solid gold cylinder into the machine. Two openings remain vacant next to it. A blade of light opens in the air! Burning symbols slash the air, like living serpents of fire.

Exterior, Cosmic Slit—Night. The edges of the cosmic slit sizzle with color; an alien galaxy sparkles on the other side. Suddenly, a work light tears loose and flies in.

Exterior, Cosmic Slit—from the Other Side—Night. The 6-foot work light tumbles by the massive Ogdru Jahad: seven egg-like monoliths of unholy origin. Within their translucent walls, horrible creatures lie slumbering. As the light sweeps by, one of the giants opens a filmy eye, and then another, and another, and another … Fleshy tentacles move lazily within their crystalline prison.

Exterior, Abbey Ruins—Altar Area—Night. Grigory screams as his body rises. Veins swell in his neck, his face distorted by ecstasy and pain.

Click. Someone shoots a photograph.

CONTROL PANEL

The control unit for the Hell-Hole Generator was designed by Production Designer Steven Scott. Wendy Partridge designed the uniforms.

HELLBOY

GERMAN SCIENTIST

MIGNOLA ON THE OGDRU JAHAD

While I had drawn the Ogdru Jahad several times in the comic, I'd never shown them clearly—never shown them outside of their crystal/cocoon/prison things. I had no real idea what they would look like. I did this drawing just to give Wayne a direction to start with.

—MM

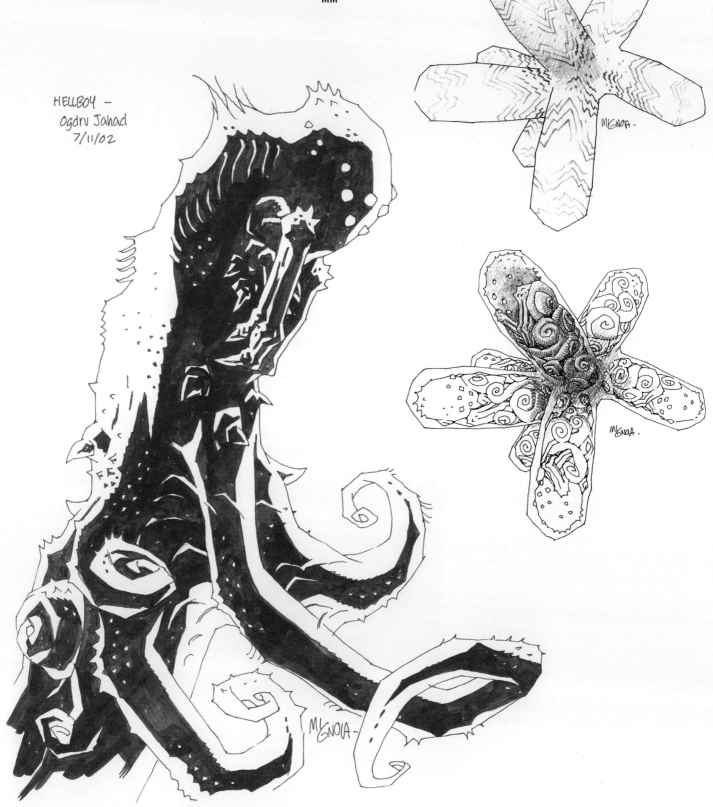

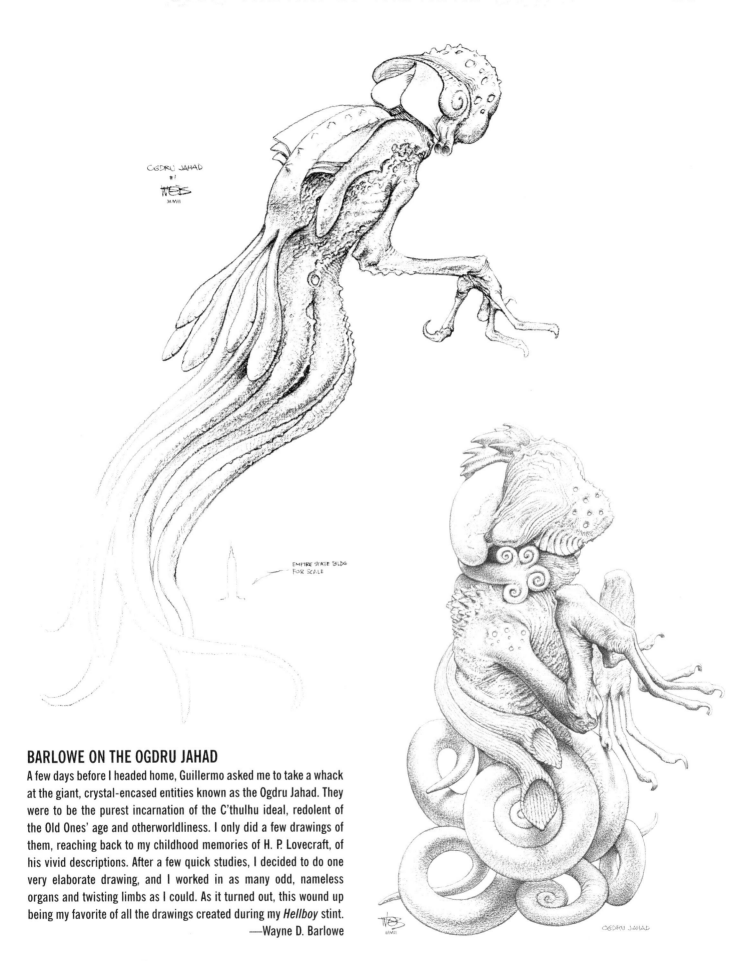

OGDRU JAHAD
#1

EMPIRE STATE BLDG
FOR SCALE

OGDRU JAHAD

BARLOWE ON THE OGDRU JAHAD

A few days before I headed home, Guillermo asked me to take a whack at the giant, crystal-encased entities known as the Ogdru Jahad. They were to be the purest incarnation of the C'thulhu ideal, redolent of the Old Ones' age and otherworldliness. I only did a few drawings of them, reaching back to my childhood memories of H. P. Lovecraft, of his vivid descriptions. After a few quick studies, I decided to do one very elaborate drawing, and I worked in as many odd, nameless organs and twisting limbs as I could. As it turned out, this wound up being my favorite of all the drawings created during my *Hellboy* stint.

—Wayne D. Barlowe

Exterior, Ruins—in the Underbrush—Night. It's Matlin, snapping for all he's worth. Whitman pulls him down and pulls out a large bayonet blade.

WHITMAN
Listen to me, you moron—you do that again, I'll carve you a new—

Too late. One of the Nazi scientists has heard them.

Exterior, Ruins, in the Underbrush—the Nazi scientist approaches. Pauses next to the box with the gold cylinders.

BROOM (*fierce whisper, to Whitman*)
Listen to me! The portal is open! We have to stop them!

Exterior, Abbey Ruins—Altar Area—Night. Grigory dangles like a marionette in a new surge of energy. Even the skeptical Von Krupt is in thrall. The Nazi scientist reaches for a second gold cylinder. But something else lands next to him: a grenade! The explosion blows him to pieces. In a few seconds, the squad of Allies storms the area.

A hail of bullets cuts down a dozen Nazis. The Allies overrun the machine gun nest as grenades explode everywhere. Von Krupt shoots wildly, hitting Broom in the leg. But Whitman's bullets rip into the old Nazi's chest. Leaving a trail of blood, Broom crawls to a dead GI and grabs a grenade from his belt.

Tchkkk! Kroenen extends two gleaming blades from twin steel bands on his wrists and takes on an entire group of soldiers, mowing through them with swords spinning like deadly rotors. The steel chops clean through their weapons.

Broom pulls the pin and throws the grenade at the generator. Click-clack! It wedges itself between two moving tie rods. Kroenen squeals and—retracting

his blades—lunges after it. The gyrating rails slice through his leather jacket. As his fingers reach the grenade, it explodes! Kroenen flies through the air, hitting a stone wall, where two long pieces of shrapnel pin him like an insect.

Another rail plunges—Fffft!, like a javelin—into the earth right next to Matlin.

ILSA
Grigory!

Exterior, Abbey Ruins—Altar Area—Night. Grigory's face is distorted, pulled like ectoplasmic taffy, his body contorting and breaking. The cosmic portal suddenly implodes! Nothing is left but a few burnt rails and the metal glove, empty and smoking. As the Allies approach, the fighting rages on. Grigory and Ilsa are gone. And for now, so is Kroenen. Embedded in the wall where he was pinned, two bloody rails, nothing more.

Exterior, Inside the Church—Night. Allied soldiers penetrate the ruins. Matlin helps Broom up.

MATLIN
It's almost over!

BROOM
No. It's not.

He picks up a sample of white, viscous goo from the outer rings of the smoking machine. Whitman approaches.

BROOM
Cordon off the area. Something came through.

WHITMAN
From where?!

Broom glances at a 13th century fresco depicting heaven and hell.

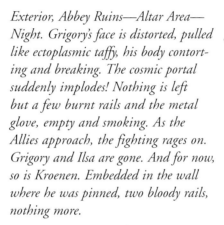

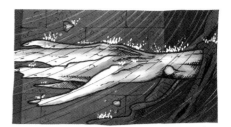

MURAL

To me there's nothing spookier than old religious paintings, so I com-
bined a few different ones for this mural that was to have been visible
near the altar. It was dropped from the finished film. The furnace-belly
hell-mouth seemed to hint at Rasputin's condition at the end of the film.
—MM

HELLBOY
Church Ruin
"Hell Mural"

M GNOA 7/24

Exterior, Inside Church Ruins—Night. Still raining. A group of soldiers spreads out, using flashlights to scour through the rubble. Every one of them has a rosary hanging from the bayonet.

Broom hastily bandages his bleeding leg. Matlin and Whitman roam over the debris. Rain pours through the broken roof.

MATLIN
Do you believe in hell?

BROOM
There is a place—a dark place where evil slumbers and awaits to return. From there it infects our dreams. Our thoughts. Grigory gave us a glance tonight—

MATLIN
Grigory—That's Russian, right?

Broom nods.

MATLIN
Thought they were on our side ...

BROOM
Grigory Yefimovich Rasputin—

MATLIN
C'mon—Rasputin?

BROOM
Spiritual advisor to the Romanovs. (*Beat.*) In 1916, at a dinner in his honor, he was poisoned, shot, stabbed, clubbed, drowned, and castrated.

MATLIN
1916? That makes him more than a hundred—

A rustling sound reaches their ears. Matlin readies a handgun as Broom scans the walls with his flashlight. Something moves, accompanied by a loud scrape. Matlin cocks his pistol and nervously approaches a crumbling statue.

HELLBOY
Baby Hellboy
room #2
MIGNOLA
7/17/02

HELLBOY
Baby Hellboy
room #3
View from inside
Church —
MIGNOLA
7/17/02

HELLBOY
Church Ruins
Study # 9

Back Wall
of the
Hellboy Junior
Room.

MIGNOLA —
7/15/02

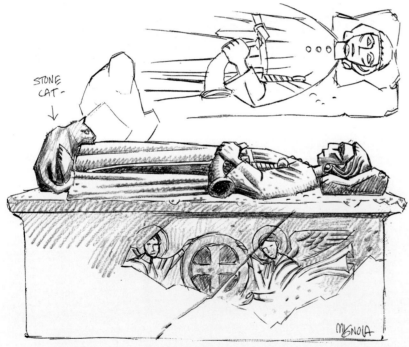

STONE
CAT —

HELLBOY — TOMB IN THE HELLBOY JUNIOR ROOM.
7/17/02   IN FRONT OF HELL WALL

HELLBOY APPEARS

I just happened to have a reference for a tomb lid with a stone cat on it. I thought this would be a perfect place for baby Hellboy to first appear, since the first time we see adult Hellboy is in his BPRD room, which is full of cats.

—MM

Screeeech! A red thing jumps into the air! Instinctively, Matlin shoots at it. The red thing leaps from arch to arch, followed by a trail of bullet hits. Whitman and other soldiers join them.

MATLIN (*to Broom*)
What the hell was that? An ape?

BROOM
No. It was red. Bright red.

WHITMAN
What are you two talking about?

MATLIN
A *red* ape.

BROOM
It's—not—an—ape—

They hear the labored breathing of a living creature.

MATLIN
It's got a big stone—in its hand—

BROOM
I think that *is* its hand.

Hissing, the thing cowers between a gargoyle and a stone saint. Whitman points his gun at the scarlet shape above. Broom stops him from firing.

BROOM
Wait—

In deep shadow, the red thing observes with bright, golden eyes veined with streaks of burnt sienna. Broom slowly fishes a Baby Ruth candy bar from his pocket. Peeling back the wrapper, he slowly waves the candy. The red thing shrinks back. Broom bites into the candy and chews, noisily smacking his lips. Offers the candy again. This time, out of the dark comes a small face, not very different from the stone demons around it. The creature extends its right arm: it's solid stone with tiny runes engraved around the thick, cylindrical wrist. Four articulated stone fingers wiggle, reaching for the chocolate.

HELLBOY
CHURCH RUINS

BACK WALL IN THE
HELLBOY JUNIOR
ROOM -

MIGNOLA
7/16/02

HELLBOY –
BABY HELLBOY
7/16/02

MIGNOLA –

THIS SKETCH IS ONLY A PLACEHOLDER
TO REMIND YOU THAT PRIMATE BABIES
HAVE BIG EARS.   WDB

Art from **Hellboy: Seed of Destruction,** *copyright 1994, Mike Mignola.*

YOUNG SOLDIER
Jesus! Would'ya look at the size of
that whammer!

*Whitman moves closer. On the wall
behind him, a shadow shows the red
thing climbing into Broom's arms.
Broom tenderly covers it with a blanket.
The stubby fingers snatch the candy.
Broom smiles.*

BROOM
It's a boy. Just a baby boy.

*Exterior, Chapel Ruins—Night. The
soldiers cluster around, curious to see it.
Matlin prepares his camera and directs
them into a group shot. Broom smiles
like a proud new father and embraces
the creature, patting him gently. Click!*

OLD MATLIN'S VOICE
Best photo of my career—

Cut to:

*Interior, Darkroom—back to Interview
#1.*

OLD MATLIN
—and no one has ever seen it.
They keep saying he's not real, but
I want to set the record straight
before I go.

**With the removal of the photographer's
interview, this sequence was covered by a
voiceover from Broom.**

*Matlin finally pulls an old 8x10 from
a battered portfolio. He smiles, full
of memories.*

OLD MATLIN
Here. The real picture, not the
retouched one in *Life* magazine.
(*Hands over the photograph.*) This is

him. The very same night we found
him. The night Broom gave him that
name. (*Beat.*) Can I say it on TV? He
called him—

*Exterior, Inside the Church—Back to
1944—Night.*

BROOM (*smiles at the creature*)
Hellboy.

*Inside the blanket, Hellboy blinks
his bright golden eyes and chews candy,
his devilish red tail twitching happily.*

Cut to:

HELLBOY—MAIN TITLE

BIOGRAPHY: DR. THOMAS MANNING

BORN IN 1945, ELDEST SON OF CONNECTICUT SENATOR PAUL MANNING AND HIS WIFE EMELINE.

BABY THOMAS WAS SWIFTLY PLACED IN AN INCUBATOR, WHERE HE BRAVELY FOUGHT FOR HIS LIFE FOR THREE WEEKS.

HE REMAINED A STRAIGHT-A STUDENT AND A STAR ATHLETE THROUGHOUT HIS SCHOOL YEARS.

AS A DEBATER AT YALE, HE PROVED HIMSELF MASTER OF STRONGLY HELD IDEAS.

HIS DEBATES OFTEN DISINTEGRATED INTO SHOUTING MATCHES OR SPITTING CONTESTS.

UPON RECEIVING A DOCTORATE IN LAW, THOMAS TOOK A POSITION WITH THE CONN. TRUST & SAFE DEPOSIT CO., HIS FAMILY'S BUSINESS.

AT AGE 23, HE BECAME MANAGER OF THE HARTFORD BRANCH OF THE GREAT AMERICAN INSURANCE CO.

HE WAS THUS COMFORTABLY ENSCONCED IN THE PRIVILEGED LIFE THAT WAS HIS DUE.

HIS FATHER'S POLITICAL CAREER, HOWEVER, WAS STILL AN INSPIRATION: THOMAS COULD NOT RESIST THE PUBLIC ARENA.

HE REMAINED A CONSERVATIVE THROUGH THE '60s (A FACT THAT HE HAS LAMENTED MANY TIMES SINCE).

HE HAS BEEN CITED, YEAR AFTER YEAR, AS ONE OF WASHINGTON'S "BEST-DRESSED POLITICIANS."

HIS VISAGE WAS FEATURED NOT ONCE BUT TWICE ON THE COVER OF "CIGAR AFICIONADO" MAGAZINE.

MANNING'S ACTIVITIES EVENTUALLY CAME TO THE ATTENTION OF PROF. TREVOR BROOM.

THE MAN'S INNATE ABILITY TO BE INSINCERE BUT EARNEST, BROOM REASONED, WOULD MAKE HIM AN IDEAL FRONT-MAN FOR THE B.P.R.D.

MANNING WAS INTRODUCED TO ABE SAPIEN AND HELLBOY IN 1984...

AND WOKE UP SCREAMING FOR NINE CONSECUTIVE WEEKS.

HIS POLITICAL CAREER CONTINUED — LEADING TO AN ILL-ADVISED RUN FOR THE SENATE IN 1996.

MANNING FOR SENATE

DURING THE CAMPAIGN, HE ATTENDED A DANCE CONTEST AT AN IMPORTANT COUNTRY CLUB...

DESPITE THE WARNINGS OF HIS STAFF, HE WENT ONTO THE FLOOR AND DANCED TWO RUMBAS AND A MERENGUE.

SHORTLY THEREAFTER, MANNING WITHDREW FROM THE SENATORIAL CONTEST.

HE HAS THE VAGUE FEELING THAT THE B.P.R.D. IS MORALLY WRONG AND POTENTIALLY DAMAGING TO HIS POLITICAL CAREER.

BUT HE HAS REMAINED AS HEAD OF OPERATIONS FOR EIGHTEEN YEARS, IN SPITE OF HIS MORE AMBITIOUS ASPIRATIONS.

Jeffrey Tambor as Dr. Thomas Manning.

Montage: Tabloid covers and news clippings screaming "Hellboy Sighting In Reno!" "Government Denial!" etc. TV newscasters read lurid copy. Springer excerpts (fistfight included) feature the show's theme: "I Was Hellboy's Bride!" Some blurry, grainy footage depicts Hellboy crossing an alley. Much like Bigfoot in the woods.

TOM MANNING (*voice over*)
Look at that. That's a costume. These people amaze me.

Manning's TV interview was also omitted.

Interior, Studio TV Host Show— Interview #2—Day. Manning is a balding, official-looking guy in a suit.

MANNING
With their conveniently blurry footage of their beloved "Hellboy." And they claim that he works for the FBI—?

SUPER ON TV:
Tom Manning, FBI.
Head of Special Operations.

Manning on a TV show à la Regis Philbin.

TV HOST
As the head of your division, you— you have seen dozens of pictures like this!

MANNING
Exactly—so, why is it that they're all

out of focus? C'mon! God knows, people manage to get good pictures at a wedding!

He shows a blurry picture.

MANNING
That's the alleged best man—?

The audience applauds.

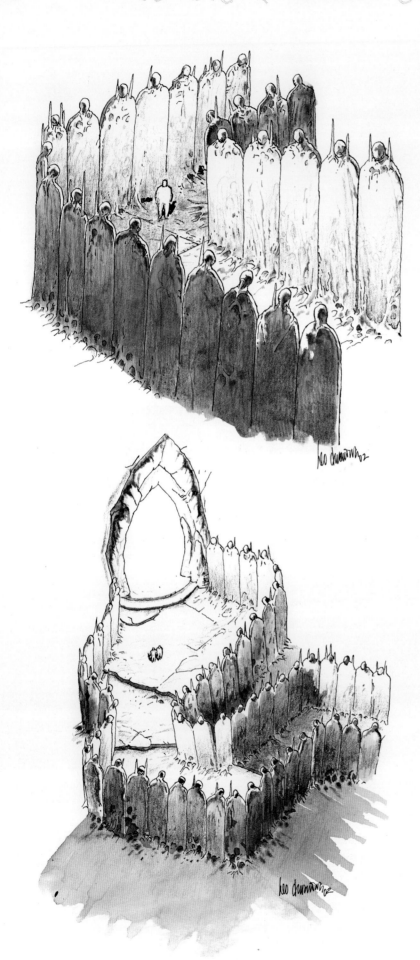

Exterior, High Mountains, Eastern Europe—Day. In the thick of a snowstorm, three figures climb the icy steps of a massive rock formation.

TITLE
Birgau Pass, Moldavia, Present Day.

Exterior, High Mountains (Set), Eastern Europe—Day. The three figures move through a narrow passage until they reach a dead end. Figure 1 stops at a symbol carved in the rocky ground and consults Grigory's leather-bound book. The symbol matches an illustration in the book. Before them, a thick wall of ice. Using a heavy steel hammer, Figure 1 breaks through.

PEASANT GUIDE
I will guide you no further.

Figure 2 produces two small gold ingots. Hands one to the Guide. Keeps the other one. The Guide examines his pay greedily: engraved in it, a swastika.

Interior, Ice Cave—Small Corridor—Day. The ice curtain collapses, revealing a rough-walled corridor. Figure 1 spots a glowing firefly. They follow it into—

Interior, Ice Cave—Main Nave—Day. A cathedral-like vault that could easily hold a stadium. From an opening somewhere above, eerie blue light streams down on a magnificent labyrinth. A few more fireflies speckle the air, winking on and off.

Interior, Ice Cave—Labyrinth—Day. The three figures move past cyclopean statues guarding the inhuman architecture. The humans are dwarfed by the monumental scale of the walkways and ramparts.

Interior, Ice Cave—Central Labyrinth Area—Day. At the center of the labyrinth the stone floor is covered in grooves radiating from a shallow stone

ICE/STONE STATUES - ICE CAVE

basin. *Figure 3 uncovers his face: he's a peasant guide.*

PEASANT GUIDE (*in Romanian*)
We shouldn't be here—

Figure 1 exchanges a meaningful look with Figure 2. Figure 1 throws two solid gold pieces at the feet of the Sherpa. On them, an embossed swastika. After a greedy moment of thought, the Peasant kneels to pick up the gold.

Tchkk! A long, shiny blade pierces the Peasant's chest from behind. He blinks twice and slumps forward. Figure 2 steps out from behind him, a long, bloody blade in his hand. The figures uncover their faces. Ilsa has not aged and Kroenen still wears the same tight gas mask. He cleans his blade in the snow and takes back the gold. Ilsa watches the Sherpa's blood as it runs in a steaming rivulet, tracing a glyph in the grooves and filling the basin.

A figure rises from the blood. A naked human shape, haloed by fireflies.

ILSA
Your eyes. What did they do to your eyes?

RASPUTIN'S JOURNAL

I must have done about twenty of these pages, although I guess you only end up seeing two in the film.

Top left: This is a reference to the Ogdru Jahad and the Christian Beast of the Apocalypse.

Top right: The firefly is a reference to a sequence that was abandoned. Originally Kroenen and Ilsa would follow a firefly into the ice cave and fireflies would form a halo or crown over Rasputin's head as he rose out of the pool of blood. That would have been something.

Opposite, top left: This is the Russian witch Baba Yaga in her mortar and pestle, an important character in the comic.

Opposite, top right: The Block from the end of the movie.

—MM

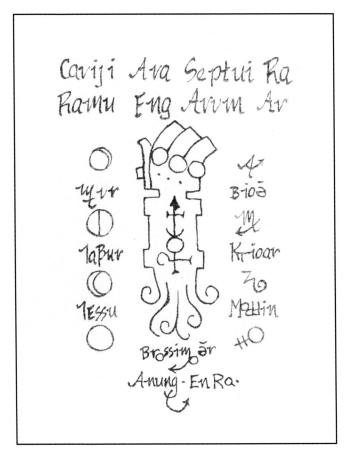

BIOGRAPHY: GRIGORY YEFIMOVICH RASPUTIN

CERTAIN ASPECTS OF HIS LIFE ARE WELL KNOWN. BORN, PROBABLY 1867, IN THE PEASANT VILLAGE OF POKROVSKOYE.

AS A YOUTH, RAUCOUS AND UNEDUCATED, MUCH GIVEN TO THE PLEASURES OF THE FLESH.

THEN ONE NIGHT, AS HE LAY IN THE WOODS, AN ANGEL CAME UNTO HIM.

THIS BEING DECLARED ITSELF ALL-POWERFUL AND APPOINTED GRIGORY ITS EMISSARY ON EARTH.

FOR THIS, GRIGORY WOULD RECEIVE ALL EARTHLY POWERS, AS WELL AS ETERNAL LIFE.

AS CONFIRMATION, THE ANGEL WOULD SOON SEND A GIANT CARVED STONE DOWN FROM THE SKY.

HIS REPUTATION AS HOLY MAN AND HEALER BROUGHT GRIGORY INEVITABLY TO ST. PETERSBURG AND THE ROYAL FAMILY.

HIS MIRACULOUS WORK WITH THE YOUNG TZAREVICH GAINED HIM ACCESS TO THE HIGHEST CORRIDORS OF POWER.

IN 1908, THE ARTIFACT PREDICTED BY THE ANGEL FELL TO EARTH IN SIBERIA.

A HUGE STONE SLAB WAS RECOVERED BY THE TZAR'S ARMY AND TRANSPORTED TO A SECRET LOCATION.

BY 1916, RASPUTIN HAD ATTRACTED NUMEROUS ENEMIES. IT WAS TIME TO ALLOW HIS OWN ASSASSINATION.

HE WAS POISONED, BEATEN, AND SHOT, HIS BODY DROPPED INTO THE ICY NEVA.

OVER THE ENSUING YEARS OF DARKNESS, RASPUTIN LEARNED CALM — AND HE SAW THE FUTURE.

HIS ASHES WERE AT LAST RECOVERED BY HITLER'S ELITE CORPS. A CEREMONY BROUGHT FORTH HIS RENEWED SELF.

HE EMERGED FULL-GROWN AS THE TRUE POWER BEHIND THE THIRD REICH.

THIS TIME HE WAS WISER: HE NEVER SHOWED HIMSELF IN PUBLIC — LESS LIKELY TO MAKE ENEMIES THAT WAY.

HE GATHERED ABOUT HIM A CIRCLE OF DISCIPLES, HIS BERLIN SALON A CENTER FOR DRUGS AND DEBAUCHERY.

KROENEN WAS HIS FAVORITE APOSTLE, ILSA HAUPSTEIN HIS MAGDALENE.

HE PROMOTED THE ILL-PLANNED ADVANCE ON MOSCOW, IN HOPES OF RECAPTURING THE PROPHETIC STONE.

THE VENTURE COST HITLER THE WAR.

MORE SUCCESSFUL WAS THE PORTAL GENERATOR, WHICH BROUGHT FORTH, IN 1944, THE SCARLET BEAST ... HELLBOY!

AND RASPUTIN WAITED IN THE DARKNESS FOR A SIGN — AND A CHANCE TO FINISH HIS WORK.

DEL TORO ON COLOR

The following is an excerpt from Guillermo del Toro's memo "to all departments and actors" regarding the light and color of the Hellboy *film from a memo entitled "Hellboy Visual Notes."*

Let me make something abundantly clear—in case you've been on Mars—NO RED!!!!!—Except for Hellboy or the atmospheres that are intimate/related to him: BROOM, LIZ, GRIGORY, and/or the colors in WWII.

There should be NO EXCEPTIONS and, except for the pre-approved sequences (PUMPKINS/HALLOWEEN, etc.), warm colors should be BANNED.

NO: Light Blues.
NO: Bright Yellows.
NO: Bright Greens.
NO: Browns.

YES: Olive green, steel blue, blue-gray, gray, earth tones, off-white, some white. All the black you can eat. And mostly any color you want from THE CORPSE paperback.

RUST is welcome in all metals! Copper should be "green" and oxidized.

COLOR PALETTE: BLACK, GREEN, BLUE, GRAY, AMBER, AND OFF-WHITE.

The MIGNOLA light is usually a very liberal transposition of the EXPRESSIONIST patterns of lighting used in German films and some early Universal monster movies.

We will use shadows and patterns on the walls and will go for some more BOLD effects with colored light and fluorescent tubes in some sets (BPRD, MENTAL HOSPITAL, etc.).

The nights will be STEEL BLUE, with the exception of the scenes around the Back Alley of the Machen Museum, the Highway crossing, and the Party at "Central Park." I don't care about consistency, I care about the colors and light designs being EXPRESSIVE.

The movie's colors are—or should be—in contrast when prudent (the green light in Broom's room with the blood-red SUNSET outside his window), since this is a movie about the varied colors and elements—Blue (Abe), Red (Hellboy), and Black (Liz), and fire, water, etc.

VERTICAL LINES OF LIGHT:

The FX department and the D.O.P. should show us a column of STEAM with colored light behind it (according to the scene) to be used as a VERTICAL element in the composition. Especially important in: HIGHWAY SCENE, BACK ALLEY SCENE, SAMMAEL'S CAVE, etc.

In the TUNNELS under Moscow, we should use the vertical and narrow tunnels to emulate the Mignola compositions in that format. And in the case of the COLLAPSED COFFIN tunnel, we should even do it DIAGONALLY.
—GdT

Art from Hellboy: Conqueror Worm, *copyright 2001, Mike Mignola.*

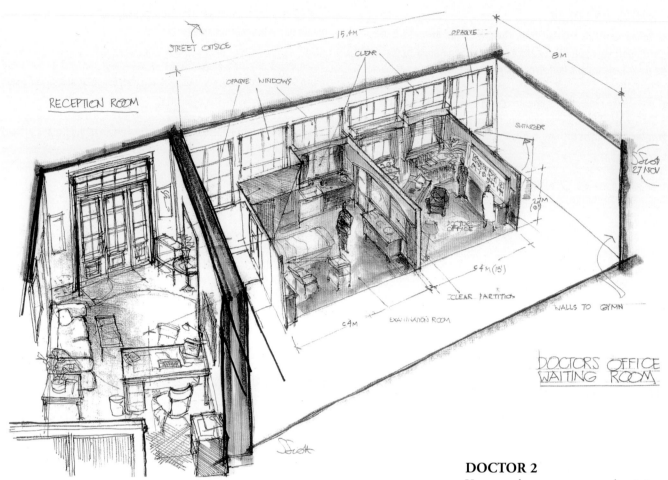

RECEPTION ROOM

DOCTORS OFFICE
WAITING ROOM

Cut to:

Interior, Doctor's Office—Day. Mechanized rollers transport x-ray films over a backlit screen. A group of 4 doctors study the pictures and exchange somber looks. Rain spatters the windows. Doctor 1 glances at the others.

DOCTOR 1
Have you told him yet?

This scene was shortened so that we never see the doctor tell Broom he's dying.

Doctor 2 looks through a glass partition at an aged but dignified Broom, 72, who slowly buttons his shirt. Hanging from his wrist, his rosary.

Interior, Doctor's Office—Examination Room—Day.

DOCTOR 2
Malignant sarcoma. In the lungs … the spine, liver …

BROOM
Approximately … how long?

DOCTOR 2
Maybe—six weeks.

Broom impassively takes in the information.

DOCTOR 2
I can arrange for hospitalization, pain management. Make the time more bearable—

Broom pensively shuffles his tarot cards.

BROOM (*shakes his head*)
I'd rather … stay home, you know. I'll be making arrangements. (*Beat.*) For my son.

DOCTOR 2
You can always get a second opinion.

Broom looks down: first card off the deck: Death.

BROOM
That won't be necessary.

Exterior, NY—Manhattan Street—Day. Leaves stir on the pavement. All the stores are decorated for Halloween. Two kids dressed as skeletons run in front of Broom, carrying a Jack-O-Lantern. Leaning on a cane, Broom exits the building and walks toward a waiting black Mercedes. The driver (Agent Lime) opens the door. Broom pauses to buy a dozen Baby Ruth candy bars from a street vendor. In an electronics store, a wall of TVs. The image of a red, blurry shape (Hellboy) fills the screens.

BROOM (*seeing this*)
Son …

TV HOST
Mister Manning, what about the "Bureau for Paranormal Research and Defense?" The FBI has been known to conceal—

TOM MANNING
That word—conceal—

TV HOST
—from the American public—

TOM MANNING
Phil—Phil— hold your little green horses. Let me tell you and the American public one thing—this Bureau for—what was it?

TV HOST
—Paranormal Research and—

TOM MANNING
—Defense, right, well—I'm here to clear this up once and for all. (*He looks at the camera.*) There—is—no—such—thing.

Broom smiles.

Exterior, BPRD Building Complex—Day. On a wooded, New Jersey hill, a low-slung, high-tech complex rests at the edge of a bluff, its foundation fused with the rock below.

TITLE
Bureau for Paranormal Research and Defense, Newark, N.J.

Exterior, BPRD Complex—Gate Entrance—Day. A dolled-up mod-style moped stops at the massive gate. Strapped to the luggage rack are two cheap suitcases. The driver, a very wet young man named Myers, touches an old fashioned buzzer under a sign reading "Waste Management." A crackling intercom voice answers.

INTERCOM VOICE
Yes?

MYERS (*shivering*)
John Myers, FBI. Transfer from Quantico.

A beat, then—Whirrr! An eyepiece and an LCD screen scanner pop out.

INTERCOM VOICE
Look at the birdie, son.

Myers looks into the eyepiece. On the screen, Myers's cornea is scanned. Two violet flashes. His ID and badge numbers appear. Clack! The gate opens.

Exterior, Uphill Road—the moped—Day. The moped putt-putts toward the building in the distance.

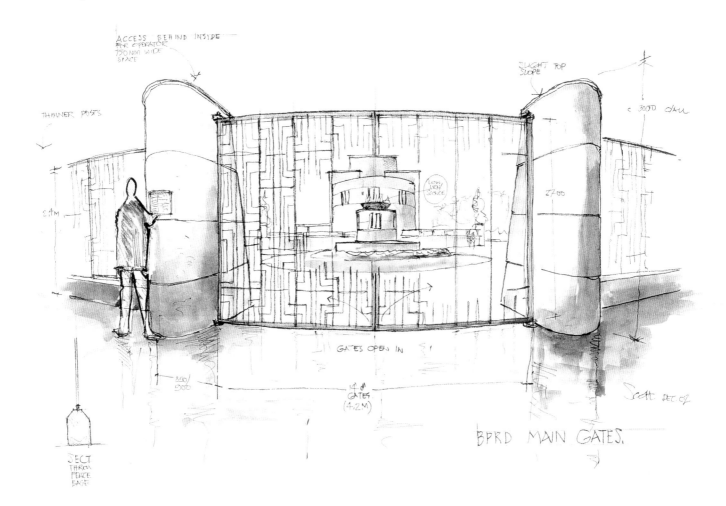

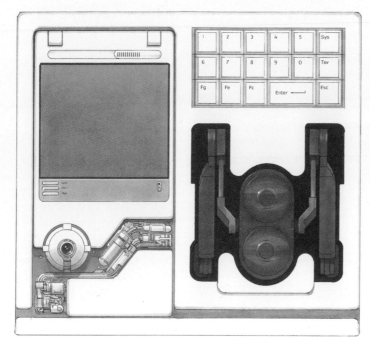

EYE CANNON SCANNER INTERFACE-
SCANNER RETRACTED   HELLBOY   ELLINGSON AUG.28.02

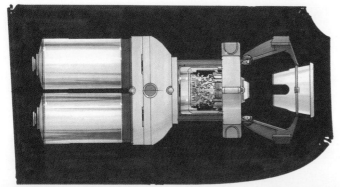

EYE CANNON SCANNER - STUDY No.1   HELLBOY   P.TRUBEY 8.2.02
(SCANNER END IN OPEN POSITION)

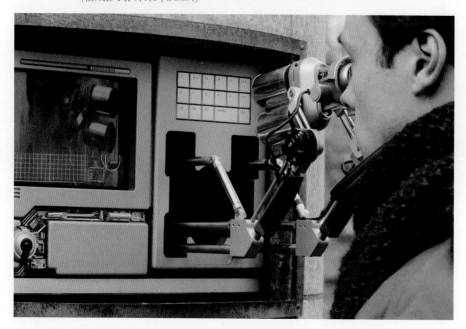

Interior, BPRD Lobby—Day. Seated at a dramatic circular desk is a solitary guard. Myers approaches.

MYERS
Hello, I'm—

LOBBY GUARD
—late. Five minutes late.

MYERS
Yes, I—

LOBBY GUARD
Section fifty-one. Step back.

MYERS
Pardon?

LOBBY GUARD
Two steps back, please.

Confused, Myers picks up his suitcases and complies. He realizes he's dead center on a giant BPRD logo: a hand holding a sword.

LOBBY GUARD
Watch your hands and elbows.

Immediately, the floor under Myers' feet starts down. He's on a small elevator.

Interior/Exterior, Open Elevator—on the way down—Day. The panel overhead slides shut. A row of safety lights comes on.

Interior, Open Elevator—Day. He's in a vast underground area with other elevators moving up and down in the distance.

Interior, BPRD—Concrete Chamber 51—Dusk. The elevator stops in a narrow, dark space. Neon lights flicker on, illuminating a circular chamber. Painted on the floor is a huge number: 51. Right in front of Myers: a magnificent oak door. Myers knocks on it. No answer. Myers enters.

BIOGRAPHY: JOHN THADDEUS MYERS

HE WAS BORN IN THE CENTER OF THE AMERICAN HEARTLAND: A KANSAS FARM.

THE DATE WAS SEPTEMBER 9, 1976.

ONE OF FIVE OFFSPRING TO PROUD AND LOVING PARENTS...

THE MOTHER: A GIFTED HOMEMAKER, THE FATHER: OWNER OF LOU'S DINER, ON MAIN ST. IN AUGUSTA, KANSAS.

JOHNNY'S WAS A TYPICAL CHILDHOOD OF THE RURAL MIDWEST...

SUNDAYS AT CHURCH, SUMMERS AT THE POND, BIG FAMILY DINNERS, QUIET EVENINGS UNDER THE STARS...

UNTIL AGE SIX, WHEN HIS PARENTS VANISHED FROM THE FACE OF THE EARTH.

THEY SIMPLY DROVE AWAY ONE AFTERNOON, NEVER TO BE SEEN AGAIN.

POLICE THEORIZED A CAR-JACKING — BUT NO TRACE OF THE COUPLE OR THEIR CAR WAS EVER FOUND.

THE FEELING HAS NEVER LEFT JOHNNY THAT THEY MIGHT RETURN ANY DAY.

THE FIVE SIBLINGS WERE TAKEN IN BY VARIOUS RELATIONS, JOHNNY BY AN UNCLE IN PONCA CITY, OKLA.

UNCLE THAD SMELLED OF GASOLINE, NICOTINE, AND PAINT THINNER.

AS A TEEN, JOHNNY SPENT HOURS ON HIS MOPED...

AND IMMERSED HIMSELF IN COMIC BOOKS. FAVORITE SUPER-HERO: THE RED CRUSADER HELLBOY.

HE FELL IN LOVE WITH A LOCAL GIRL NAMED LAURA. THEY PLANNED TO MARRY.

BUT SHE YEARNED TO LEAVE PONCA CITY — WHICH SHE DID AT LAST. JOHNNY PREPARED TO FOLLOW HER.

THEN ONE DAY, HE FOUND HIS UNCLE COLLAPSED ON THE WORKSHOP FLOOR.

YEARS OF GAS FUMES AND UNFILTERED CIGARETTES HAD TAKEN THEIR TOLL. WITHIN WEEKS THAD WAS DEAD.

WHEN JOHNNY CAUGHT UP WITH LAURA, IT WAS TOO LATE. THE BIG CITY HAD CHANGED HER HEART.

AT A RESTAURANT IN KANSAS CITY, MO., THEY CALLED IT QUITS.

WITH MONEY FROM HIS UNCLE'S ESTATE, HE PUT HIMSELF THROUGH COLLEGE: STRAIGHT A'S, DEAN'S LIST, MAGNA CUM LAUDE...

AND FROM THERE TO THE F.B.I. AS A GENUINELY GOOD GUY, HE COULD ENVISION NO OTHER PATH.

BPRD - ELEVATORS   HELLBOY   7·19·02   ELLINGSON

B.P.R.D. COMPLEX
STUDY #4
APRIL 2002

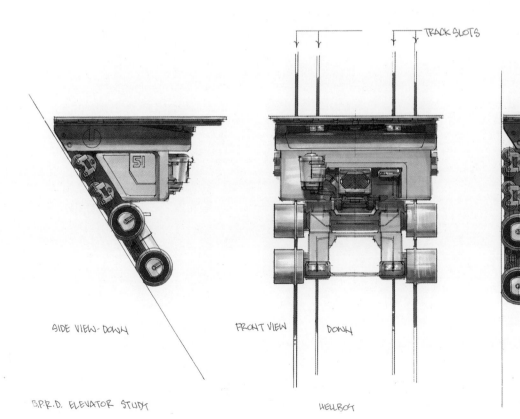

TRACK SLOTS

SIDE VIEW-DOWN

FRONT VIEW DOWN

SIDE VIEW UP

B.P.R.D. ELEVATOR STUDY

HELLBOY

 7·22·02 ELLINGSON 2002

Rupert Evans as John Myers.

BROOM'S OFFICE

Interior, Broom's Office (Full Aquarium)—Dusk. Myers looks around, fascinated: books. An office made of them. The soft glow of green-shaded reading lamps bathes everything in an intimate, warm light. One entire wall is a thick pane of glass, the wall of a huge tank of water. A voice crackles through an intercom next to the tank.

VOICE
Turn the pages, please.

Myers jumps, then moves closer to the glass.

VOICE
Over here … if you don't mind?

In the tank, Abe Sapien, a fish-man, glides in and out view.

MYERS
Jesus Christ!

Myers looks at four book stands facing the glass. Each supports an open volume. He leans close to the glass, peering intently.

Abe reappears. He is slender, dolphin-gray, with dark patterns streaking his soft skin. Bright blue eyes shine with intelligence. Behind a thin wound-like mouth, gills are bubbling. Myers points at the books.

MYERS
These—? You're reading these—?

Abe nods. Through a side door, Broom enters.

BROOM
Four books at once. Every day—as long as I'm here to turn the pages. (Smiles.) My name's Broom. Professor Trevor Broom.

Myers extends his hand in greeting—

MYERS
Sir, I'm—

Bam! Abe presses his webbed hand against the glass, closes his eyes—all three lids. Abe's voice surges from the speaker.

ABE
Agent John T. Myers, Kansas City, 76. "T" stands for Thaddeus, mother's older brother. Scar on your chin happened when you were ten, you still wonder if it's ever going to fade away.

MYERS
How did it—

BROOM
He. Not "it."

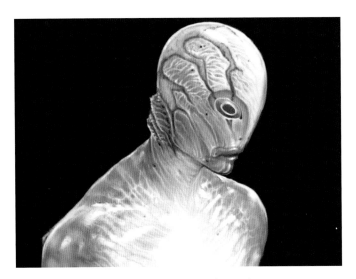

Sculpture by José Fernandez with Photoshop color pattern by Steve Wang.

Nigel Booth, Steve Wang, and Doug Jones as Abe Sapien, in the first full makeup test.

Cut to:

Interior, BPRD—Freak Corridor "A"—Night. Myers and Broom walk down a corridor. The walls are lined with glass cases containing occult artifacts. Myers eyes a mummified hand, a clay golem, a sumptuous pagan altar …

BROOM
1937, Hitler joins The Thule Society—a group of German aristocrats obsessed with the occult. 1938, he acquires the Spear of Longinus, which pierced the body of Christ. He who holds it becomes invincible.

He gestures at an ancient lance. Next to it: a silver and gold reliquary.

BROOM
Hitler's power increases tenfold.

They go through a series of pneumatic doors.

BROOM
In 1943, President Roosevelt decides to fight back. The Bureau for Paranormal Research and Defense is born.

Workmen are replacing two of the doors. Big dents from an oversized fist have deformed the 2-inch thick metal plates. Myers stares.

BROOM
1958, the occult war finally ends when Adolf Hitler dies.

MYERS
1945, you mean. Hitler died in '45.

BROOM (*enigmatic smile*)
Did he, now?

They reach a final door. Stainless steel, like a bank vault. Waiting there is Agent Clay, a burly guy in a suit, with a cartful of beef and mashed potatoes. A dinner pile at least 4 feet high.

BROOM
Agent Myers, this is Agent Clay. Follow his lead.

Broom hands Myers two Baby Ruth bars and walks away.

MYERS
You're not coming?

Broom signals "no."

BROOM
I hand-picked you from a roster of over seventy academy graduates. Make me proud.

The door closes behind him.

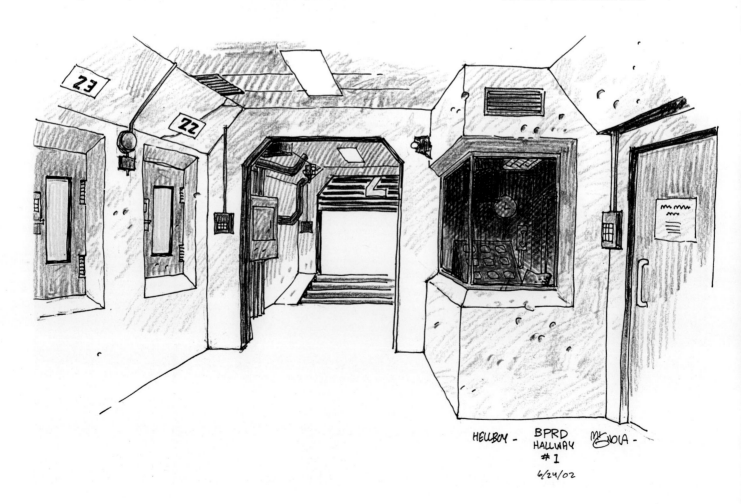

HELLBOY - BPRD HALLWAY #1
6/24/02

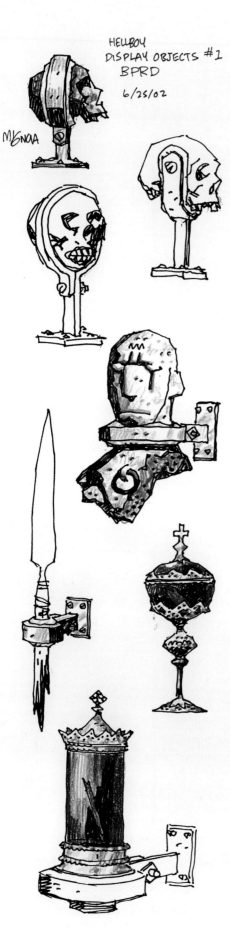

HELLBOY
DISPLAY OBJECTS #1
BPRD
6/25/02

MIGNOLA

CLAY
They're not speaking. Professor Broom had him grounded.

MYERS
Grounded? Who's grounded?

CLAY
Okay. You saw the fish man, right?

Myers nods.

CLAY
Well, come on in and meet the rest of the family.

Clay uses an odd-shaped electronic key to unlock the door. Three solenoid locks turn. Two steel vertical pistons open up.

Interior, Hellboy's Den—Night. Clay pushes the cart into a solid concrete bunker, windowless, austere except for a few samurai suits of armor and weapons. Dozens of cats wander around; others are curled up on the furniture. There are Zippos everywhere, from every era. On a sofa (made from the bed of a pickup truck) is a heap of blankets and comic books. All in all, a mega bachelor pad.

CLAY (*sotto voce*)
He gets fed six times a day. He's got a thing for cats. You'll be his nanny, his keeper, his best friend. He never goes out unsupervised—

MYERS
Who?!

Clay points at a torn comic book: Hellboy, The Uncanny. Myers picks it up, looks at the cover: it shows Hellboy—in a US uniform, fighting a monstrous ape. Myers watches, amazed, as a bright red tail waves in and out of a pool of light about ten feet away. One of the cats playfully paws at it.

MYERS (*sotto voce*)
You're kidding—

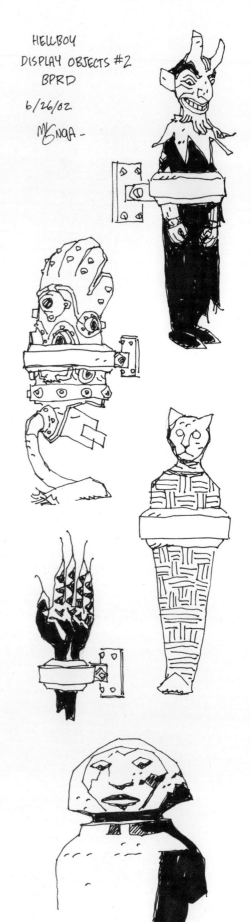

HELLBOY
DISPLAY OBJECTS #2
BPRD
6/26/02

MIGNOLA

Fake comic cover by Mignola; colors: Dave Stewart; design: Cary Grazzini.

HELLBOY
HELLBOY'S
ROOM

Bedroom & Bath

TOM
WAITS

MIGNOLA
8/30/02

HELLBOY'S ROOM

I knew this would be too dull for del Toro, but I always thought Hellboy's room would be just like an over-cluttered single guy's apartment—nothing fancy. I certainly never imagined he'd sleep in the back of a truck.

—MM

WOOD

GLASS

DROP DOWN TAIL FLAT

CHROME

Scott
APRIL 03

HELLBOY's TRUCK BACK

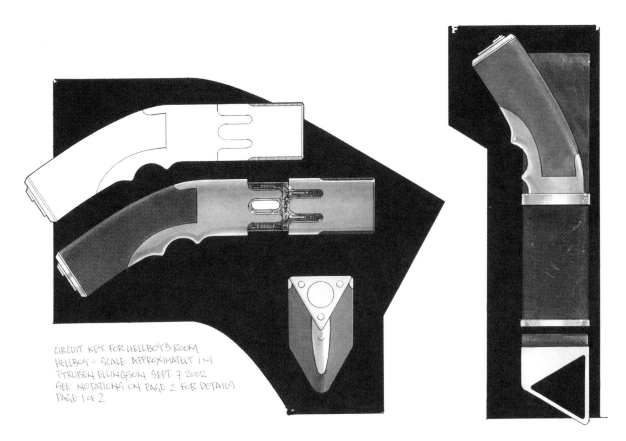

CIRCUIT KEY FOR HELLBOY'S ROOM
HELLBOY - SCALE APPROXIMATELY 1 to 1
T.TRUBEN ELLINGSON SEPT. 7 2002
SEE NOTATIONS ON PAGE 2 FOR DETAILS
PAGE 1 of 2

HELLBOY'S ROOM

DOOR

 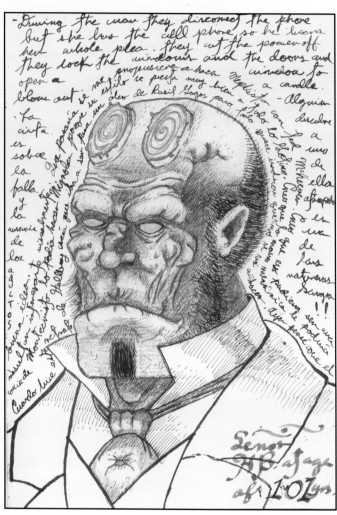

Pages from del Toro's diary.

HELLBOY
Those comics—They never got the eyes right.

The voice is a deep baritone, chesty and powerful.

MYERS (*to Clay, sotto voce*)
Oh, Jesus! Hellboy—? Is real—

CLAY (*sotto voce*)
Yup. Sixty years old by our count. But he doesn't age like we do—think dog years. He's barely out of his teens.

Myers gasps, seeing a monumental figure in the shadows, exercising with a 300 lb. stainless steel dumbbell. Crimson biceps like cooked hams. Chomping an unlit cigar stub.

HELLBOY
What's with the hair, Clay? Finally got those implants?

Agent Clay blushes as he hides his scalp.

CLAY
It'll fill in. Where do you want your dinner, Red? By the couch?

On a nearby pile of junked TV sets, a loop of Fleischer cartoons and home movies cycles endlessly. One subject appears over and over: an attractive young woman with a pale face and raven-black hair.

HELLBOY
Who's the squirt?

CLAY
Agent Myers is your new liaison.

HELLBOY
Got tired of me?

CLAY
Nah. I'll be around, Red, just back in the field.

Bang! Hellboy lets the dumbbell drop. Instinctively, Myers jumps.

HELLBOY
I don't want him.

CLAY
Manning says I'm too soft on you. (*Sotto voce, nudging Myers.*) The candy. Give him the candy.

HELLBOY
BACK SYMBOL
MIGNOLA
8/5/02

HELLBOY
Hand Study
#2
6/27/02
MIGNOLA —

HELLBOY
Hand Study
#1
6/27/02
MIGNOLA

← THUMB
SIDE

HELLBOY'S BACK

A discarded idea for a back symbol. I always thought this was a little like Hellboy having a bar code.

—MM

Ron Perlman as Hellboy.

HELLBOY'S MARKINGS

Hellboy's markings were one of the first things I did on the film. Del Toro felt that the plain stone hand in the comic would be too boring-looking on film (and he was right, of course), so he asked me to come up with "Mignola-like" magic symbols. We decided to carry the symbols up the arm and onto the chest, as if whatever marked the hand wasn't too careful and carved up the flesh as well as the stone.

At one point I was left alone with a beautiful clay sculpture of Hellboy and told to mark it up with scars and bullet holes. I was desperately afraid Rick Baker was going to walk in and start yelling at me for ruining the sculpture.

—MM

BIOGRAPHY: HELLBOY

HIS STORY BEGINS WITH HIS MOTHER — WHO WAS BORN IN 1631, IN EAST BROMWICH, ENGLAND.

ADEPT IN THE FEMININE ARTS, IMMERSED IN GERMAN LITERATURE, SHE DREAMED OF SPIRITS AND MAGIC.

SHE CALLED FORTH A HIGH-RANKING DEMON AND HAD INTIMATE RELATIONS WITH HIM.

TERRIFIED AND ASHAMED, SHE SPENT THE REST OF HER LIFE IN DEEP REPENTENCE.

UPON HER DEATH, THE DEMON RECLAIMED HER BODY.

WITHIN HER STILL LIVED THEIR SPIRITUAL SON, AWAITING TO INCARNATE AND FALL TO EARTH.

SHE LAY DORMANT, LIKE AN INSECT, UNTIL THAT FATEFUL AUTUMN NIGHT IN 1944...

WHEN HER CHILD WAS SUMMONED FORTH BY GRIGORY YEFIMOVICH RASPUTIN.

THE CREATURE WAS TAKEN BY PROF. TREVOR BROOM TO AN ARMY BASE IN NEW MEXICO.

IT WAS BROOM WHO NAMED HIM... HELLBOY! HE GREW FAST AND WAS INCREDIBLY INQUISITIVE.

HE SHOWED REMARKABLE RESISTANCE TO PAIN. HIS STONE "GLOVE" PROVED IMPERVIOUS TO ANALYSIS.

HE DISPLAYED A STRONG CONNECTION TO ANIMALS. FOR A TIME, HE COULD "TALK" TO THE BASE MASCOT.

BROOM WAS ASKED BY THE GOVERNMENT TO CONCEAL HELLBOY'S EXISTENCE FROM THE WORLD.

NEVERTHELESS, CERTAIN CELEBRITIES FOUND THEIR WAY TO THE ATTRACTION.

THE EARLY '50s WAS AN ACTIVE TIME FOR THE B.P.R.D., AS HITLER WAGED HIS SECRET WAR FROM SOUTH AMERICA.

THE BUREAU MOVED INTO NEW HEADQUARTERS. HELLBOY'S ROOM WAS SET DEEP INTO THE CLIFF WALL.

BROOM KEPT HELLBOY'S ORIGINS A SECRET FROM HIM UNTIL ONE NIGHT IN 1959.

HELLBOY WAS JOLTED: HE VOWED NEVER TO PROBE INTO THE SUBJECT.

MOST SENSITIVE WAS HE TO BEING WATCHED, STARED UPON, OR PHOTOGRAPHED.

HE REMAINED THE ONLY NON-HUMAN OF THE B.P.R.D. UNTIL 1978, WHEN ABE SAPIEN JOINED THE ORGANIZATION.

WHEN, IN 1988, LIZ SHERMAN JOINED THE B.P.R.D., HELLBOY FELL IN LOVE.

FROM THAT MOMENT ON, HE KNEW THE MEANING OF PAIN.

Myers remembers he's holding the Baby Ruths.

MYERS
Oh. Uh. Hello. I—I have these. For you.

HELLBOY (*realizing*)
Father's back? (*Clay nods.*) Still angry?

CLAY
Well, you did break out—

HELLBOY
I wanted to see her. (*Grunts.*) It's nobody's business.

CLAY
It is. You got yourself on TV again.

HELLBOY
"Myers," huh? You have a first name?

CLAY (*sotto to Myers*)
Try not to stare. He hates when people stare.

MYERS
Uh—oh—John. (*Sotto.*) Staring at what?

CLAY
His horns. He files 'em. To "fit in."

MYERS
His what?!

Hellboy finally enters the light. He's awe-inspiring, with chiselled features, patterned red skin, and deep-set golden eyes. Involuntarily, Myers recoils. In spite of himself, Myers is staring at the horn stumps.

HELLBOY
Whatcha looking at, John?

MYERS
Oh—n-no—I—
An alarm sounds, and a red light blinks on the wall. Myers looks around, bewildered.

HELLBOY (*to Clay*)
Hey, hey, hey. They're playing our song.

CLAY
We're on the move.

HELLBOY (*to Myers*)
C'mon, Champ! Happy Halloween! You're taking me for a walk!

Cut to:

Exterior, Machen Library—Night. An imposing four-story structure, all pillars and pediments. A Halloween banner advertises Magick: The Ancient Power.

TITLE
The Machen Library, Manhattan.

Chaos near the entrance: policemen, TV reporters, mounted police. Loud protests from the reporters as a line of black sedan cars are waved through.

BLONDE REPORTER
—the NYPD has yet to issue a statement. We've got SWAT vans, paramedics, you name it … and now here's—a garbage truck— (*Double take*)—a garbage truck?

Trailing behind the cars, a garbage truck. On its side a mirrored sign reads: Squeaky Clean, Inc. Waste Management Services.

Interior/Exterior, Garbage Truck— Library Street Entrance—Night. An agent is driving the truck, with Myers at his side.

Exterior, Machen Library—Street Entrance—Night. The crowd parts like the Red Sea for the garbage truck. Dozens of faces are reflected in the truck's mirrored logo. A mounted policeman rides past the mirrored sides of the truck.

Interior/Exterior—Garbage Truck Lab—Library Crowd—Night. The mounted policeman is visible as he rides by. The mirrors are see-through. The back of the truck is a fully equipped crime lab, crammed with hi-tech gear and low-tech talismans. Abe fits a respirator over his face. It looks like a mechanized Elizabethan collar. Valves bubble and hiss as he inhales liquid through his mouth and out his gills. Hellboy looks out onto the crowd.

HELLBOY
Look at them ugly suckers, Blue. One sheet of glass between them and us.

ABE
Story of my life.

HELLBOY
I break it, they see us, Happy Halloween. No more hiding. (*Nostalgic.*) Outside. I could be outside—

ABE
You mean, outside … with *her.*

Hellboy straps on a huge utility belt heavy with amulets, rosaries, horseshoes. From an ashtray he grabs a handful of stogie stubs. Lights one, puts the rest in a pouch.

HELLBOY
Don't get psychic with *me.*

ABE
Nothing psychic about it. You're easy.

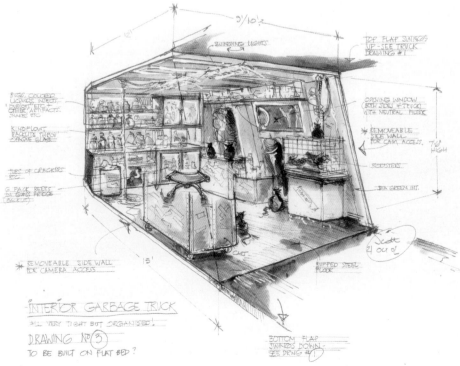

ABE'S GOGGLES

The very first design I addressed was Abe's goggles and gill cap collar. Guillermo wanted these items to look like they were constructed in the '30s or '40s, and to appear believably functional.

These devices are kind of the reverse of a human scuba suit, the goggles keeping Abe's eyes immersed in water and the collar providing a means for water to flow through his gills and keep him breathing.

In working up the design, function came first. I created shapes that would cover the right parts of the head and then tried to come up with an interesting way to connect those to a reservoir of water.

The asymmetrical lens that appears on one side of the goggles is an element that del Toro asked me specifically to include in the design. It echoed the vampire Ninja goggles created for *Blade 2*, which had a third luminous lens on one side as well.

—TE

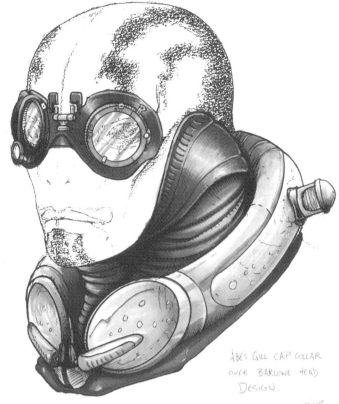

ABE'S GILL CAP COLLAR
OVER BARLOWE HEAD
DESIGN.

SIMEON WILKINS
8/7/02

Ty Ellingson designed the goggles for Abe Sapien and had storyboard artist Simeon Wilkins redraw them over one of Barlowe's studies of Abe's head, creating the unusual collaboration above between the three artists.

From del Toro's diary.

ABE'S GILL CAP COLLAR
FORM STUDY

TYRUBEN ELLINGSON
HELLBOY 06·21·02

EASTER ISLAND STATUE /
TOTEM POLE?

INT. MACHEN LIBRARY
ENTRANCE HALL

Hellboy unlocks a steel box (stenciled on its lid: "The Good Samaritan") and extracts the meanest-looking, custom-built, double-barrel, blue-finished handgun ever made. A veritable cannon.

HELLBOY
How am I ever gonna get a girl? I drive around in a garbage truck.

ABE
Liz left us, Red. Take the hint.

HELLBOY (*hefting the gun*)
We don't take hints.

Exterior, Courtyard / Loading Dock Machen Library—Night. The garbage truck pulls into an interior courtyard and stops. FBI/BPRD teams spread through the area, expelling uniformed cops and securing the doors. Three agents—Quarry, Stone, and Moss—close a gate, sealing off the area.

STONE
All areas secured.

From a nearby roof, Agent Lime signals all clear.

CLAY (*into a handheld radio*)
Seal the doors. Red and Blue are coming in.

The truck stops. Clay pulls a lever. Myers watches as the dumpster loader hinges down like a drawbridge, revealing Hellboy and Abe.

CLAY
Okay, boys, let's synch up our locators.

Abe, Clay, and Hellboy activate lights on their belts. They beep and blink. Hellboy starts walking.

Interior, Machen Library, Main

Lobby—Night. As BPRD agents clear the area, Clay, Myers, Abe, and Hellboy march through the main lobby. On view, various display cases. Two banners flank the marble staircase.

CLAY (*reading a report*)
At nineteen hundred hours an alarm tripped. B&E. Robbery. Six guards dead—

HELLBOY
Hold on—hold on—I thought we checked this place. Fakes, and reproductions.

BROOM
Apparently not everything was fake.

Broom stands at the base of the marble staircase.

HELLBOY (*surprised to see him*)
Father …?

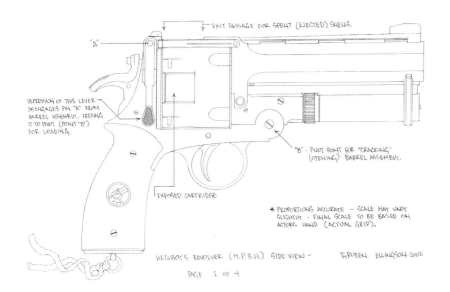

EXIT PASSAGE FOR SPENT (EJECTED) SHELLS.

"A"

DEPRESSION OF THIS LEVER DISENGAGES PIN "A" FROM BARREL ASSEMBLY, FREEING IT TO PIVOT (POINT "B") FOR LOADING.

EXPOSED CARTRIDGE

"B" - PIVOT POINT FOR "CRACKING" (OPENING) BARREL ASSEMBLY.

* PROPORTIONS ACCURATE - SCALE MAY VARY SLIGHTLY - FINAL SCALE TO BE BASED ON ACTORS HAND (ACTUAL GRIP).

HELLBOY'S REVOLVER (M.P.B.H.) SIDE VIEW -   T. RUBEN ELLINGSON · 2002

PAGE 1 OF 4

DUO-LOAD BULLETS   HELLBOY   T. RUBEN 07-06-02

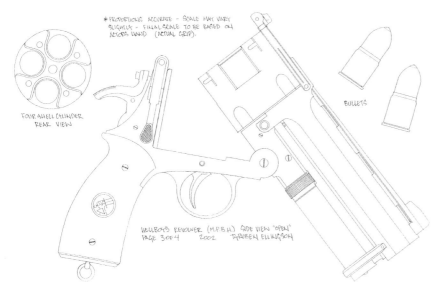

* PROPORTIONS ACCURATE - SCALE MAY VARY SLIGHTLY - FINAL SCALE TO BE BASED ON ACTORS HAND (ACTUAL GRIP).

FOUR-SHELL CYLINDER REAR VIEW

BULLETS

HELLBOY'S REVOLVER (M.P.B.H.) SIDE VIEW "OPEN"
PAGE 3 OF 4   2002   T. RUBEN ELLINGSON

HELLBOY'S "SIDE BY SIDE" STUDY No.1 T. RUBEN 07-01-02

SAMARITAN

I like revolvers. They have cool moving parts and a vibe that says, "I'm a tool for the working man." When approaching the design of Hellboy's gun, I felt it would be cool to head in the direction of a massive snub nose.

As the design of the gun progressed, Mike started telling me how Hellboy draws his gun quite a bit, but hardly ever fires it. "He mostly uses it to hit things with."

The idea of this gun functioning as a hammer started to show up in the new design. The barrel got fatter and longer, and the cylinder bigger and chunkier. And when it was time to render the final design, lots of dings, dents, and scratches were added to underscore the idea that whether this master-blaster shot you or clobbered you, it was most certainly going to hurt.

—TE

HELLBOY'S GUN (MPBH) SIDE VIEW CLOSED   JULY 16 02 T. RUBEN ELLINGSON

HELLBOY'S COAT

HELLBOY
COAT STUDY
#2
6/28/02

Also one of the first things I did. I had come up with an idea for how the right sleeve could be done—so Hellboy could get the thing over his big right hand—and I wanted to get my idea in before Wendy (the costume designer) came in with any ideas. The shoulder flaps were del Toro's idea.

—MM

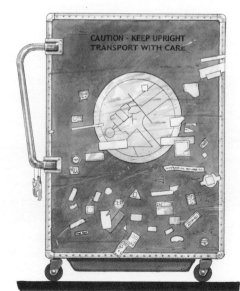

BPRD MUNITIONS CART - AUG. 29. 2002
SCALE 1.5" = 1'0"

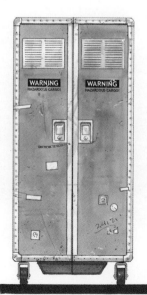

HELLBOY
T.TRUBEN

Myers observes as the red Goliath sheepishly averts his gaze from that of the fragile old man.

Interior, Main Corridor / Machen Library (Set)—Night. They approach an oversize set of brass doors. Abe removes a leather glove from his hand. Fwap! He spreads his webbed fingers on the door. He closes his three eyelids and concentrates. Two agents arrive with a rolling munitions case. Myers observes as Hellboy opens it and looks over a potpourri of bullets of all colors and shapes.

BROOM
A 16th century statue was destroyed. Saint Dionysius the Aeropagite.

HELLBOY
Who wards off demons.

BROOM
Smuggled into this country by an overzealous curator. The statue, however, was hollow—

HELLBOY
A reliquary—

BROOM
A prison. The Vatican deemed its contents dangerous enough to include it on the List of Avignon. Of which we hold a copy.

Hellboy selects a clip full of bullets and a speed loader.

HELLBOY
Would'ya look at these babies? Made 'em myself. Holy water, silver shavings, white oak—the works.

ABE (*pulling his hand away*)
Behind this door. A dark entity— Evil, ancient, *and* hungry.

Abe quickly starts scanning a few leather-bound volumes of ancient magic.

HELLBOY

Oh, well. Lemme go in and say "hi."

As Hellboy opens the big doors, a flickering amber glow illuminates him. He steps inside.

Interior, "Magik Exhibition" Hall— Night. Blue emergency lamps are on. The exhibits are destroyed; piles of debris are burning. Hellboy walks past a fallen display case. He moves around cautiously. A couple of large carvings and statues startle him. On the floor: boots, half chewed. Bitten belts and shreds of uniforms and hats.

HELLBOY (*whispers into radio*)

Blue, it stinks in here—Finely aged roadkill.

The sickening sound of snapping bones and mastication reaches his ears. Hellboy reacts to a smell, raises his eyes to discover …

A huge pale creature hangs from the ceiling, chewing slowly. Sammael: equipped with powerful arms, a head full of tentacles and two well-muscled hind legs. Most of its face is hidden, but the jaws are shiny with blood.

HELLBOY

Hey. Stinky. Kitchen's closed. (*Beat.*) Whatcha havin'? Six library guards, raw? Plus belts and boots? Man, you're gonna need some heavy fiber to move that out—

ABE (*in earphone*)

Red, I found something—

Interior, Main Corridor / Machen Library (Set)—Night. Abe has found a small, medieval engraving of Sammael in one of the books.

ABE

There's not much here. The entity's name is Sammael, the desolate one, son of Nergal—

BIGGER THAN LIFE
From del Toro's memo "Hellboy Visual Notes."
In many Mignola sets, DARKNESS engulfs everything and light HIGHLIGHTS only the important sculptural details. We usually showcase a BIGGER THAN LIFE ELEMENT (the giant furnace, the giant clock, etc.).

—GdT

INT. MAGIK EXHIBITION

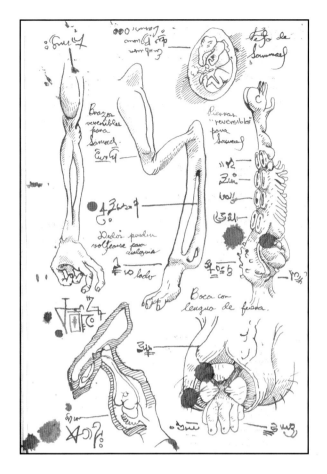

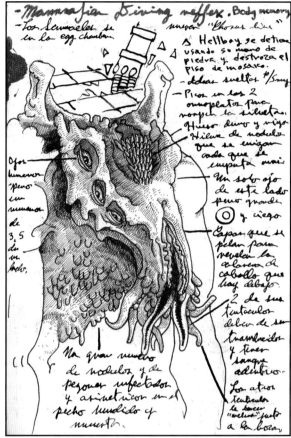

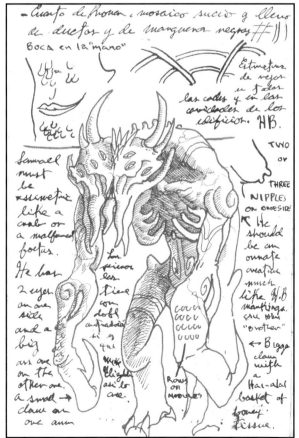

Opposite: This painting by Wayne Barlowe was commissioned by del Toro as a way to breathe life into the project years before filming would begin. The painting reflects the early idea of putting Hellboy's giant hand on the left arm rather than the right, as it is in the comics. This would allow the actor full use of his right hand. The fact that Ron Perlman is ambidextrous allowed the filmmakers to preserve the Right Hand of Doom.

This page: Sammael sketches from del Toro's diary.

MIGNOLA ON SAMMAEL

My creature designs were deemed "too nice." Del Toro would often comment, "I want to have a drink with them."

—MM

HELLBOY
"Sammael1"
6/20/02

- HELLBOY -
"SAMMAEL 4"
6/21/02

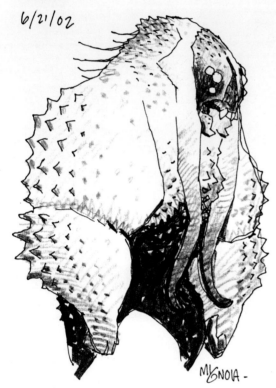

HELLBOY
"SAMMAEL"
6
6/21/02

HELLBOY
"SAMMAEL ▦"
5
6/21/02

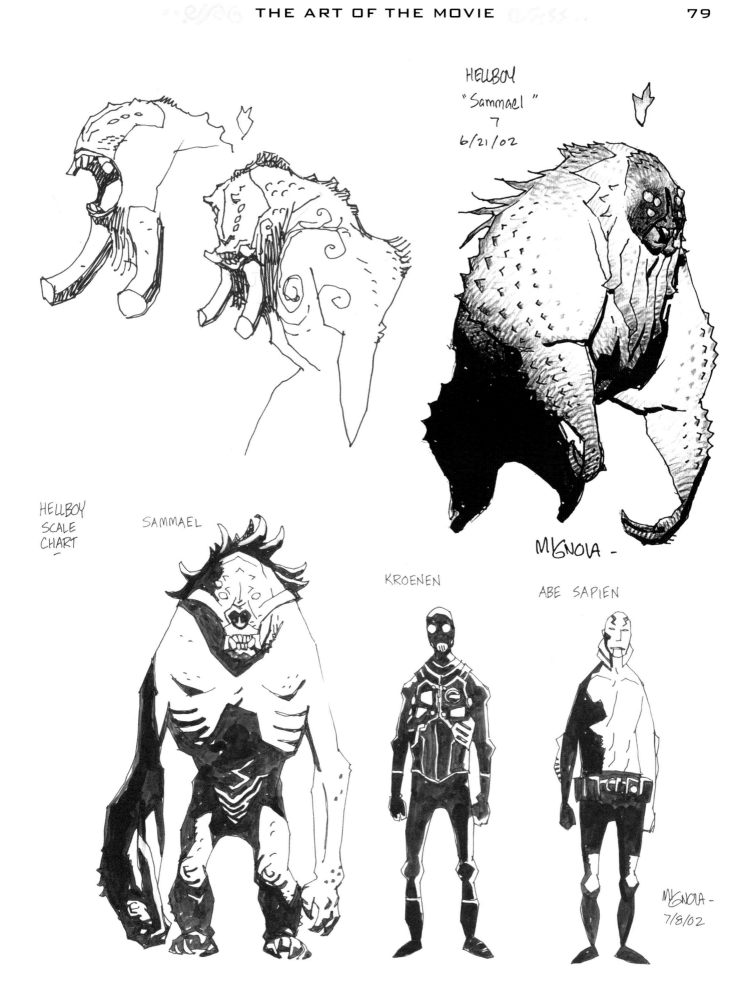

HELLBOY
"Sammael"
7
6/21/02

M¹GNOLA -

HELLBOY
SCALE
CHART
-

SAMMAEL

KROENEN

ABE SAPIEN

M¹GNOLA -
7/8/02

UNFLYABLE · WINGS !!

SAMMAEL

from NIRASAWA

o He has tattoos
the whole body

TAIL with CLOWS

Top of Hands
coloured Red!
with thorn.

SAMMAEL FACE A

WITH · 3D-TATTOO
PIASING
&
RINGS

o skin-white
o Hair-Red

SAMMAEL
FACE B

o skin-purple
o Hair-Brown

SAMMAEL FACE B

Radical departures by Yasushi Nirazawa (above) and Katsuya Terada (opposite).

terra

Sammael
2

BARLOWE ON SAMMAEL

Working with Guillermo del Toro has to stand as one of the high points of my career. He is an extraordinarily visual director whose on-screen aesthetic must be considered unique among his peers. Understanding his desire to make imagined film characters as interesting and surprising to the viewer as possible is critical to beginning any design curve with him, and after working with him on *Blade 2* I pretty much knew what to expect.

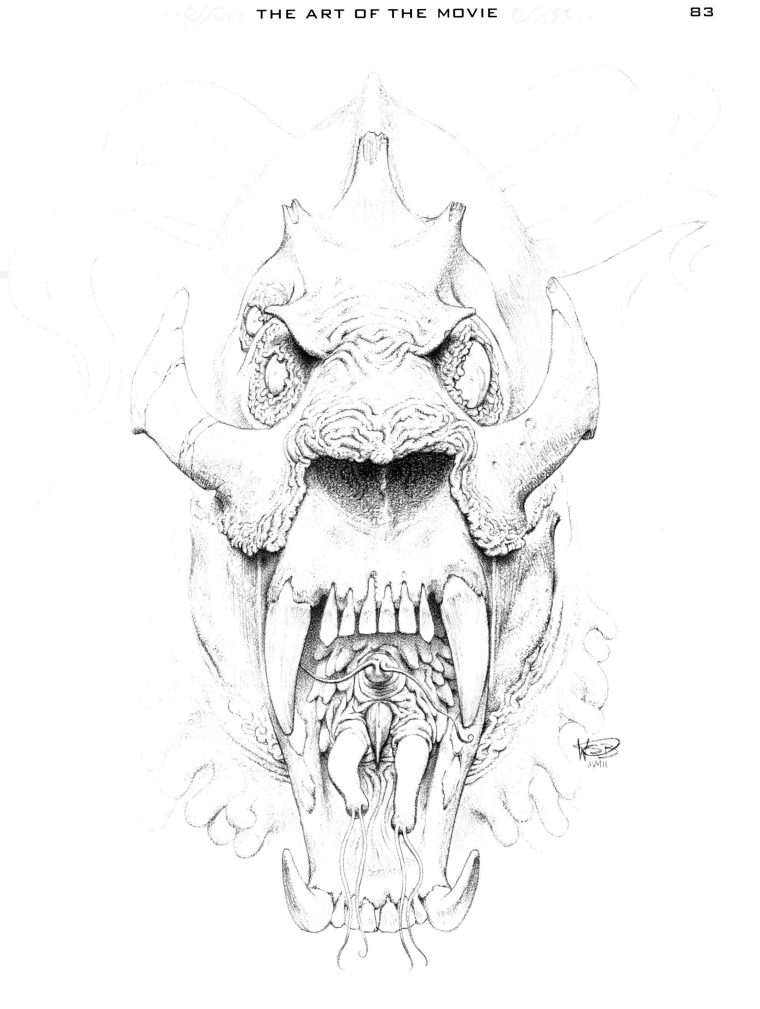

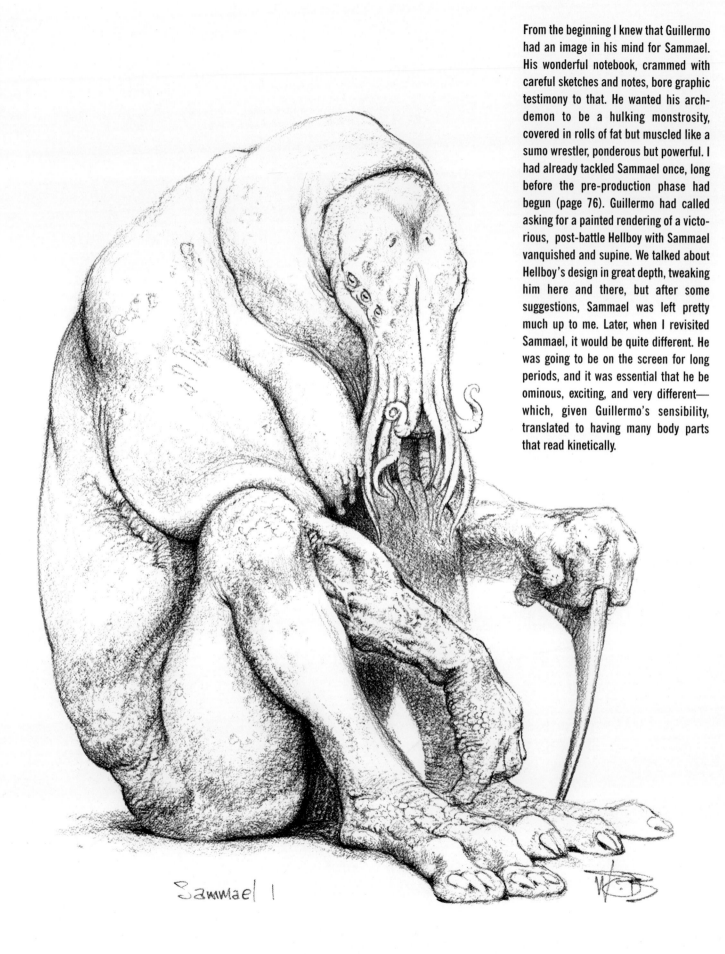

Sammael 1

From the beginning I knew that Guillermo had an image in his mind for Sammael. His wonderful notebook, crammed with careful sketches and notes, bore graphic testimony to that. He wanted his arch-demon to be a hulking monstrosity, covered in rolls of fat but muscled like a sumo wrestler, ponderous but powerful. I had already tackled Sammael once, long before the pre-production phase had begun (page 76). Guillermo had called asking for a painted rendering of a victorious, post-battle Hellboy with Sammael vanquished and supine. We talked about Hellboy's design in great depth, tweaking him here and there, but after some suggestions, Sammael was left pretty much up to me. Later, when I revisited Sammael, it would be quite different. He was going to be on the screen for long periods, and it was essential that he be ominous, exciting, and very different—which, given Guillermo's sensibility, translated to having many body parts that read kinetically.

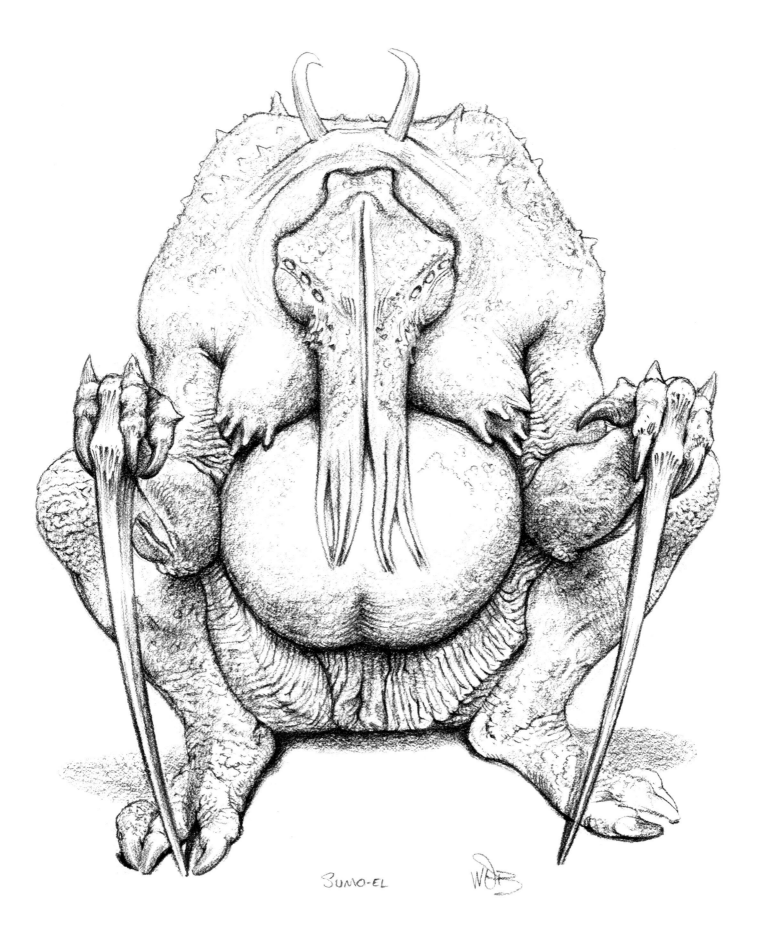

SUMO-EL

The initial parameters included a C'thulhu-like head festooned with lots of dangling bits and tentacles, scimitar-like fingers, and a large paunch; gone were the wings from the original painting, but the multiple eyes remained. It all sounded intriguing to me. I thought the idea of breaking from the norm—the predictable, heavily muscled villain—was refreshing. And so I began what would turn out to be something of a personal quest, a search with the director for the proper balance between the horrific and the unorthodox. Our goal was to scare the audience with a nightmare creature unlike any they had seen before.

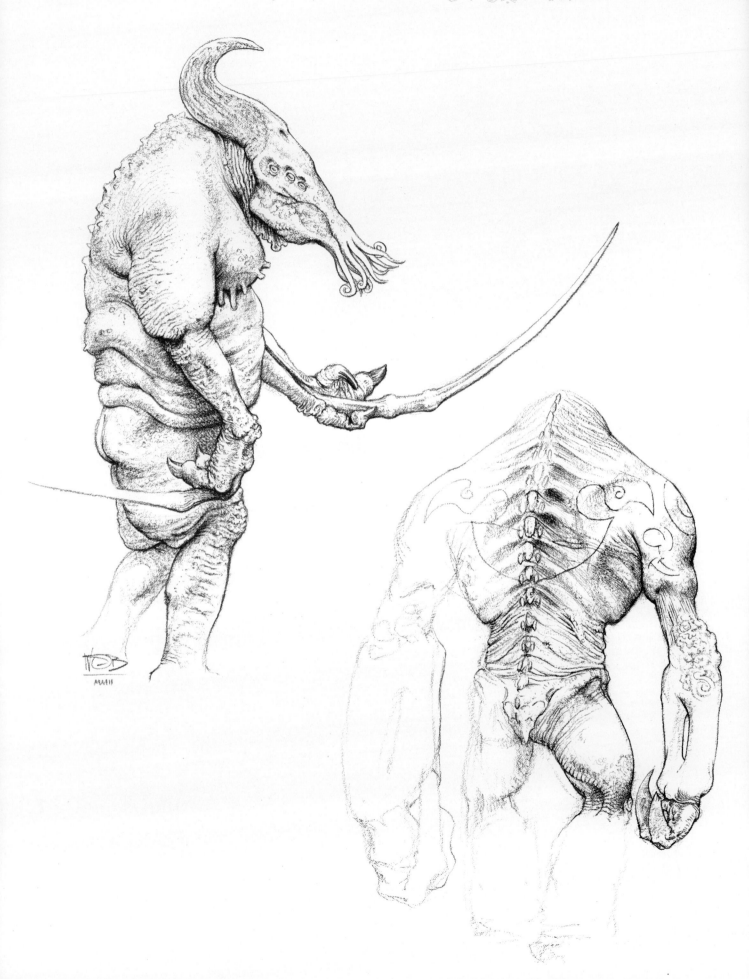

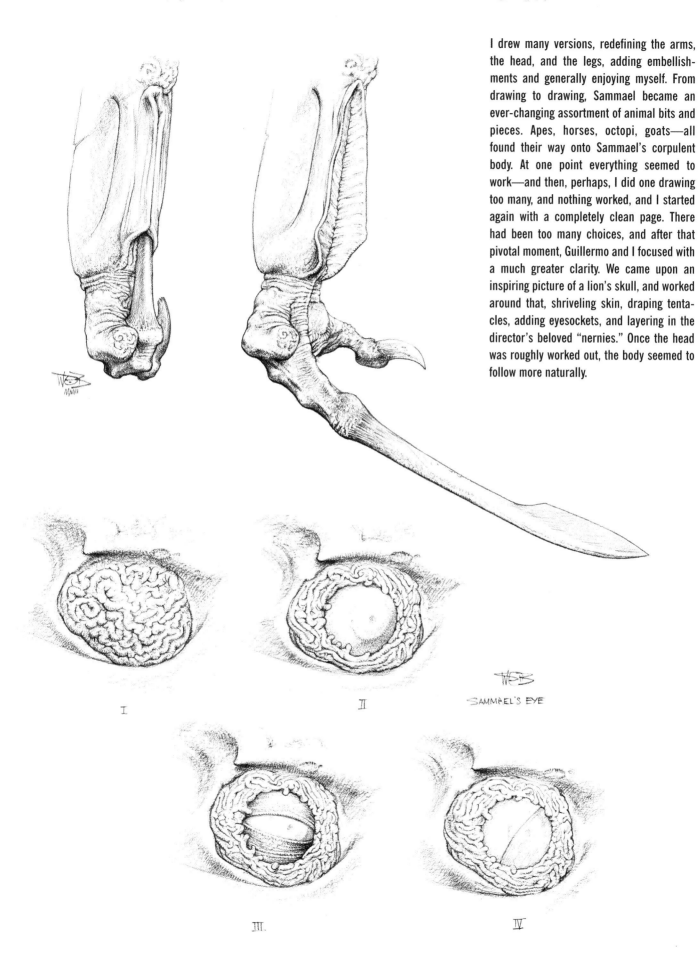

I drew many versions, redefining the arms, the head, and the legs, adding embellishments and generally enjoying myself. From drawing to drawing, Sammael became an ever-changing assortment of animal bits and pieces. Apes, horses, octopi, goats—all found their way onto Sammael's corpulent body. At one point everything seemed to work—and then, perhaps, I did one drawing too many, and nothing worked, and I started again with a completely clean page. There had been too many choices, and after that pivotal moment, Guillermo and I focused with a much greater clarity. We came upon an inspiring picture of a lion's skull, and worked around that, shriveling skin, draping tentacles, adding eyesockets, and layering in the director's beloved "nernies." Once the head was roughly worked out, the body seemed to follow more naturally.

SAMMAEL'S EYE

I

II

III.

IV

In a creative sense, Sammael is very much the director's child; I am merely the surgeon who managed to wrest him—using a pencil, not forcep—from the dark incunabula of Guillermo's mind.

—WB

Del Toro wanted to change the legs on Barlowe's otherwise final Sammael drawing, and asked Mignola to do it, resulting in this unique collaboration.

MMIII

SAMMAEL

Sammael study
Smaller legs—

MIGNOLA'S SAMMAEL

I did this drawing based on Wayne's final design, just to satisfy my curiosity, to see the character rendered in my style. I wanted to see what it would look like if he appeared in the comic.

—MM

HELLBOY
SAMMAEL
7/8/02

MIGNOLA
AFTER BARLOWE

Interior, "Magik Exhibition" Hall—Night. Sammael releases himself, lands on the floor. Part of the neck is exposed: white, slimy skin, cracked like old marble and criss-crossed with blue veins.

HELLBOY
Hold it—(*Beat.*) Hey, Sammy, whaddayasay we work this out? Peacefully. I'm not a great shot, but—(*Raises his gun*)—"The Samaritan" here, uses really big bullets, so whaddyasay we work this out?

Sammael stands and turns around—Crack-kk! His waist twists him 360 degrees! Screeching, Sammael leaps away! Hellboy shoots. The high-caliber ammo rips a few columns apart and finally catches Sammael. The bullet goes through it and destroys a statue and a large window behind him. The monster squeals and goes down. With a rattling cough, it grows still.

HELLBOY
That's all for you, Sammy.

ABE'S VOICE (*in earpiece*)
Red—you need to hear the rest of the information—

Hellboy turns away for a moment. Puts his gun away, like a gunslinger.

HELLBOY
Nah—he's taken care of.

Interior, Machen Library—Exhibit Corridor Doors—Night.

ABE
No, listen this—Sammael, the desolate one, lord of the shadows, son of Nergal—

Interior, Machen Library—"Magik Exhibition" Hall—Night.

ABE'S VOICE
—hound of resurrection—

HELLBOY
See? I don't like that—

ABE'S VOICE
—hound of resurrection?

Hellboy looks back at the corpse: it's gone!

ABE'S VOICE
—harbinger of pestilence, seed of destruction—

HELLBOY
Skip to the end, willya? How do I kill it—?

ABE'S VOICE
It doesn't say—

Bammm! From out of nowhere, Sammael appears and swings an arm! Hellboy CRASHES into the brass doors!

Interior, Machen Library—Exhibit Corridors—Night. The doors bulge and crack under Hellboy's impact. Abe and Broom backpedal fast. Myers pulls out his gun, and starts looking for another way in. Broom observes this, pleased.

Interior, Machen Library—"Magik Exhibition" Hall—Night. Sammael lashes out with a massive punch. Hellboy goes K-krash! K-krash! through six glass cabinets, then hits a window, falling—

Exterior, an Alley—Behind Machen Library—Night—two stories down, landing sideways in an industrial garbage bin. Hellboy fights to stay conscious. Blood drips from his mouth.

GRIGORY'S VOICE
Child …

Hellboy looks up: standing in the alley, like an apparition, is Grigory, in a black suit and overcoat, his eyes shielded by pitch-black sunglasses.

GRIGORY
All grown up, I see.

Hellboy's in shock, confused.

HELLBOY
That voice—

GRIGORY
I sang the first lullaby you ever heard, my child. I ushered you into this world. (*Beat.*) I alone know your true calling, your true name.

HELLBOY
Don't tell me, it's Zeppo.

Hellboy catches sight of his big gun, lying on the ground. He goes for it, but Bammm! Sammael lands before him.

GRIGORY
I can see that you're still young and don't know your place. (*Turns to Sammael.*) Teach him.

Before Hellboy can reach the weapon—Wshhhp! A 7-foot tongue lashes out from Sammael's mouth like a whip. It's arm-thick, with yellow sacs billowing from its sides. It wraps around Hellboy's right arm. Hellboy falls to the ground, writhing, grinding his teeth. The tongue squeezes and pulls. Smoke pours from Hellboy's skin.

Exterior, an Alley—Behind Machen Library—Night. Then—Bang! Bang! Bang! Myers appears at the end of the alley, firing round after round into Sammael's tongue. Amber blood explodes in the air. The tongue recoils with an infernal squeal! Hellboy manages to roll away.

Myers goes for Hellboy's gun … and grabs it! He takes cover behind the trash container. Hellboy is there.

HELLBOY
What do you think you're doing?

Myers proudly shows him the gun.

MYERS
Helping you—I just—

HELLBOY
No one *ever* helps me. It's *my* job.

He grabs his gun and tries to reload, but his arm hurts too much.

HELLBOY
Damn—Okay. Here—

He hands him the gun and a fresh clip. Reaching into his belt, Hellboy extracts a vacuum-sealed packet. He throws it at Myers.

HELLBOY
Then load this.

In the packet: a single bullet.

HELLBOY
It's a tracking bullet. Crack the pin. Load it.

Klang! The tongue punches through the steel like a ramrod. Again and again … Hellboy and Myers can barely dodge it. Myers cracks a safety pin. The glass head on the bullet glows like a chemical flare.

MYERS
Jeez … What the hell is that?

He's looking at Hellboy's smoking arm. Inside a bloody gash, a big, black stinger is gleaming. Hellboy pulls it out, then steps on it. It pops like a ripe grape.

HELLBOY
Lemme go ask—

Hellboy steps from behind the container. Sammael's tongue instantly wraps around the gun's muzzle. Bam! Bam! Hellboy shoots repeatedly. His face lit weirdly green as the tracking bullet lodges within the gun. Then—Bam!

KBS-13A ○ 13A
WARNING! AVOID EXPOSURE TO SUNLIGHT
SHELL CONTENTS: ST-F
MANUFACTURED IN JAPAN

Package Made from Recycled Board
Elaborado en Cartón Reciclado

0 88698 85771 7

BULLET PACKAGE — TGRUBEH
SPECIAL LOAD
HELLBOY AUG 2002

PUMPKIN STANDS

Inside gun shot. The glowing bullet flies through the barrel and out toward—

Exterior, Alley—Sammael, still in mid-air. It hits him square in the chest: an explosion of green goo! With a shriek, the thing leaps over a wall. Hellboy scrambles after it.

Exterior, Loading Alley—Night. On the empty sidewalk, Hellboy sees a trail of glowing goop. He hits full stride, following it around a corner. Myers lands a second later, cradling his arm, chasing after him.

MYERS
Wait! No, what are you doing?

Loading Dock / Alley. Sammael dashes by, followed closely by Hellboy, running

full tilt. A ten-wheeler backs up, effectively blocking their way. A few workers load pumpkin boxes in it.

WORKER 1
What the hell is that?

Without slowing down, Sammael jumps onto the trailer, denting the roof then jumping off and into a crowded carnival area. A small carousel and refreshment stand flank a pumpkin patch. Full of curiosity, Sammael pauses a second to inspect a trick-or-treater dressed as a golden dragon. Hellboy catapults himself onto the trailer's roof.

3 WORKERS (*chorus*)
Whoa-whoa-whoa—

Hellboy jumps and lands heavily on top of the driver's cab: Crash! The driver is

almost crushed under the steel. He screams, showered by thousands of glass shards. Myers is a few steps behind.

MYERS (*into headset*)
We'll hit the street in a minute. We're heading toward civilians …

He squeezes between the vehicle and the alley wall. The vendors are yelling at him.

MYERS
Yeah, yeah, crazy costume, huh? Trick or treat!

Exterior, West Side Street—Night. Sammael runs past a group of trick-or-treaters, and jumps straight into the street. Cars swerve, avoiding a collision as Sammael lands on the opposite sidewalk. The trick-or-treaters scream.

Hellboy appears. He too dives straight into the traffic as Myers follows. He runs into the road … and a 4X4 speeds straight at him! Seeing this, Hellboy runs back, and lands next to Myers, holds out his stone hand and stops the 4x4 dead in its tracks. The impact somersaults the car over them both. It lands with a thud on the street, air bags exploding. Myers almost faints. Other cars stop, tires squealing and horns blaring. A major traffic jam.

HELLBOY
Are you okay?

Myers opens his eyes, nods.

HELLBOY
Good. Stay here.

He moves after Sammael.

Exterior Alley—Night. Hellboy follows the glowing goop into an adjacent alley. At the far end he sees a metal grate has been moved. Sammael's gone. He comes up to the opening, then jumps in.

Exterior/Interior, Stunt Tracks Tunnel— Night. He lands on a subway track. Sammael is a few yards away. Seated.

HELLBOY
Waiting for me, Sammy?

A train horn blares. A headlight approaches! Hellboy smiles and puts away his gun.

HELLBOY
Uh-oh—between a rock and a hard place—

But Sammael sprints toward it!

HELLBOY
Aw, crap—

Sammael unhinges a long, scythe-like bone from his forearm, then jumps at the front car—

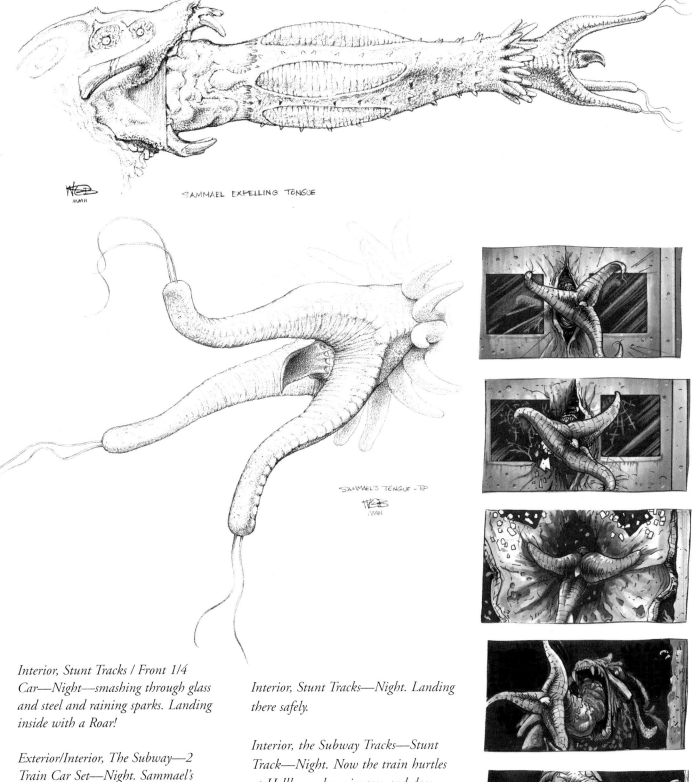

SAMMAEL EXPELLING TONGUE

SAMMAEL'S TONGUE-TIP

Interior, Stunt Tracks / Front 1/4 Car—Night—smashing through glass and steel and raining sparks. Landing inside with a Roar!

Exterior/Interior, The Subway—2 Train Car Set—Night. Sammael's tongue punches through the doors as he races through one, two passenger cars and out the—

Stunt track rear 1/4 car—rear of the train, back onto the tracks.

Interior, Stunt Tracks—Night. Landing there safely.

Interior, the Subway Tracks—Stunt Track—Night. Now the train hurtles at Hellboy, who grimaces and does his best.

Interior, Stunt Tracks Front 1/4 Car. He leaps, but Humpf! He's hit! His legs rattle over the tracks.

Interior, Undercarriage—Stunt Tracks—Front 1/4 Car—Night. Inches from the wheels, he punches his stone hand through the steel floor and grabs a handhold. Steam and sparks explode everywhere. The train driver grabs a fire extinguisher and starts slamming it against Hellboy's head.

HELLBOY
Hey! Hey! I'm on your side!

Bammm! He goes under!

Interior, Stunt Tracks—Front 1/4 Car. The train whizzes overhead, grazing his horn stumps, making sparks fly! After the train passes, Hellboy sits up, forehead smoking. Sammael is gone. A trail of goop is glowing. He follows it, until it ends abruptly. He looks ahead: no trace of Sammael … Then a fat drop of glowing goop hits his hand.

HELLBOY
Aw, I forgot—

He looks up. Sammael hangs from the ceiling, then drops. Then the creature lifts Hellboy in a ferocious bear hug. Hellboy twists around and cracks open the jaws of the creature, like King Kong and the T-Rex. Sammael staggers back and—in an impossible maneuver— re-knits his jaws together! Then he uses his bone scythe to tackle Hellboy and— Tchakkkk!—pin his shoulder down. A deep wound. Sammael's mouth starts to open! Hellboy looks at the sparking third rail a few feet away. Sammael's tongue rears back, a snake ready to strike.

HELLBOY
Screw you.

Hellboy grabs the rail. An electrical discharge consumes both creatures and burns the frame like flashpaper. Hellboy lets go, his hand and body smoking. Sammael—very crispy—is convulsing in a cloud of smoke. He grows still.

Wreathed in smoke, Hellboy shakes off the shock and uses a flame on his arm to light a cigar.

HELLBOY
I'm fireproof. (*Puffs smoke, kicks the body.*) You weren't.

Exterior—West Side Highway—Night. A huge traffic jam clogs the highway. The totalled 4X4 is being towed away. Several TV crews interview witnesses. Myers—his arm freshly bandaged—signs a police form. His radio beeps.

HELLBOY (*voice over*)
Myers? How's your arm?

MYERS
My arm is fine. Where are you?

Myers moves away from the police officers.

MYERS (*sotto voce*)
Where are you?

Interior, Subway Tracks—Stunt Track—Hellboy walks away from the smoking Sammael carcass.

HELLBOY
I just fried Stinky. Tell Father I'll be home. He shouldn't wait up.

Exterior, West Side Highway—same.

MYERS
Wait—Wait—You can't go anywhere—I gotta go with you—

Interior, Subway Tracks—Stunt Track.

HELLBOY
No, no, no, it's fine—I do my job, I take a break.

MYERS (*voice over*)
No. Stop. Don't do this—Listen to me—Tell me where you are—

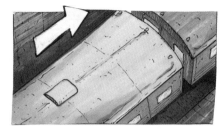

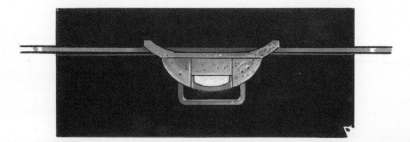

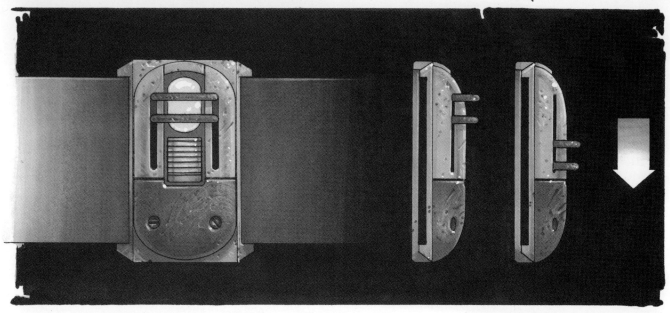

TOP VIEW   SIDE VIEWS ↓

BPRD LOCATOR DEVICE
HELLBOY - AUG 21 2002
T. TRUBEN ELLINGSON
PAGE 1 OF 2

BPRD LOCATOR DEVICE - FRONT VIEW (EXACT SCALE TO BE BASED ON BELT WIDTH)

HELLBOY
Myers?

MYERS (*voice over*)
Yes?

HELLBOY
Goodbye.

He turns off his belt locator and moves away into the darkness of the tunnel. In the foreground: black light escapes from Sammael's charred body.

Interior, Main Abandoned Baths Alcove—Night. An abandoned shower room. A series of sinks and stalls, lined with dirty white tile. A phonograph nearby plays Wagner. Kroenen stands next to it. Ilsa is nearby, a straight razor glinting in her hand. She stands over

Grigory—his back to us—lovingly shaving her master's scalp. She grabs two glass eyes from a table. Places them in Grigory's sockets—his back to us—as he turns, a glass eye shifts lazily into position. He opens his hand: in it the pale black light that escaped from Sammael's body. He cradles it like a precious stone.

GRIGORY (*smiling*)
Sammael has fulfilled his destiny … Die in peace and be reborn again and again …

He closes his fist.

ILSA
Only seven more days to the eclipse, Grishka …

Rasputin stands, his neck and shoulders

rising, engorged by moving flesh beneath his human skin. Ilsa stares in fascination.

GRIGORY
The child will be there. And so will we all—Won't we?

Behind him, in the darkness of a tunnel: two Sammael silhouettes appear. Cut to:

Exterior, Machen Library Entrance—Night. A sleek black limo drives past the crowd and stops outside. FBI agent Tom Manning emerges.

Interior, "Magik Exhibit" Hall—Night. Manning and Broom walk through the mess. A crew is cleaning up. The dead guards are carried out.

BIOGRAPHY:
ILSA HAUPSTEIN

AUGUST HAUPSTEIN, OWNER OF A MUNICH CHEMICAL LAB, AND HIS WIFE BERTHA PRODUCED THEIR FIRST CHILD — ILSA — IN 1902.

AUGUST EXPECTED HIS FIRST-BORN TO BE A SON, SO HE EDUCATED THE GIRL TOWARD A LIFE STRICTLY "FEMININE."

HE ORDERED HER TO A CONVENT SCHOOL, TO LEARN THE SKILLS USEFUL TO SECURING A PROPER MARRIAGE.

BUT THE ABUSE SHE ENDURED AT THE HANDS OF THE SADISTIC NUNS TURNED HER IN AN OPPOSITE DIRECTION.

AWAKENED TO THE HORRORS AND PLEASURES OF SIN, SHE ONE NIGHT RECEIVED THE VISION OF A BRIGHT ANGEL.

THE BEING PREDICTED THAT A MAN WOULD APPEAR AND MAKE ILSA HIS BRIDE. FROM THEM BOTH WOULD SPRING FORTH A NEW AGE.

FROM THAT NIGHT, SHE WAS FREE — THE MASTER OF HER OWN DESTINY.

ONE EVENING, A DOSE OF ATROPA BELLADONA FOUND ITS WAY ONTO THE HEAD NUN'S DINNER PLATE.

AS SHE MATURED, ILSA WAS A BRILLIANT STUDENT OF THE SCIENCES: BOTANY, PHYSICS, CHEMISTRY.

SHE WAS ALSO A REBEL AND HEDONIST, TAKING LOVERS OF BOTH SEXES, SEEKING EVERY STIMULUS AVAILABLE.

HER OCCULT STUDIES BROUGHT INTO HER CIRCLE SEVERAL MEMBERS OF THE NAZI ELITE — AMONG THEM HEINRICH HIMMLER.

AN ARDENT PARTY MEMBER, SHE APPEARED IN PUBLIC AT THE 1934 NUREMBURG RALLY.

IN 1940, SHE ENGINEERED THE DEATH OF HER FATHER, FOR WHOM SHE CARRIED AN ABIDING HATRED.

SHE THEN APPLIED A LARGE PORTION OF HER FAMILY'S FORTUNE TO THE GERMAN WAR EFFORT.

AT A RECEPTION, SHE WAS INTRODUCED TO GRIGORY RASPUTIN. SHE RECOGNIZED HIM FROM HER VISION.

HER MASTER, HER LIBERATOR, SHE SUBMITTED TO HIM COMPLETELY.

ILSA ROSE QUICKLY WITHIN THE NAZI RANKS, LEAVING IN HER WAKE COUNTLESS ATROCITIES.

SHE WAS DEFINITELY KNOWN TO BE A PART OF THE "HELLBOY INCIDENT" OF 1944.

SHORTLY THEREAFTER, SHE VANISHED WITHOUT A TRACE.

SHE HAS BEEN SEEN SPORADICALLY SINCE THAT TIME, BUT HAS SOMEHOW MANAGED TO ELUDE CAPTURE.

HER BEAUTY HAS REMAINED UNCHANGED OVER THE DECADES.

NOW CONNECTED TO SEVERAL TERRORIST SECTS, SHE HAS DECLARED: "I WOULD CUT OPEN THE WORLD TO SEE IT BLEED."

MANNING
Every time the media get a look at him, they come to *me*. I'm running out of lies, Trevor.

BROOM
I thought you liked being on TV.

MANNING
I do. (*Beat.*) How many escapes? This year alone—five!

BROOM
Tom—he's our guest, not a prisoner.

MANNING
Your "guest" happens to be six foot five, bright red, and is government funded.

BROOM
He's just going through a phase—

Manning moistens and lights a fine cigar, using a kitchen match.

MANNING
A "phase"? What do you think this is, "The Brady Bunch"? These … *freaks*—

Abe Sapien listens while pacing the exhibition hall, palm open.

MANNING (*lowers his voice, tense*)
These freaks, Trevor, they give me the creeps. And I'm not the only one. You're up for review. You and your petting zoo.

BROOM
I know where to find him. I'll get him back.

Manning watches as Abe finds a sharp dagger embedded in the floor.

MANNING
Hey, fishstick—Don't touch anything—

Abe silences him.

ABE
I need to touch it to "see" …

MANNING
See what?

ABE
The past, the future, whatever this object holds.

MANNING (*eyes Broom*)
Is he serious?

ABE
Don't worry about fingerprints. I never had any.

Abe holds the dagger in his hand, turns to Broom.

ABE
They were over here, Professor.

MANNING
Oooh! Who was here? Nixon? Houdini? You mind sharing your mystic insights?

Broom examines the dagger: a Ragnarok symbol crowns the hilt. The dragon and swastika.

BROOM
Show me, Abe … show me.

He solemnly extends his hand. As soon as Abe takes it, the room … Morphs to:

Interior, "Magik Exhibit" Hall—Flashback. Hours earlier: the place is intact. Both Abe and Broom witness spectrally as a guard checks an alarm monitoring unit. Hearing a ticking sound, he shines his light into a dark corner: no one's there. But after the guard moves on, a spidery form emerges from the pool of shadows on the floor.

It's Kroenen, encased in shiny black latex from head to toe. On his chest, a close-fitting harness comprised of softly ticking gears. He approaches a glass case which holds an ancient wooden statue of an Eastern Orthodox saint. Then, on the glass, a reflection: Ilsa.

BIOGRAPHY: KARL RUPRECHT KROENEN

BORN IN MUNICH IN 1897, YOUNG KARL RUPRECHT WAS BLESSED WITH ANGELIC FEATURES AND A HALO OF BLONDE HAIR.

AS A CHILD, HE TOURED THE CAPITALS OF EUROPE. AUDIENCES THRILLED TO HIS FINE, PURE, SINGING VOICE.

AS HE GREW, HE LEARNED THE VALUE OF PAIN AND SELF-DISCIPLINE.

EACH DAY, HE WHIPPED HIMSELF WITH A FRESH BRANCH OF OAK—THERE FINDING A STRANGE ECSTASY.

PUBERTY ENDED THE CAREER OF THE "MUNICH SONGBIRD." HE LOATHED HIS AWKWARDNESS AND LONGED FOR PERFECTION.

HIS AFFINITY FOR ALL THINGS MECHANICAL LED HIM TO THE DESIGN OF CLOCKS, TOYS, AND COMPLEX AUTOMATA.

KROENEN WAS CERTAIN THAT THE FUTURE OF HUMANITY LAY IN THE MARRIAGE OF FLESH AND MACHINE.

HE UNVEILED A MECHANICAL CHERUB CAPABLE OF SINGING AN ENTIRE MOZART ARIA WITHOUT INTERRUPTION.

HE CONDUCTED A SERIES OF BRUTAL EXPERIMENTS TO "ENHANCE" HIS FACE, ONLY TO DEFORM IT HORRIBLY.

HE FASHIONED A TIGHT-FITTING MASK, WHICH FILTERED OUT GERMS. KROENEN WAS OBSESSED WITH PURITY.

HE MET GRIGORY RASPUTIN IN 1930 AND QUICKLY BECAME HIS MOST LOYAL DEVOTEE.

HE ADVANCED STEADILY IN NAZI RANKS AND JOINED THE S.S. IN 1933.

HIS SKILL AT FENCING WAS LEGENDARY. HE DESIGNED AND FABRICATED HIS OWN SWORDS.

THE FUHRER ENTRUSTED HIM TO CREATE A FENCING PROGRAM FOR ARYAN YOUTH.

AS COMMANDANT AT AUSCHWITZ, KROENEN SERVED WITH DISTINCTIVE ENTHUSIASM.

THE NUREMBURG COURT, WHICH INDICTED HIM IN ABSENTIA, CHARGED HIM WITH "BLOOD-LUST."

HE PAINSTAKINGLY DEVELOPED HIS PORTAL GENERATOR, WHICH WAS AT LAST PUT TO THE TEST IN OCTOBER OF 1944.

AFTER THIS, HE WAS NEVER SEEN AGAIN.

RECORDS WERE FOUND OF HIS EXPERIMENTS TO FUSE STEEL AND BONE.

PILES OF CHILDRENS SHOES LAY NEXT TO THE FURNACE OF HIS HOME IN VIENNA.

IN 1956, AN UNMARKED GRAVE WAS FOUND IN ROMANIA. DENTAL RECORDS IDENTIFIED THE REMAINS: KARL RUPRECHT KROENEN.

MANY, HOWEVER, DO NOT BELIEVE THAT HE IS DEAD... CHIEF AMONGST THEM: KROENEN HIMSELF!

KROENEN'S VEST

Kroenen's vest is pure del Toro, by way of super-genius Ty Ellingson. Del Toro walked in knowing exactly what he wanted this character to be. I thought it was fascinating to see a character of mine turned into something I never imagined—it was great.

—MM

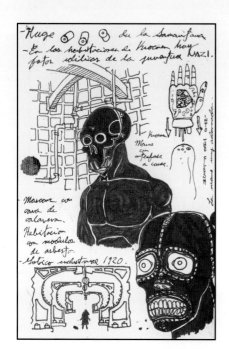

From del Toro's diary.

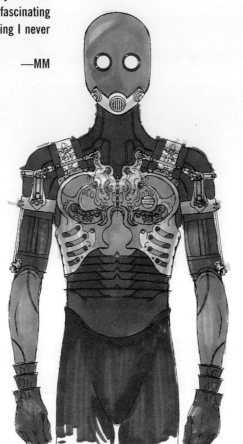

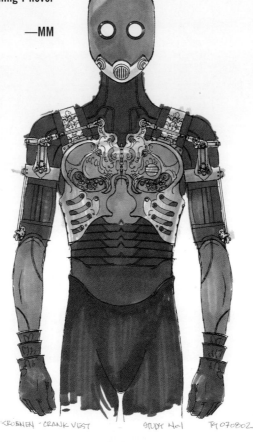

KROENEN - CRANK VEST　　STUDY No.1　　TY 070802

SANDOVAL/02

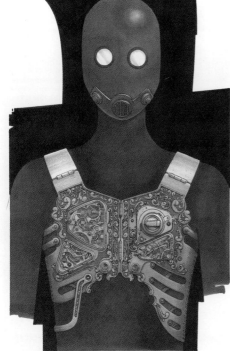

KROENEN'S CLOCKWORK VEST No.3　HELLBOY　R.RUBEN ELLINGSON 6.29

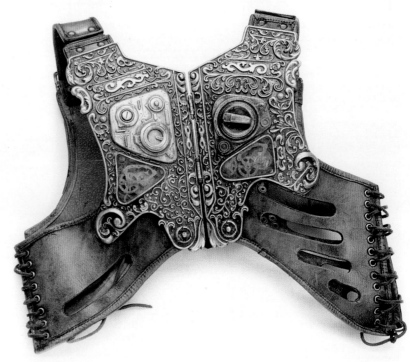

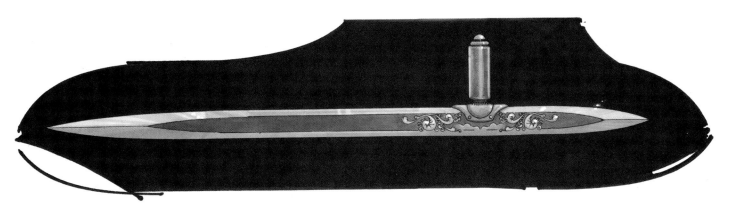

KROENEN'S BATON SWORD   HELLBOY   P.RUBEN ELLINGSON
* EXACT SCALE TO BE BASED ON ACTORS ARM

ILSA
Move.

She uses her hammer to destroy the glass case. The alarm shrieks. Warning lights come on. Kroenen pulls out a double-ended Blade. It spins, like a giant bone saw, slicing across the statue. No apparent damage until—Crackkkkk!—a diagonal line appears and the top half falls.

Kroenen reaches for a small crank embedded in his chest and winds himself up. Ilsa reaches into a hollow portion in the wooden statue and removes a large reliquary jar containing golden sand.

Six guards hurry in. They point their flashlights and guns at Kroenen.

GUARD 1
You! Don't move! Hands up!

Kroenen starts shaking, as if in a seizure and readies two twin blades. A bullet tears into Kroenen's arm, spewing forth an explosion of dust. He turns. The guards shoot again. Kroenen maneuvers the steel, deflecting the bullets which ricochet wildly and finally hit three of the guards. They fall silently to the floor. Kroenen dispatches two more in a flurry of knives. The last guard raises his gun.

GUARD 6
Don't—

Something is clearly stopping him. His hand breaks, twisted by an unseen force! The flesh on his neck pushes upwards, held by an invisible force. He starts floating in mid-air. The blinking lights of arriving police cars tint the windows red and amber. They outline a figure formerly submerged in shadows. Grigory. He gestures with both hands, as if holding an imaginary doll.

His arm muscles twitch under his skin, shifting, changing, gaining strength. With a quick gesture Grigory twists the lower and upper parts of the guard's body in opposite directions. With a wet crunch, the guard's shadow on the wall goes limp. Grigory looks at Ilsa.

GRIGORY
Ready the welcome, my love—

Ilsa opens the reliquary jar and pours a circle of sand onto the floor.

GRIGORY
Salt. Gathered from the tears of a thousand martyrs. Restraining the essence of Sammael, the hell hound, the seed of destruction.

Grigory slices the air with his open

hand, creating fleeting glyphs ... and a small black flame dances on his open palm. He deposits it in mid-air, at the center of the circle.

Then, the sand begins to move, like liquid mercury. Lines fuse into a pile. It melts and bubbles, growing and foaming. Bones are formed, tendons and ligaments join together, growing, growing, into Sammael. It roars! Cut to:

Interior, Machen Library—Night. Abe snaps out of it. Broom is pale. He steps away, wincing, enduring a bolt of pain in his side. Abe holds him. Motions for the others to stay back. He extends his open palm and "feels" the air near the old man's back.

ABE
Professor …? You—are very sick—

BROOM
I don't want Hellboy to know—

Broom turns around, gently pushes Abe's hand away.

BROOM
Sixty years ago, Abe, they tried to destroy the world. And they are back—in my lifetime, they are back. To finish the job.

EXTERIOR BELLAMIE
HOSPITAL - GARDEN AREA

NEW FRONT
ENTRANCE

GAZEEBO

Cut to:

Exterior, Central Park—Night. A small nighttime Hallowe'en celebration. Lanterns hanging from the trees, couples drinking and listening to pop music on picnic tables. On a bench, a young guy pulls out a cold six pack of beer and passionately kisses his girlfriend. As he shuts his eyes, a bright, red tail neatly snatches the six-pack.

Behind the bench, Hellboy smiles.

Exterior, Bellamie Mental Hospital—Night. Dry leaves fly up in a gust of wind. A small army of emergency vehicles roars down the deserted streets, right past a brick 1940s hospital, behind a high wall topped with barbed wire. The mesh-covered windows are decorated with paper skeletons and jack-o'-lanterns. A topiary garden surrounds the building.

Watching from atop the wall is Hellboy. One sleeve of his overcoat is soaked in blood. He keeps an eye on the second-floor windows. Hanging from his tail: the six pack of beer.

Interior, Bellamie Mental Hospital Corridor—Night. Doctor Marsh, a female psychiatrist, moves down a line of patients, distributing pills. Behind her, a lithe young woman in a patient's gown carries the medicine tray. This is Liz Sherman, age 26, her pale skin contrasting with her raven-black hair and piercing dark eyes. A scar mars her forehead. Three thick rubber bands circle her wrist.

Near a window, a Down's Syndrome patient senses something.

DOWN'S PATIENT (*pointing*)
There's a big red guy down there!

DOCTOR MARSH (*readying more pills*)
That's fine, darling, Santa's not here for another month.

DOWN'S PATIENT
Not Santa. Big and red. With gold eyes. And he has beer!

Hearing this, Liz stops. She closes her eyes, tugs at one of the rubber bands on her wrist and lets it snap against her skin. She winces and peers out the window. The garden below seems empty.

BIOGRAPHY: LIZ SHERMAN

BORN IN 1974, FOR HER FIRST FOUR YEARS SHE SPOKE NOT A SINGLE WORD. HER PARENTS WORRIED.

THEN ONE EVENING IT ALL CAME OUT IN A DELUGE: FROM TOTAL SILENCE TO FULL ARTICULATION IN A FEW HOURS.

HER FATHER, EFFICIENCY EXPERT FOR SEVERAL LARGE COMPANIES, MOVED THE FAMILY AROUND THE COUNTRY.

LIZ FOUND IT DIFFICULT TO MAKE FRIENDS. SHE WAS TOO INTENSE, TOO INTELLIGENT.

THE FIRST FIRE OCCURRED WHEN SHE WAS SEVEN, IN THE FORM OF MYSTERIOUS SCORCHED PATCHES ABOUT HER BEDROOM.

NO CAUSE COULD BE FOUND. LIZ COULD ONLY REMEMBER THAT SHE HAD DREAMED OF FIRE THAT NIGHT.

THE PHENOMENON REPEATED ITSELF SEVERAL MORE TIMES. HER PARENTS WORRIED.

ONCE, HER HANDS BURST INTO FLAMES IN THE SCHOOL YARD.

HER MOTHER AND FATHER HAD FURIOUS ARGUMENTS AND EVENTUALLY DIVORCED. THEY DIDN'T BLAME LIZ: SHE BLAMED HERSELF.

SHE TOOK UP PHOTOGRAPHY, BECAUSE, "THINGS STAY STILL IN PICTURES."

HER WORLD CHANGED WHEN SHE WAS ELEVEN: AN ENTIRE COURTYARD ENGULFED IN FLAMES.

AMONG THE FATALITIES: HER OWN MOTHER. LIZ WAS THE SOLE SURVIVOR, YET SHE REMEMBERED NOTHING.

SHE SPENT HER TEEN YEARS ON THE STREET, LEARNING THE HARD CODE OF SELF-RELIANCE.

AT AGE 17, SHE MET PROF. TREVOR BROOM, AND WAS PERSUADED TO JOIN THE B.P.R.D.

SHE QUIT AND WAS WOOED BACK A DOZEN TIMES. SHE WAS QUITE THE STAR OF THE BUREAU.

SHE MET OTHERS LIKE HERSELF — EQUALLY AT ODDS WITH NORMALITY.

OVER THE YEARS, SHE FOUND SOLACE IN HELLBOY. THEY SHARED A LOVE FOR SILENT MOVIES AND OLD CARTOONS.

THEY SETTLED INTO A COMFORTABLE FRIENDSHIP, LIZ BEING UNABLE TO ABANDON HERSELF TO ANYTHING MORE.

THEN CAME THE "PITTSBURGH INCIDENT" OF 2002. SIX BUREAU AGENTS ON ASSIGNMENT IN AN ABANDONED FOUNDRY.

SUDDENLY: A MILE-WIDE FIREBALL OF ENORMOUS DEVASTATION. THE ONLY SURVIVORS: LIZ SHERMAN AND HELLBOY.

BRANDED AN ARSONIST, CLASSIFIED AS A LIVING WEAPON OF MASS DESTRUCTION, SHE AGAIN TOOK TO THE ROAD.

BUT THIS TIME IT WAS MORE DIFFICULT.

Exterior, Bellamie Mental Hospital—Garden Area—Night. Liz steps out a side door into the hospital garden. Hanging from her neck: an old Polaroid camera. She follows a trail of blood to a large, thorny bush. As she circles it …

LIZ
Back so soon?

Visible in the branches, a leg and part of Hellboy's overcoat. His tail emerges, dangling the six-pack.

HELLBOY
Uh, I brought beer.

Liz shoots a Polaroid.

LIZ
To wash down my lithium pills?

(*Beat.*) I may get a few perks, H.B. But I'm still a patient.

Shyly, he climbs out from the bush. She sees the bloody arm.

LIZ
You better have that looked at.

HELLBOY
Just a scratch. (*Shrug.*) I wanted to see you.

Liz sighs.

Exterior, Bellamie Mental Hospital—Garden Area—Night. Hellboy's sitting on a bench, next to Liz.

HELLBOY
We miss you at the Bureau. Abe's crazier every day. And Father's still

mad at me—(*Liz smiles.*) Come back, Liz. Come back. I—

LIZ
No. Not this time, H.B. It's been months since I've had an episode. And you know what? I'm learning to control it.

Around her right hand a faint blue aura of fire blooms, crawling over her fingers like a velvet haze. She stares at the pale flame.

LIZ
I'm learning where it comes from. (*Beat.*) And for once in my life I'm not afraid.

She clenches her fist and puts the flame out.

BELLAMIE GDN

EXISTING TREE.

LIZ
Looks like your ride is here.

The garbage truck and the two black sedan cars have pulled into the hospital grounds. A dozen agents climb out of the vehicles.

HELLBOY
The Nanny Squad.

Angle—the cars—continuous. Clay starts toward Hellboy, but Myers stops him and turns to Broom.

MYERS
Sir, may I go first?

CLAY (*to Broom*)
Not so fast. He barely knows him—

BROOM (*cuts him off*)
Then he should make it his business to change that.

Angle—the bench—continuous. Liz stands up, puts her hand on his shoulder.

LIZ
Listen, H.B. I've got a chance out here. If you truly care about me, don't come back anymore.

Hellboy smiles sadly. She walks away.

HELLBOY
Goodnight, then.

LIZ
Goodnight.

She doesn't turn back.

HELLBOY
Yeah, I gotta go, too. Lots to do—

Feeling light-headed, he stands up. On the bench and at his feet, a pool of his own blood. He sees Myers tentatively approaching.

Perlman as a wounded Hellboy with Selma Blair as Liz Sherman.

HELLBOY
What took you so long?

MYERS
C'mon, time to go home. Tape you up.

HELLBOY
What are you, a Boy Scout?

MYERS
No. I never was.

HELLBOY (*weak*)
Could've fooled me. Go away.

Hellboy drops to his knees. Clay, Quarry, and Moss reach him. Help him up.

CLAY
C'mon, champ. You look a little woozy, there.

HELLBOY
This—? This is nothing. You know what'll kill me? (*Points at the doorway.*) Her.

Liz stands at the hospital door and sees

Hellboy keel over. A few of the agents help him to the vehicles. Myers looks back at Liz. They hold each others' gaze, their unfamiliar faces filled with curiosity. Eventually, she goes inside.

Interior, BPRD Medical Bay "A"—Night. In the depths of the BPRD infirmary, Hellboy lies flat on a stainless steel table. Broom sits alongside him. Abe peers through a magnifier at Hellboy's wounded arm.

ABE
You were burned by some organic acid.

HELLBOY
I'm lucky that way.

Using a scalpel, Abe probes the gash. Hellboy lets out a grunt.

BROOM
Son. About Rasputin—

HELLBOY
Don't worry. I'll get him soon enough—

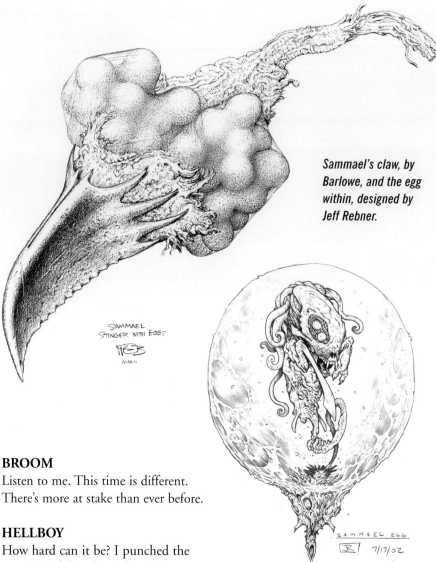

Sammael's claw, by Barlowe, and the egg within, designed by Jeff Rebner.

BROOM
Listen to me. This time is different. There's more at stake than ever before.

HELLBOY
How hard can it be? I punched the crap out of that thing that he sent—ouch!

BROOM
I worry about you.

HELLBOY
Me? C'mon—

BROOM
Well, I won't be around forever, you know?

HELLBOY
Oh, stop that—(*Grimaces in pain.*) Damn! Be careful, there—

ABE
Red. How long was it latched onto you?

HELLBOY
I dunno, maybe five seconds—ow!

MYERS
You want me to hold him down?

HELLBOY (*snickers*)
That's right, Stud, hold me down.

ABE
Professor …

Broom moves to Abe's side of the table. Abe is poking at the depths of the wound.

BROOM (*sharp, to Hellboy*)
Don't look! Turn around.

HELLBOY
Is it bad?

Broom comes closer, eyes wide: inside the wound on Hellboy's forearm, nestled like ticks, are 3 translucent eggs. Hellboy jumps as Abe plucks the first one out. Abe deposits it in a glass container.

ABE
Touched you five seconds. Laid three eggs.

HELLBOY
Didn't even buy me a drink.

Interior, Medical Bay. Examination Table—Later. The computer beeps having finished an analysis. On a monitor, an enlarged color image of one of the throbbing eggs.

ABE
The eggs are very sensitive to heat and light. They need a humid, dark environment to breed.

Abe picks up an egg with a pair of tweezers, passes it on to Hellboy, who sports a bandage on his arm.

MYERS
Down there. Did you ever lose track of him?

HELLBOY
Well, let's see—there was that moment, when I had a train on top of my head—

Broom frowns, worried.

BROOM (*to Hellboy*)
We can't risk it—You'll go back to the tracks tomorrow with a group of agents, search the area, top to bottom.

Myers observes, repelled, as inside the egg a small foetal thing wiggles.

Interior, Broom's Office—Night. Myers stands by Broom's desk as the old man places a new set of books on the reading stands in front of the fish tank.

MYERS
I'm in way over my head, I know that much.

BROOM
You're doing fine.

At the last book stand, Broom glances at Abe, who is sitting in the shadows near the door.

MYERS
No, I'm not. He respects Clay. Not me. I don't know why you chose me, Sir. But I'm not qualified.

Discouraged, Myers heads for the door.

BROOM (*very quiet*)
I'm dying, Agent Myers.

Shocked, Myers looks over at Broom.

BROOM
And as a father, I worry about him. (*Directly to Myers.*) In medieval stories, Agent Myers, there's often a young knight, inexperienced but pure of heart …

MYERS
Oh, please. I'm not "pure of heart."

ABE
Yes, you are.

BROOM
What I ask from you is—have the courage to stand by his side after I'm gone. Help him find himself. Who he must be. (*Beat.*) He was born a demon … You will help him become a man.

Interior, BPRD Archive / Conference Room—Night. Dozens of Hellboy clippings flash by: tabloid headlines along with intimate images of Hellboy as a kid. H.B. at 7, at 12, dressed as a human for Halloween, Broom by his side.

Myers works at a computer workstation. He brings up a small photograph in an

old issue of The Enquirer. *The headline: "Arson Suspect Now Working For Secret Government Agency" There's a photo of a woman, taken with a telephoto lens. Another clipping: young Liz, 11, and a photo of a tenement building burned to the ground: Tragic Explosion.*

A Quicktime interview pops up. LIZ, in her early twenties. A caption reads: Elizabeth Sherman, first interview, BPRD, Pyrokinetic. She has a Polaroid camera in her hands. Shoots one at the lens.

LIZ
I don't like the term "firestarter." I just don't. And "Pyrokinesis" sounds like psychosis or something. I dunno— maybe that's right. Not being able to let go—(*Shrug.*) Scary. Sometimes you hear so-and-so lost control and just exploded. (*Beat.*) They're lucky it isn't true. (*Looks at the camera.*) With me—it is.

Interior, Bellamie Mental Hospital—Corridor—Night. Two strolling orderlies shine their flashlights inside the rooms on both sides of a long corridor.

ARCHIVE ROOM
3 SIDED SET

CONT. : BLAST BUBBLE RETRACTS

CONT. : BLAST BUBBLE EXPANDS & DISSIPATES AS A SECOND BLAST BUBBLE
SURROUNDS LIZ

BLAST "BUBBLE" MOVES FORWARD & INCINERATES FRONT HALF OF THE KIDS

LIZ EXPLODES

Interior, Hospital—Liz's Room, Min. Security Ward—Night. A flashlight beam sweeps Liz's room. It illuminates a corkboard covered with hundreds of Polaroids depicting scenes of everyday life. When the beam of light crosses her face, she turns slowly, still asleep. As the light fades, the shadows in the room grow deeper. Grigory emerges from a dark corner. He gazes down on the bed, extending his right hand.

GRIGORY
The Master is calling your name now, my girl. We are all part of his plan. You must return to the child … So, once again …

He gently caresses the scar on her forehead. Under his skin, a hideous movement, a writhing rearrangement of muscles. His fingers start to glow.

GRIGORY
… dream of fire.

Liz convulses. A small ripple of heat rises from her forehead.

Flashback to: Exterior, Tenement Building Courtyard—Day. Somewhere in a smokestack city, grown-ups and kids hang banners and prepare a ragged birthday party in a cement courtyard.

Angle—Liz—continuous. Sitting on some tenement steps, Liz, age 11. Sullen, alone, a gold crucifix hanging on her chest. A woman—Liz's mother—comes down the courtyard steps, carrying a basket of apples.

MOTHER (*to Liz*)
Liz! Liz! Come on, darling, give Mummy a hand.

Nearby, under a balloon archway, munching candy-coated apples … three kids giggle and point at her.

BLONDE KID
Freak!

Liz turns to see them.

BLONDE KID (*to his friend*)
See? She knows her name.

Liz shies away from them.

BLONDE KID
Go home, you freak. We don't want you here.

They start throwing stones. One hits the steps. Another misses her by inches. A third hits her in the shoulder. Scared, Liz turns, but a rock catches her full on the face. She falls down, blood trickling from her forehead, splattering the pavement. She starts sobbing.

Another rock sails across, but this time, in mid-air, it catches fire and turns to ash. A ripple of heat starts crawling up Liz's hands. Soon a pale blue flame rings her entire arm.

LIZ (*sobbing*)
Not again, please, not again …

Firelight glints off the crucifix.

Exterior, Tenement Courtyard—Day. Mother is dunking the apples in a pot of caramel. A heartbreaking cry reaches her ears.

LIZ
Mommy! Mommy!

Mother sees …

Exterior, Tenement Courtyard—Steps—Day. Liz: outlined by licking flames!

LIZ (*panicked*)
Mommy! Help me! I'm burning!

Mother screams, horrified.

LIZ
Help meee!

She then explodes. A white-hot supernova engulfs the courtyard. Her mother's body burns like flash paper. Then the rest of the people are—

THE BLAST BUBBLE EXPANDS AND …

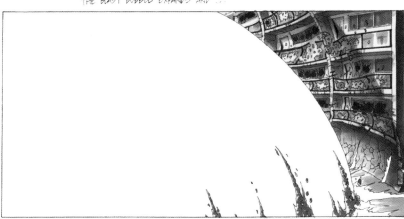

CONT.: BLAST BUBBLE & CONCAVITY CONTINUE TO EXPAND

WIPE ON LIZ IN THE CENTER OF THE BLAST BUBBLE AS IT CONTINUES TO EXPAND

BLAST FILLS FRAME

LIZ's ROOM
AT BELLAMIE
HOSPITAL
APPROX 12' WIDE x 18' DEEP
+ALCOVE AREA
OMIT GUARDROBE & RVG.

'CELL' PADDED DOOR

CORRIDOR

DARK ALCOVE AREA?

OMIT

OMIT RVG

GRIGORY'S ALCOVE

Scott
JAN 03.

SECURITY HUT
BELLAMIE HOSPITAL

7'.6" HIGH

8'

Scott
27.1.03

The entire tenement courtyard—devoured by an explosion of atomic proportions. Benches, people, trees. Everything. The four surrounding apartment blocks collapse as a shock wave hits like a wrecking ball.

The frame whites out. And at ground zero there is but one figure left standing: Liz … a little girl, still crying.

Flash Forward to: Interior, Bellamie Hosp.—Liz's Room, Minimum Security Ward—Night. Liz screams, her back arching, her body now in flames. Her chest glows, silhouetting organs and ribs. The rubber bands on her wrist vaporize.

Interior, Bellamie Mental Hospital—Min. Sec. Ward—Night. The glow from Liz's room streams into the corridor.

Interior, Bellamie Mental Hospital—Security Room—Night. In their glass kiosk, two orderlies are listening to the radio and sharing a pizza. A red light flashes repeatedly on a panel. They silence the radio, grab their batons and get up. A low rumble shakes the room. Through the vibrating glass window they see—

Corridor Miniature / Composite—a ball of flame pushing inexorably through the corridor. The inside of the glass booth is absolutely silent, making the vision both terrifying and strangely serene.

ORDERLY
Oh my—

Interior, Bellamie Mental Hospital—Security Room (Set)— Night. As the glass explodes, the fire roars, drowning everything. The orderlies hit the floor, taking cover under a shelf.

Exterior, Bellamie Mental Hospital (Miniature)—Night. The top floor blows

DEMOLISHED HOSPITAL

up. *Flame pours out of every window, showering glass into the streets below.*

Interior, BPRD—Freak Corridor "A"— Day. Myers pushes the breakfast cart. On it, three dozen pancakes and a mound of bacon and toast. He opens the door to Hellboy's den.

Interior, Hellboy's Den—Day. Inside, Hellboy is leaning over Broom, glaring at the old man.

HELLBOY
How many buildings does she have to burn? She belongs here!

BROOM
That's not how she feels. She may *never* feel it.

Myers enters, deliberately clearing his throat. They ignore him.

BROOM
It's her choice—(*Beat.*) She's human—

HELLBOY
Oh, as opposed to—?

Broom grows silent. Hellboy stomps over to a mirror and—using a hand-held belt sander—savagely shaves his horns. Sparks fly every time he goes at the round stumps.

HELLBOY
Mmmh—"Pamcakes." We're going out—

MYERS
Professor, that girl you were talking about—

HELLBOY (*whirls around*)
Hey. You—think twice—

MYERS
I think I can help—Talk to her—I can bring her back.

HELLBOY (*chuckles*)
What landed you this job, pushing "pamcakes"? Punctuality? What was your area of expertise?

Myers murmurs.

The last two lines of this scene were omitted to leave it more open ended.

HELLBOY
What was that?

MYERS
Hostage negotiations.

Hellboy's face lights up.

HOSPITAL

HOSPITAL

Digitally animated matte paintings were created for the film by Deak Ferrand.

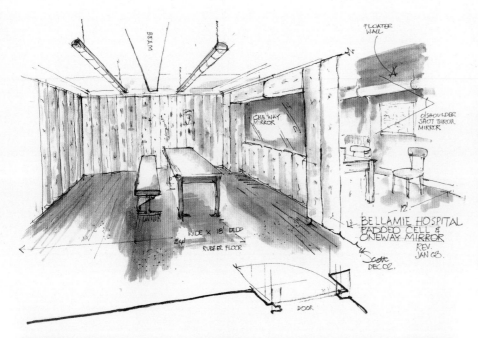

Exterior, Bellamie Mental Hospital—Day. Part of the building is demolished. Repair crews and firemen are still hosing down smoldering piles of debris. Myers arrives in a taxi cab.

Interior, Bellamie Mental Hospital—Max. Security Wing—Day. Myers looks at Liz through a see-through mirror. She sits on a bench inside a padded cell. A security camera and monitor records her constantly. A worried-looking Dr. Marsh stands alongside him.

DOCTOR MARSH
She's been like this since it happened. There were no casualties. But it's put a big dent in our Thorazine supply … (*Dubious look at Myers.*) Are you sure you want to go in?

Myers nods, loosens his tie and enters.

Interior, Bellamie Mental Hospital—Padded Cell—Day. Liz doesn't acknowledge Myers' presence. He kneels and looks up at her.

MYERS
Miss Sherman? I'm Agent Myers, FBI.

Liz turns away.

MYERS
Miss Sherman? I'm Agent Myers, FBI. (*No response.*) The hospital called us. They don't feel they're capable of caring for you any longer, and—

Silence.

MYERS
Liz—can I call you Liz? It's a beautiful name—

LIZ (*sighs*)
60% of the women in this world are named "Liz."

MYERS
It's still impressive by my standards— My name's John.

She looks at him. He offers his hand. She looks away.

MYERS
Dr. Broom asked me to invite you back to the Bureau. No special precautions, no security escorts. You and me in a taxi. Like regular folks.

LIZ
Doesn't sound like him.

MYERS
Miss Sherman, he's asking you back, but it's entirely your choice.

Liz turns to the 2-way mirror. Both their reflections are there.

LIZ
Choice, huh? That's cute. I've quit the Bureau thirteen times. I always go back. (*Snaps two rubber bands.*) Where else would I go?

Cut to:

*Interior, Beam Tunnel Area—
Benjamin Institute—Day. An explosion
of sound and light as a subway train
passes through a dank tunnel. Then,
light beams sweep the encrusted walls
and steel columns. Clay and some
BPRD agents hold flashlights. Two
of them—Moss and Quarry—carry
flamethrowers. Hellboy and Abe bring
up the rear.*

*Interior, Storage Room—Day. They
enter a store room piled high with filing
cabinets, typewriters, and school desks. A
turn-of-the-century mural depicts happy
boys doing charitable acts. A Latin
phrase ("Viriliter Age") encourages them
to behave like men.*

QUARRY (*reads a map*)
We're in the cellar of the Benjamin
Institute. Turn-of-the-century orphanage. Closed since they moved the
sewers in '51.

*Abe removes his gloves, hyperextends
his palm and senses the air. Then the
surface of the water.*

ABE
There's a pulse. And it's coming from—

*Debris and dust seem to float from the
water's surface and toward Abe's hand.*

ABE
—there.

*They point their flashlights at a
bulkhead.*

ABE
A cistern on the other side. Most of
the eggs are there.

*They move some filing cabinets and
stare at a blank concrete wall.*

AGENT QUARRY
No way in.

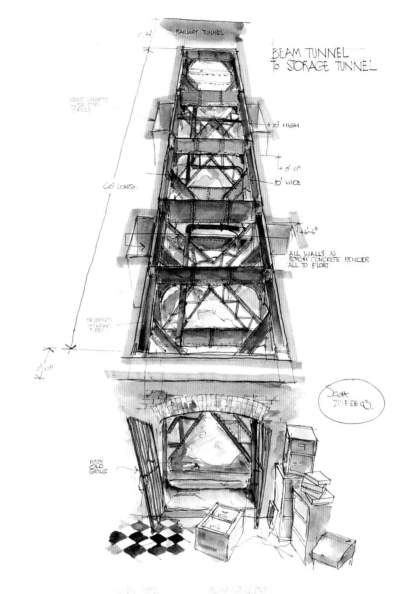

Kronen's Quarters

CLAY
We should go back and request permission to—

Bammm! Hellboy's stone hand racks the concrete. He starts pounding, again and again, like a jack hammer. Cut to:

Interior, (Set/Location Built Sugar Factory) Furnace Room—Day. Makeshift living quarters tucked below a maze of furnace ducts. Scores of old clocks fill the room with ticking. At a desk, Kroenen calmly repairs a mechanical hand: his own. His face is partly exposed. Under his leather mask, horrible lidless eyes glitter over a skull-like grin, made of raw gums and taut skin.

As Hellboy's pounding reaches his ears, he rises, like a spider whose web has twitched. The mechanical hand rattles blindly on the table. He opens an ancient leather folder and extracts an engraving depicting Sammael. Carefully places it on the table. Then he opens a drawer and, from an envelope, takes two torn pieces of paper. He puts them in a pouch in his belt.

Interior, Storage Room—Day. The wall collapses under Hellboy's attack.

HELLBOY
Are you coming or not?

Clay smiles uncertainly back. Hellboy moves in.

CLAY (*to Quarry and Moss*)
You two, check this dump, then join us—

Interior, Abandoned Shower Room (Set)—Day. A large oval room of rusting metal, with pipes spilling water through a large grate on the floor. Abe studies it, senses something, and nods. With superhuman effort, Hellboy lifts it. Hundreds of roaches pour out.

Del Toro demonstrates his obsession with bugs.

KROENEN'S HAND

Quite often del Toro would come into my office and say, "I have an idea and you're going to hate it." One day it was, "What if Kroenen had a mechanical hand?" I thought about it for a couple of minutes, then tried to sell del Toro on a scene where the hand springs out (still connected to the wrist by a chain or a wire) and stabs a guy.

—MM

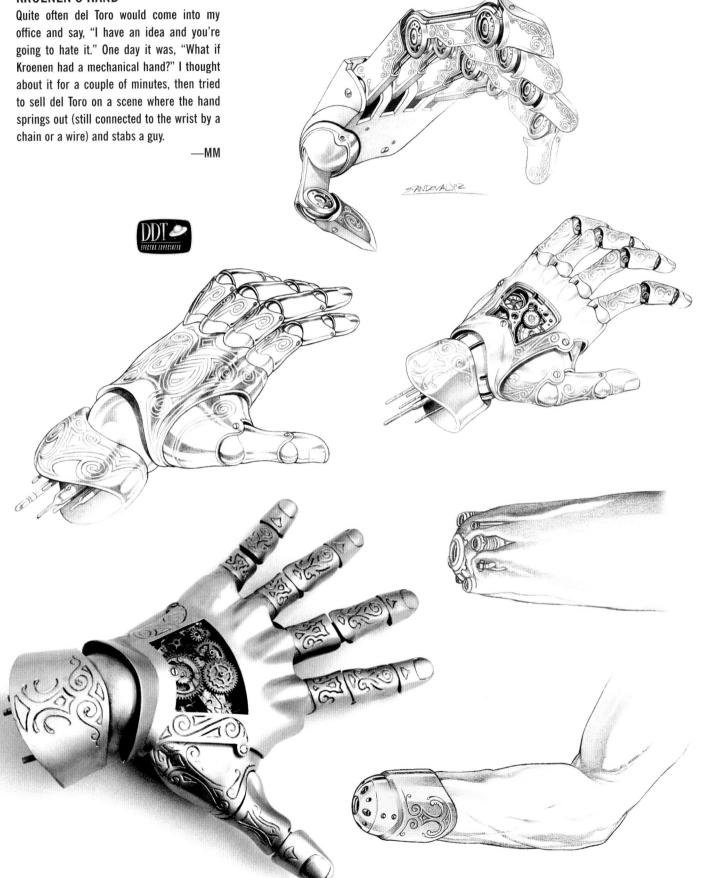

HELLBOY
Pipe room study #1
MIGNOLA
7/25/02

SHOWER ROOM/GRATE

In an earlier draft of the script, the shower room was Kroenen's lair instead of the boiler room. Del Toro and I worked out this strange image of Kroenen's masks hanging in the frames of broken mirrors, hanging over a room-length urinal.

—MM

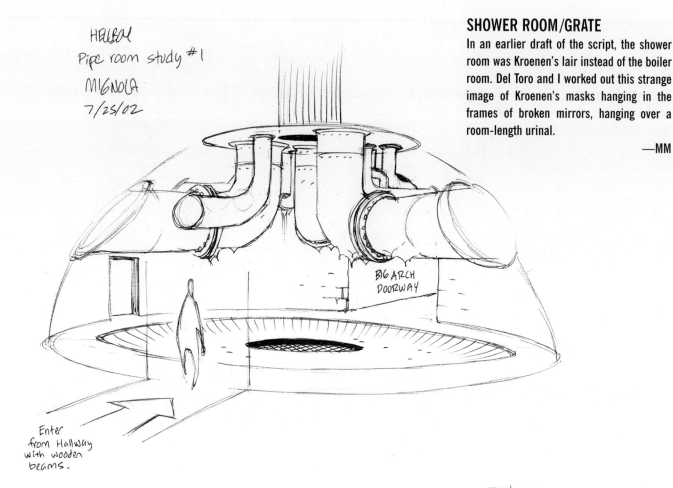

BIG ARCH DOORWAY

Enter from Hallway with wooden beams.

HELLBOY
Kroenen's Living Quarters
(underground Bath/shower)
room.
Study #2

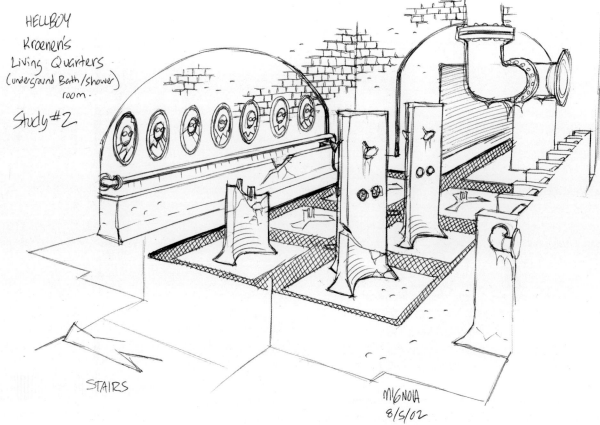

STAIRS

MIGNOLA
8/5/02

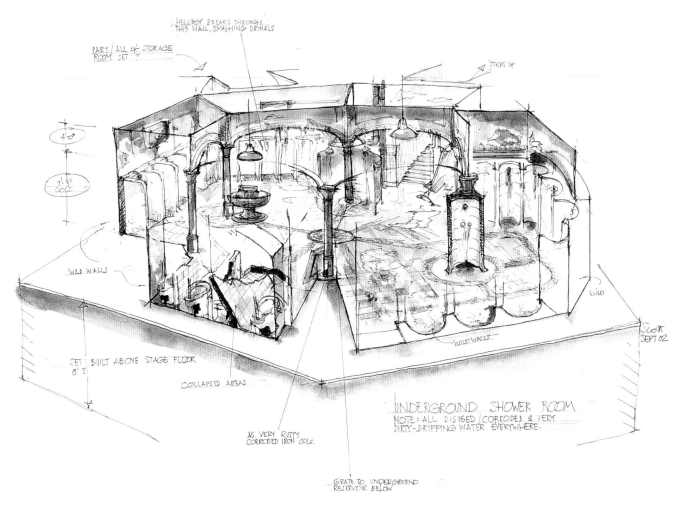

ABE
I'm glad I'm not human. This place would be an embarrassment.

Below, a vast cistern. Abe drops in two chemical flares.

Interior, Underwater—Chamber (Set Tank)—Day. The flares sink, illuminating floating office furniture and torn paper …

Interior, Underwater Chamber 2 (Location: R. Warehouse Cellar). In the lower depths, they pass shadowy industrial ruins. Settling on the bottom they reveal the hulk of a waiting Sammael.

Interior, Abandoned Shower Room (Set)—Day. Abe pulls off his breathing apparatus. Activates the locator on his utility belt. Hellboy does likewise. Beeep! The devices synchronize. Hellboy extends a metal reliquary containing a small bone.

HELLBOY
There you go, Doctor. This should cover your tailfin—On loan from the Vatican, a bone from Saint Dionysius. Ugh. Looks like a pinky.

Abe ties the reliquary around his hand.

ABE
Remind me why I keep doing this.

HELLBOY
Rotten eggs and the safety of mankind.

ABE
Oh, right—

As transparent nictomembrane lids cover his eyes, Abe dives.

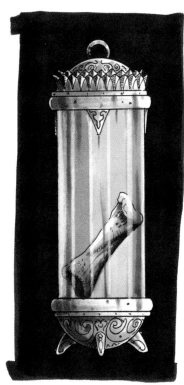

The reliquary, designed by Simeon.

Interior, Underwater Chamber 2—(Location R. Warehouse)—Day. Underwater, Abe finds an entire control room. 1940s magazines float by, like paper jellyfish. The amber light of the chemical flares gives the room an eerie otherworldly feel.

Interior, Abandoned Shower Room (Set)—Day. Waiting above, Hellboy chews a Baby Ruth and pokes around. Finds a pile of children's shoes covering some yellowing albums. In the albums, a myriad of sad faces, the orphans from the past. Some of the faces have been cut out. There's an unfinished letter to Father Christmas, dated 1866. Clay stands below a grate, admiring his hair implants with a hand mirror.

CLAY
See? It's thicker. Isn't it? It's not that doll-hair thing—

Suddenly, something moves. Hellboy shines his light into an adjoining tunnel. Kroenen is standing there, like a deer caught in headlights.

HELLBOY
Son of a—!

The figure darts away. Hellboy tears after it, gun in hand.

CLAY
Red, wait!

Clay tries his radio. Static.

CLAY
Red's on the move! I'll cover him!

He pulls out his gun and runs after Hellboy.

Interior, Tunnel Labyrinth (Set)—Day. Clay arrives at an intersection of sewer tunnels. The glow of Hellboy's flashlight is visible somewhere ahead, his booming footsteps rapidly receding. A veritable labyrinth.

CLAY
Damn it, Red.

Interior, Underwater Chamber 2 (Location R. Warehouse)—Day. Abe nears the bottom of the cistern. As his feet touch bottom, a cloud of silt fogs the water. He picks out a translucent egg!

Suddenly, something big glides by. Abe turns: sees nothing. He places the egg in a glass canister. Now eggs are floating everywhere, undulating in the water like amber fireflies. Abe swims slowly, collecting them one by one. Some of them are snugly wedged between two rusty machines. Abe's reliquary gets caught in a lever and snaps loose! It lands on a grate on the floor. Abe swims down and tries to grab it, but it falls through. Abe curses and stands up, only to find himself face to face with Sammael!

The monster rakes Abe across the chest; dark blue blood begins to flow. Abe shoves himself into a long, concrete fissure. Sammael can't fit through, but the tongue darts out, missing Abe by inches. Sammael scratches at the walls, trying to reach deeper, screaming in rage. Abe screams too, emitting a trail of bubbles.

Interior, Abandoned Shower Room—Day. The bubbles burst on the surface. Watching them is a second Sammael.

Interior, Intersection (Location /Built Sugar Factory)—Day. Hellboy stops, disoriented. No trace of Kroenen. He sniffs the air, then steps through a non-descript portal.

Interior, (Location/Built Sugar Factory) Furnace Room—Day. Hellboy stands in Kroenen's quarters. An array of gas masks dangle from ducts overhead. Glued next to the walls are dozens of old photos of children.

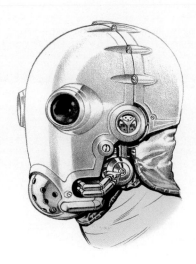

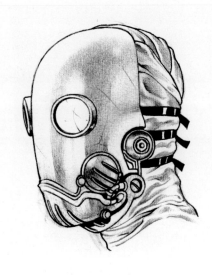

SANDOVAL\02

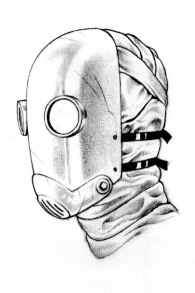

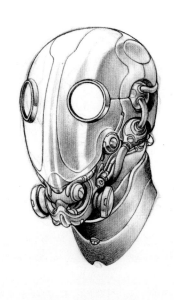

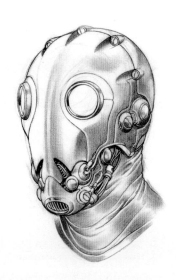

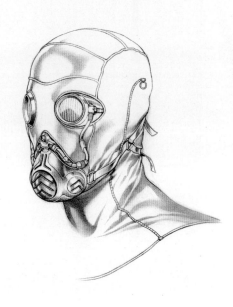

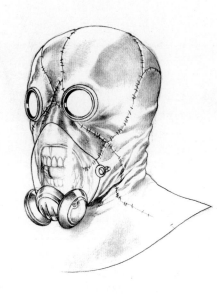

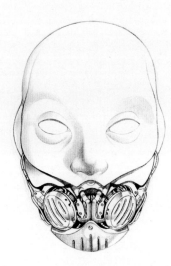

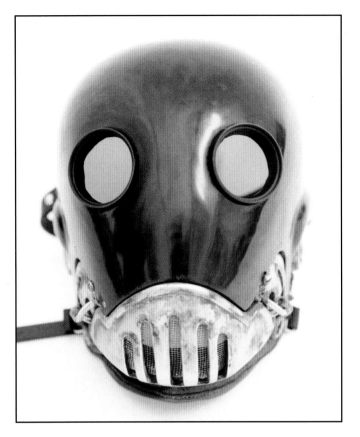

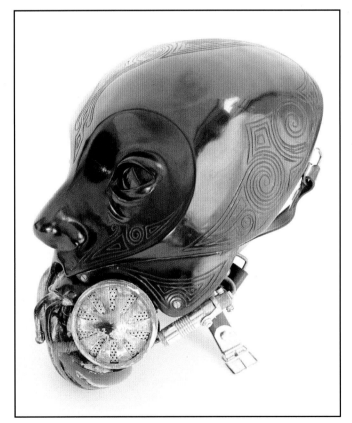

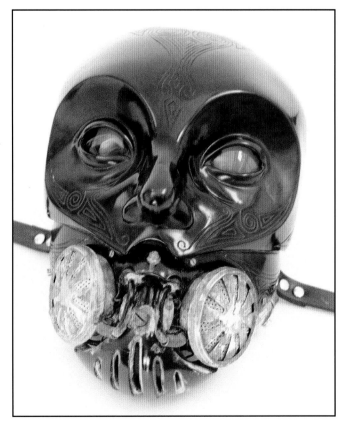

DDT Special Effects in Spain, headed by the artist Sandoval, created most of the art relating to Kroenen, and also constructed the various masks.

SUBWAY STATION

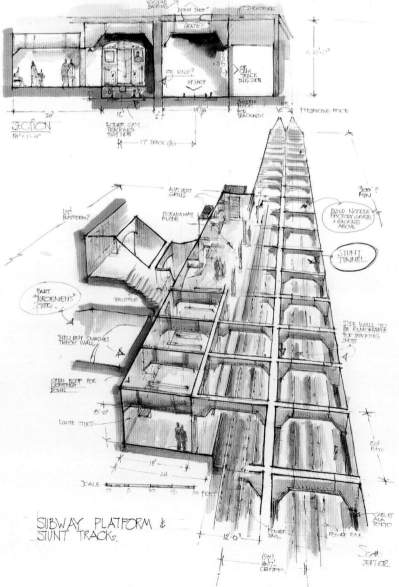

SECTION

SUBWAY PLATFORM & STUNT TRACKS

He discovers the Sammael engraving.

HELLBOY
"Sammael—seed of destruction.
Death becomes the fertile ground."

*Suddenly: drool drops from above:
Sammael hangs from a beam.*

HELLBOY (*turning*)
Didn't I kill you already?

*Sammael lunges, hurling Hellboy
through an open service shaft and it's a
long way down. When Sammael leaps,
Hellboy throws him over the edge.
Sammael , however, grabs Hellboy's tail
and pulls him over the side.*

*Interior, Service Shaft (New Location
Set)—Day. They crash through pipes,
wiring and ducts and slide off down a
duct and into—*

*Interior, Service Shaft 2 (Set)—same—
another passage. There they bounce off
of dripping water pipes and jutting steel
I beams, until they finally break
through a mesh/insulation ceiling and
directly onto—*

*Interior, Subway Platform Station—
Day. Full of people. The two fighting
creatures land on the ticket booth—in
an explosion of coins, glass and steel!
Some bold New Yorkers in the crowd
start picking up handfuls of change.
The dust clears, revealing a large crater
in the platform floor.*

*Sammael hits Hellboy. The Red Giant
lands on a line of turnstiles, uprooting
them all. Sammael flies through the air,
unfolds its bone scythe. Hellboy rolls
away. Sammael misses: the tip imbeds
itself in the floor and then—Tchakkk!—
in a concrete column. Sammael pulls,
bringing down part of the ceiling. More
screams from the fleeing public.*

*A mezzanine above Hellboy collapses,
bringing the ceiling, steel cables and*

office furniture down onto the red giant. Sammael takes a step toward the crowd and roars. Then—Bam! A desk flies up into the air. Hellboy's stone hand emerges, triumphant.

HELLBOY
Hey, Chunk-face!

He climbs out of the crater. Sammael growls.

HELLBOY
You can do better than that. Big monster like you.

Hellboy rips off one of the turnstile bars and hits Sammael again and again.

HELLBOY
See? It hurts! You shouldn't hit people!

Sammael blocks the last hit and throws the bar away. It embeds itself in the tile wall. Sammael punches Hellboy, a hard uppercut. Hellboy flies up, crashing through the plate glass of a second mezzanine above the platform. He skids on the tile floor, scraping a jagged line with his stone hand. He slides past a group of bystanders and into a row of backlit subway ads. He lands in a shower of glass and debris on a wooden bench, breaking it in two. Sammael climbs up into the mezzanine.

Hellboy gets up—his back bristling with glass shards—and hears a wail: a young girl is pointing at a box of kittens abandoned on a bench.

YOUNG GIRL
My kittens! My kittens!

HELLBOY
Aw, crap.

Sammael charges! Hellboy scoops up the box, holds it high! Using his bone blade, Sammael pulverizes the bench. Next, Sammael slashes at Hellboy, scattering a

dozen shrieking citizens. Illuminated by sparks and shorting lamps, Hellboy advances, blood dripping from his forehead and nose.

Hellboy starts to reload, but—Sammael's tongue shoots out. Hellboy throws the kitten box in the air and traps the tongue with his stone hand—

HELLBOY
Second date. No tongue!

—while catching the box with his tail. The kittens are fine. Using the tongue, he throws Sammael out a glass window. Sammael dangles above the tracks, but he re-joints himself and grabs a hand-hold on the train wall above the tunnel. From here, he pulls on Hellboy, sliding him toward the jagged glass. Sammael pulls harder, enters the tunnel.

Hellboy fights to free himself, but his sweaty face is millimeters away from being sliced by the glass. All seems lost, when—Whaaa! A train appears out of nowhere heading straight for Sammael.

It splatters the thing against the tunnel wall and plows on. Sammael's body sprawls motionless at the side of the tracks.

Interior, Subway Platform—same.

HELLBOY
I hope that hurt.

He gives the cats to the young girl—

YOUNG GIRL
Thank you—

HELLBOY
My job.

Interior, Subway Tracks (Next to Station)—same. Hellboy approaches Sammael, whose remains are wreathed in black flame. A huge crowd looks on from the end of the platform.

HELLBOY (a whisper)
This time. Stay dead, willya?

He moves away. The black flame flickers out.

Art from Hellboy: Seed of Destruction, *copyright 1994, Mike Mignola*

SIMEON WILKINS: HELLBOY STORYBOARD ARTIST

This is a true story.

I moved to Los Angeles to try my hand at drawing storyboards for film. I had seen what they were like on DVDs, and thought I could do something like that. I just didn't actually know how to get the job.

I worked in a video store in Hollywood for almost a year. During my last week at work, I met Guillermo del Toro. He had shopped there before, and even recognized me. I had told him how much I enjoyed *Blade 2*, and that I'd heard he was going to do *Hellboy* next. He said they were just starting pre-production, and, for some reason, I blurted out, "Do you need a storyboard artist?" He gave me a thoughtful glance, and then gave me his email address so that I might send him some samples. As if that alone didn't make my day, I clumsily offered to show him some of my comic work. After looking through my portfolio, Guillermo offered me a week of work on the picture.

I was there for eight months as the principle storyboard artist.

There I was, sharing an office with brilliant designers like Wayne Barlowe, Ty Ellingson, and, of course, Mike Mignola. Some might think drawing a character a hundred times over while that character's creator is in the room would be nerve wracking … and it was, but Mike was very respectful of all the work that was going on for this project. I was able to share an office with him again in Prague, as I finished up my work. I learned more about art and comics and storytelling and monsters in those walks to the office and around the city of Prague than I ever could have hoped for. Mike's work is inspiring, and actually talking to him over a beer sends the mind a-reeling. Thanks, Mike.

As for del Toro, there's never been a bigger fan of *Hellboy*, and never a more focused mind. He would do quick sketches and describe scenes to me so thoroughly that all I needed was to put pencil to paper. He knew exactly what he wanted, yet was completely open to my ideas. His exuberance and generosity were elevated by his faith in his artists. I had never touched a gray-tone marker before *Hellboy*, but Guillermo knew I could handle them. He's a tremendous man to work for, and I'd love nothing more than to be a part of every picture he makes.

It's strange, with the movie so close to release. I see stills here and there, and they are amazing. I see shots that I know I boarded, and I'm awestruck that this is really happening. Like Mike used to say in the office, "This is just so *weird*." It is weird, but it's so beautiful. A storyboard artist couldn't possibly ask for a better first job. Here's hoping for the sequel.

—Simeon Wilkins

Guillermo del Toro reviews a storyboard sequence.

FIGHTS

From del Toro's memo "Hellboy Visual Notes."

The fights in it have to be almost a throwback to the harder knuckle boxing scenes in the 1970s à la Eastwood or Bronson (see HARD TIMES) and we will avoid MARTIAL ARTS except for the occasional KROENEN scene.

We will keep the camera moving with the characters as they fight. Follow the punches like a three-camera referee in a dirty fight.

These are BIG THINGS fighting against ONE ANOTHER. POWER, SPEED, DRIVE, and MASS need to be emphasized. Part of the beauty of Hellboy is the "ouch" factor in his injuries.

—GdT

RAW POWER, ENERGY OVER "Grace"

LIKE MY SEX LIFE

Interior, Underwater Chamber 2 (Location R. Warehouse)—Day. Under the water, black light blooms within two of Sammael's eggs as a fantastic metamorphosis starts. The embryos burst out, gyrating in the water, swelling and distending.

Interior, Underwater Chamber 2 (Location R. Warehouse)—Day. Badly wounded, Abe peers from his hiding spot. Sammael's not there. He quickly swims to the surface, his weird blue blood trailing behind him. The water boils with energy and black light.

Interior, Abandoned Shower Room (Set)—Day. Abe staggers out of the pool and hides behind a crumbling shower stall. Behind him, two shapes come to the surface. Shaking, Abe pushes his belt locator and collapses. Cut to:

Interior, Subway Tracks (Near the Station)—Day. Hellboy's locator belt crackles to life. Blue.

HELLBOY
Abe—?

Interior, Beam-Supported Underground Tunnel/Storage Room—Day. Back in the tunnel, Quarry and Moss move filing cabinets and rotten boxes full of files. One of them gives out and papers spill all over.

MOSS
Jesus—

Their locators light up.

QUARRY
Abe—

Suddenly—a noise! The agents leap up and sweep their flashlights over the columns ... Nothing there.

QUARRY
Moss, what the hell was that?

HELLBOY
Hallway (with wooden beams)
leading from Subway to Pipe Room

View from Pipe Room
Looking towards Subway

MIGNOLA
7/25/02

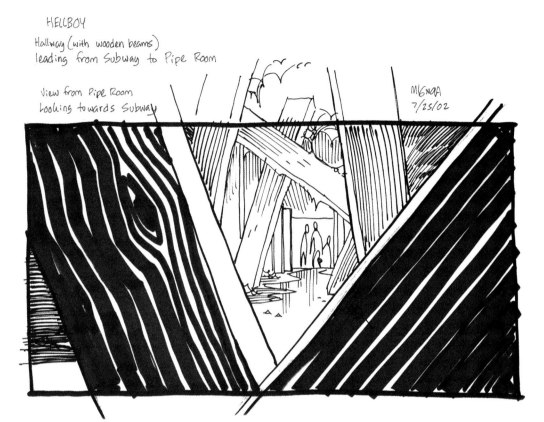

HALL OF BEAMS

I did a lot of drawings like this—in this case I am very much del Toro's wrist. He tells me what he has in mind and I try to make sense of it and put it on paper. Drawings like these would be useful tools for del Toro to communicate his ideas to the Production Designer.

—MM

SHAFTS ABOVE FOR LIGHT

WATER

FLAMETHROWER TUNNEL
(OFF STICKER ROOM)

Then, two silhouettes cast long shadows. Powerful footfalls boom like thunderclaps. Agent Quarry raises his gun and fires at the dark shapes. Useless: the things plow on. Moss hurriedly straps on his flame thrower. After a few seconds, a green light beeps, ready. The muzzle of the flamethrower vomits a 30 foot long gout of fire into the blackness.

The men pause: silence! Quarry turns on his flashlight, hand trembling.

QUARRY
Whatever it was—

Bam! Sammael's tongue uncurls from the shadows and lands on Quarry's face, pulling him into the dark. His flashlight bobbles and strobes, lighting up a nightmare: two Sammaels stand in the tunnel. One of them gleefully squeezes Quarry. The man's screams are muffled by the creature's fleshy lips wrapping around his head.

Moss runs as fast as he can, jumping and tumbling through an obstacle course of beams. Turning, he readies the flamethrower. The second Sammael lands on Moss's back, breaking his spine. Cut to:

Interior, Abandoned Shower Room (Set)—Day. Hellboy enters to find Abe, bleeding but alive, leaning against the tile, blue blood all around him. Hellboy tries his walkie-talkie. Turns on his locator. It sparks. It's damaged and broken.

HELLBOY (*into his walkie-talkie*)
We need an ambulance. Now! Over!

Interior, Center of the Tunnel Labyrinth (Set)—Day. Clay stumbles around, lost. He stops under a grate.

HELLBOY'S VOICE (*on the walkie-talkie*)
Who's there? Clay? Come in, someone.

CLAY
Clay, Code 30, this is Clay, over …

Behind Clay, Kroenen drops down from an overhead pipe, through shafts of gray light. He brings forth his customary long blade. Clay turns in time to see Kroenen coming at him. He fires. Kroenen stabs. Twin rivulets of blood run from Clay's nostrils.

Interior, Tunnel Labyrinth—Connecting Shower Room (Set)—Day. Hellboy hears the gunfire, starts running.

Interior, Center of the Tunnel Labyrinth (Set). Clay falls to the floor. Kroenen stands there, unfazed by Clay's bullets in his chest. Dust pours from his wounds and piles up neatly at his feet. He hears Hellboy coming. He places the knife on the floor, then lies down and plays dead.

Hellboy appears at the end of the tunnel. He glances at Kroenen's body, then quickly checks for a pulse on Clay. Hellboy looks demolished. Smash cut to:

The entire taxi scene was omitted from the final film.

Interior, taxi cab (moving) / exterior, BPRD adjacent avenue—day. An ethnic pop song blasts from the taxi radio. Liz pokes her head out of the window and shoots a Polaroid snapshot. She passes it to Myers:

LIZ
It feels good to be outside! It's been so long …

He can't hear her over the music. Myers knocks on the bulletproof acrylic divider.

MYERS
Hey! The music!
Turn down the music!

DRIVER
Yeah, yeah, music!

He merely changes the radio station; the music stays at the same volume. Myers looks back at Liz. She is halfway out the window, sitting on the door.

MYERS
Jesus! That's not—That's not safe, Miss Sherman—Miss Sherman?

She takes another Polaroid and passes it down to him. Myers looks at the Polaroid, then smiles. He climbs out of the other window, hands her the photograph.

MYERS
Nice view—

He waves at her. For the first time, she smiles.

MYERS
A smile, huh? That's good.

She takes his picture. With the cold morning wind blowing Liz's hair and the sun on her face, she looks beautiful.

LIZ
Don't get used to it.

Myers taps his fingers on the roof, to the beat of the music. He can't take his eyes off her. They drive toward the BPRD

Interior, BPRD Medical Bay—Day. Unconscious, Abe floats in a special tank. LED strips read water temperature, pH level, etc. He's encased in a bio-cast: a cybernetic healing unit wrapped around his thorax and right arm. A web of tubes and hoses keeps him in place. Shirtless and bandaged, Hellboy sits and studies him, as if in a trance.

ABE'S TANK
Another of my "too quiet," low-tech drawings. Abe in a can …

HELLBOY

ABE SAPIEN
IN HIS TUBE
6/24/02

MIGNOLA—

… The more high-tech version of Abe's tank by Ty Ellingson.

—MM

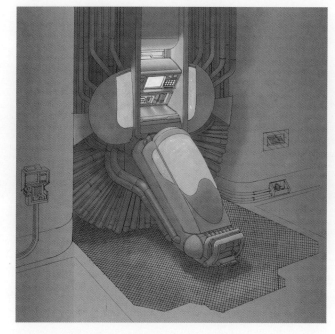

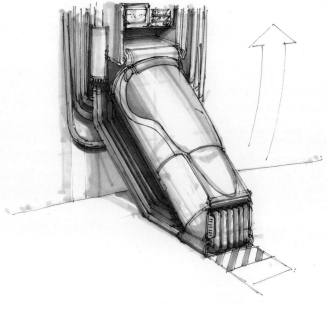

ABE'S RECOVERY TUBE   HELLBOY STUDY No.1   TYRUBEN

MANNING'S VOICE
He'll make it—

Hellboy turns, Manning is there.

MANNING
But not everyone was so lucky. (*Beat.*) Two agents died today. Clay probably won't survive the night. You're reckless.

HELLBOY
I knew those men better than you did—

MANNING
Ah, I see. That makes it all all right then.

He turns to leave. Hellboy gets up.

HELLBOY
No, it doesn't make it right, but I stopped that creature, didn't I?

MANNING
That's what you do. That's why we need you. You have an insight. (*Beat.*) You know monsters.

HELLBOY
What are you trying to say?

MANNING
In the end, after you've killed and captured every freak out there— there's still one left—you.

HELLBOY (*a deep sigh*)
I wish I could be more gracious but—

Bam! He smashes a metal locker with his stone hand and raises it above his head. Manning cowers, realizing that Hellboy's rage is a dangerous thing.

Interior, BPRD—Main Hall Area— Day. A new space. Office corridors radiate out from a brass BPRD logo on the floor. A few agents monitor computer stations and tactical glass boards. Liz and Myers walk in, carrying her suit-

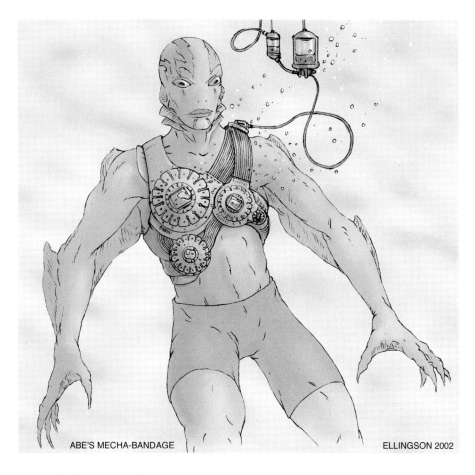

ABE'S MECHA-BANDAGE   ELLINGSON 2002

cases. She looks around and sees Broom coming down the hall.

BROOM
Welcome back.

LIZ
It's only for the weekend, Professor Broom. Then I'll be on my way—

BROOM (*impeccable courtesy*)
Come and go as you please. (*Beat.*) Find your way back. We've made quite a few changes—

Crash! Liz screams and Myers draws his gun. Smashing through a glass partition, the mangled steel locker lands in the middle of the hall in a rain of glass and aluminum studs. Next, Manning appears, retreating but unharmed.

MANNING (*gasping*)
I want that thing locked up, starting now—Now! You hear me?!

He flees.

LIZ (*to Broom*)
Nothing's changed. Home, sweet home.

Mortified, Broom hurries after Manning. Hellboy calmly steps through the hole in the wall.

HELLBOY (*seeing her*)
Liz? Liz!

She spins on her heel and walks off. Hellboy turns to Myers.

HELLBOY
You! You did it, buddy—

Myers holsters his gun and follows Liz. Hellboy is all alone now.

HELLBOY (*oblivious*)
Woo hoo!

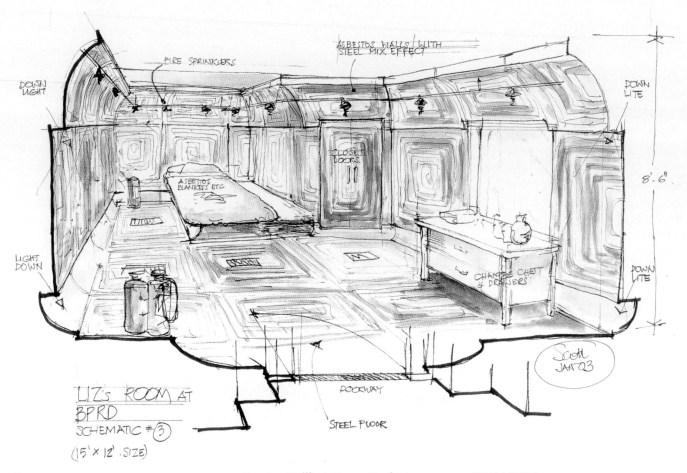

LIZ'S ROOM AT BPRD
SCHEMATIC #③
(15' × 12' : SIZE)

Cut to:

*Interior, BPRD—Liz's Room—Day.
A familiar cell. Fireproof insulation
covers the walls. Liz throws her bags
on the bed. Myers lingers in the doorway. She reflexively pulls on one of
the rubber bands on her wrist, then
lets it snap.*

**This scene was omitted, so Liz's room,
designed by Steven Scott, is never seen in
the film.**

LIZ
A little something I learned in therapy.
I'm depressed—(*Snaps a rubber band.*)
One rubber band. I'm impatient—two
rubber bands …

He sits by her side on the bed.

MYERS
I'll get you a fresh pack.

*Interior, Hellboy's Den—Dusk. A cat
bats at a ball of paper. On it, two words
are visible: "Dear Liz." Hellboy's tail
scoops up the paper and throws it in a
brimming wastebasket. He's sitting at a
stainless steel desk, deep in concentration,
writing with evident difficulty. The
floor around him is covered with more
crumpled pages. In the background, the
projector is showing* Duck Soup. *Myers
pushes in a cartload of chili.*

MYERS
Where do you—

HELLBOY
Shh! Just a second.

Myers sets the tray on the table.

HELLBOY
Myers, you're a talker. What's a good
word—a solid word for "need"—?

MYERS
"Need" is a good, solid word.

HELLBOY
Nah, sounds too needy.

MYERS
Start in, you got nachos coming.

*As he goes out, Liz appears in the
doorway. Hellboy quickly stops writing.*

LIZ (*notices the small feline army*)
Oh, my God … Look at them all!
Who had babies? C'mere, Tiger …!

*Liz plays with a cat. Hellboy lifts
the piece of paper, which looks like a
postage stamp in his stone hand.*

HELLBOY
Um … Liz—I—there's something
I'd like you to—something I *need* you
to hear.

LIZ
Well. Is it long? I'm going out, but—

HELLBOY
Out? *Out* out?

LIZ
For a cup of coffee, but go ahead, read.

HELLBOY
You're going alone?

LIZ
No. Myers is taking me.

Hellboy stands up, walks toward her.

HELLBOY
Him! Why him? Why not me?

Myers walks back in pushing a tray of nachos.

MYERS (*to Hellboy*)
Hey, your chili's getting cold—

HELLBOY (*sits back down*)
Not hungry.

LIZ
What did you want me to hear—?

Hellboy folds the paper.

HELLBOY
It's nothing. Just a list—It's not finished—

LIZ
Oh, okay then. Maybe later then.

She leaves. Myers smiles.

MYERS
Anything else you—

HELLBOY (*snappy*)
Not from you.

MYERS
Well good n—

HELLBOY (*furious*)
Good night.

Cut to:

Interior, BPRD Medical Bay—Night. Under a sheet, Kroenen's cold, naked body lies on a slab. Broom talks into a tape recorder.

BROOM
The subject—Karl Ruprecht Kroenen—

The visible areas of the body make us grateful for the sheet covering the rest.

BROOM
—Suffered a masochistic compulsion known as surgical addiction.

The silver hand and harness lie on a table.

BROOM
Both eyelids were surgically removed along with his upper and lower lips, making speech impossible. The blood in his veins dried up decades ago. Only dust remains. (*Looks at an x-ray film.*) Four pulverized vertebrae. A steel rod inserted into his pelvis held him up. (*Beat.*) What horrible will power could keep a thing like this alive?

He finds the small pieces of paper Kroenen planted in his pouch.

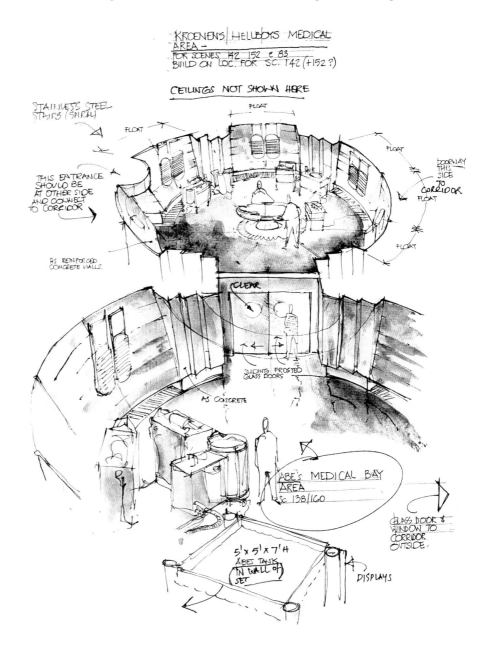

The ruins of New York by Deak Ferrand.

ABOMINATION

7/19/02

Interior, Broom's Office—Night. Startled, Broom snaps out of it—

GRIGORY
If only you had him destroyed sixty years ago, none of this would come to pass. But, then, how could you have known?

Broom is speechless.

GRIGORY
Your God chooses to remain silent. Mine lives within me.

Rasputin stands, the flesh of his neck and shoulders heaving and twitching beneath his human skin.

GRIGORY
In the frozen waters of the Malaya Nevka, in the darkness of the void—every time I died and crossed over, a little more of the Master came back with me. He disclosed to me the child's true name … Would you like to know it?

BROOM
I know what to call him. Nothing you can say or do will change that. I call him son.

Discreetly, Broom removes his rosary and places it on the book. Kroenen settles in behind him.

BROOM
I am ready.

GRIGORY
Good. Now, I'll add two crumbs more. (*Kroenen displays his knives.*) Grief and revenge …

Kroenen's knife goes in. Cut to:

Exterior, Building Rooftop—Night. The pigeons flutter on the rooftop. The pigeon kid sits by Hellboy's side.

John Hurt as Professor Trevor Broom.

KID
Just go down there and tell her how you feel! (*Hellboy shakes his head: no.*) My mom says—

HELLBOY
It's not that easy, okay? (*Beat.*) Plus, you're nine. You're not old enough to give me advice.

KID (*shrugs*)
Who are those guys?

Hellboy turns and sees two of the black BPRD Sedan cars rounding the corner. Agent Lime bounds out of one of the vehicles, grabbing Myers, talking rapidly. Liz screams, covers her ears.

HELLBOY
Something's wrong—

Interior, BPRD Hallway—Night. Agents and Bureau employees are crammed into Broom's office doorway. Hellboy, face contorted by grief, pushes through.

Interior, Broom's Office—Night. The room is full of forensics people taking pictures, picking up evidence, etc. Tom Manning is there. Seeing Hellboy, he respectfully steps back.

Broom's fragile body lies slumped in his chair. At his feet, a pool of blood. Liz enters, then stifles a whimper. With tears in his eyes, a disbelieving Hellboy looks at Liz, then at his dead father. He holds Broom's body close to his chest.

HELLBOY
Father—I'm back. I'm back. I'm back.

Manning herds everybody out. From the door, Liz blinks back tears as the red giant kneels by the body: a dog with a lost master.

HELLBOY
I wasn't here. You died alone—

Dissolve to:

Exterior, BPRD Building—Day.
It's raining like hell. The pallbearers,
Manning and Myers among them, load
Broom's casket into a hearse. Flanking it

are two rows of BPRD agents. The hearse
doors close and the vehicle pulls away.

Watching like a gargoyle from a distant
roof: Hellboy. Rain bounces off his wet
overcoat. Liz observes him, worried.

Selma Blair as Liz Sherman.

LIZ'S VOICE
He hasn't spoken to anyone in three
days. Not a word. He doesn't eat, he
doesn't sleep …

Interior, Medical Bay—Day. Abe,
conscious now, but still in the cast,
floats upside down, solving a Rubik's
Cube. Liz stands by the tank.

LIZ
I've never seen him like this. Never.
(*Beat.*) Should I stay? With him,
I mean?

She smiles faintly.

ABE
Listen—I'm not much of a problem
solver … (*Displays the cube.*) Three
decades and I've only gotten two
sides. (*Beat.*) But I know this much—
if there's trouble, all we have is each
other. And I'm stuck here. (*Beat.*)
So— take care of the big monkey
for me, will you?

Their hands almost touch, separated
only by the glass.

Interior, BPRD Conference Room—
Dusk. A projection screen shows the
enhanced image of the piece of paper
with Cyrillic characters.

MANNING
We've collected and destroyed
thousands of eggs. No trace of
this "Sammael" or this "Rasputin"
character. But we have this address—

In a meeting room, Manning stands
at a polished obsidian desk. A group
of agents—Myers among them—
listens attentively.

MANNING
Sebastian Plackba #16. Volokolamsk
fields, fifty miles from Moscow.
We leave as soon as we get clearance
and equipment—

MANNING
Hellboy's coming. (*Beat.*) But I'll be in charge this time. Either we wrap this up or I'm closing this freak show for good.

Myers spots Liz walking past the conference room.

Broom's Office—Dusk. Hellboy stands before Broom's desk, pensive, his naked chest bandaged. Liz watches him from across the room. He finds Broom's rosary on top of the book. Reads the underlined phrase on the page.

LIZ
Hi—

He turns to her. She slowly comes toward him.

HELLBOY
Hi.

LIZ
I've changed my mind. I'll come to Moscow. If you—are still going—

Hellboy nods, then clears his throat.

HELLBOY
I am. (*Beat.*) But—I have something to say, too. (*Beat.*) I never had the guts before—

He looks her in the eye.

HELLBOY
But I understand what you don't like about me. I do. What I am makes you feel out of place—out there—

LIZ
Red, I—

HELLBOY
Listen. I'm not like Myers. He makes you feel like you belong. And—that's good. It really is. I—

A grieving Hellboy (Perlman) observes Broom's funeral.

wish I could do something about this—(*Points at his own face.*) But I can't. (*Beat.*) I can promise you only two things … One—I'll always look this good. Two—I won't give up on you. Ever.

LIZ
I like that …

HELLBOY
Good.

Cut to:

Exterior, Moscow Warehouse—Day.

TITLE

Topockba Steel Mills, Moscow.

A wasteland of rust and decay. Rotting warehouses line the street like dead steel watchdogs. No one's around but a few lonely sentries. A limo and motorcycle caravan are waved through the security gates.

Interior, Moscow Warehouse—Dusk. A metal door trundles back and the limo and escort motorcycles enter. A fleshy

Russian General—Lapikov—gets out of the limo. Then Ilsa and Grigory.

GENERAL LAPIKOV

I have accumulated many objects of great interest. Preserving our heritage.

The warehouse contains a world of bric-a-brac: a towering marble Lenin head, Old Master paintings, tanks, warheads, missiles, etc.

GENERAL LAPIKOV

Many—like me—believe Mother Russia to be very close to a historic rebirth.

They stop before a cargo container.

With a butane torch, a soldier melts away the lead Kremlin seal, then opens the doors.

GRIGORY

Rebirth? I like that.

Interior, Moscow Warehouse—the Container—same. A massive stone monolith of polished marble.

This scene was omitted, so the Block is not actually seen until the climax.

LAPIKOV

Twenty tons of stone. This thing fell from the sky into Tungaska forest.

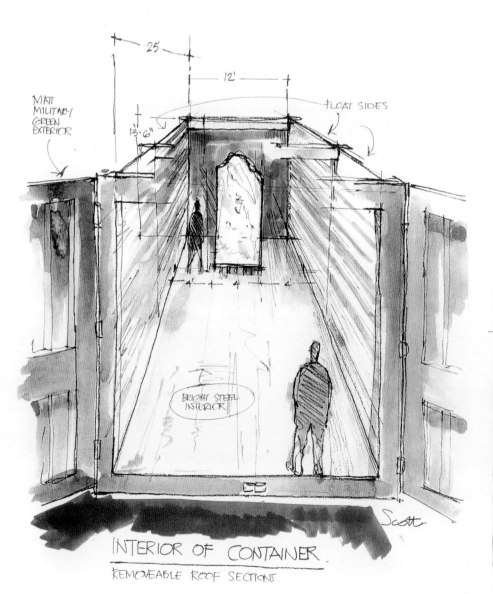

INTERIOR OF CONTAINER

REMOVEABLE ROOF SECTIONS

Biddy Hodson as Ilsa Haupstein.

HELLBOY
THE BLOCK

MIGNOLA —

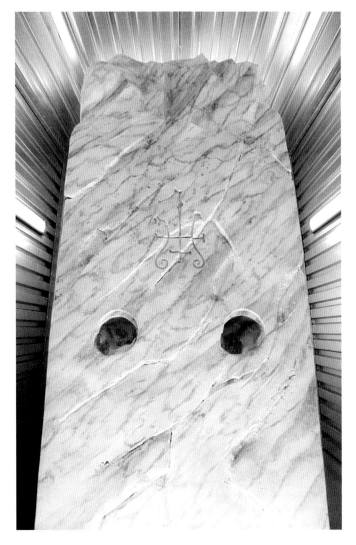

The Block in the container.

GRIGORY
June 30th, 1908. It burned hundreds of square miles of forest. The Romanovs took possession of it immediately. The Czar guarded it jealously—I have wanted it for ages.

Grigory's fingers brush over its smooth, perfect surface. At the center, two circular imprints that match Hellboy's four-fingered stone hand.

GRIGORY
Now, finally, it's mine.

GENERAL LAPIKOV
You are aware, of course, there's no way you'll get it out of Russian territory.

ILSA (*curtly*)
He is aware.

Ilsa brings out a chrome box, full of gold.

GENERAL LAPIKOV
It's a pleasure doing business with you. Perhaps you have other interests.

Grigory's voice drips with serene brutality.

GRIGORY
Enjoy the bright metal you've earned. There will be no further transactions. (*Beat.*) Only closure.

Cut to:

Exterior, The Night Sky (Matte Shot)— Night. A massive cargo plane slices the white eye of a full moon. A map details the plane's journey over the Black Sea.

TITLE
Russian Airspace—Black Sea.

Interior, Cargo Plane—Night. As the plane engines drone, Myers supervises BPRD agents Lime and Stone, who stencil a large crate: Fragile! Live Cargo.

Hellboy and Liz stand around a brightly lit work table. Hellboy shows them the medieval illustration of Sammael.

Ioſedech pontifex tili⁹ Azarie egreſſus eſt quãdo tranſtulit dominus iudam et hieruſalem per manus
Nabuchodonoſoz. Et ductus eſt cum alijs captiuus in babilonē; dicunt aliqui iſtum fuiſſe Eſdrã ſcri
bam et ſacerdotem aut forſan ipſius fratrem.

Uentos compeſcet verbo. mareq̃ furies ſedabit. pedibus mare calcans. Ambulans ſuper vndas. Infirmi
tatem hominibus ſoluens. repellens multos dolores.
Item alia Sibylla que dicitur fuiſſe berithrea ait. In vltima etate humiliabit de⁹ humanabit ples di
uina. Iungebatur humanitati deitas. Iacebit in feno agnus. et puellari officio educabitur deus et ho
mo; Eligetq̃ ſibi ex piſcatoribus et eiectis numerum duodenarium.

HELLBOY

"One falls, two shall arise." So—you pop one, two come out. You kill two, you get four. You kill four, you're in trouble. We have to nail 'em all at once. *And* the eggs.

MANNING

When we do—No mumbo-jumbo. Double-core Vulcan-65 grenades.

Manning shows them a set of grenade belts.

MANNING

We've installed a very handy timer. Set it, walk away. Cable pulls the safety pins, Kaboom! Easy to clean, easy to use—

HELLBOY (*interrupts*)

Those things never work. Never.

MANNING

Each of us gets a belt.

HELLBOY (*shrugs it off*)

I won't take 'em. They never work.

Manning looks at Hellboy, irate.

MYERS

I'll carry his—

Hellboy wraps Broom's rosary on his wrist.

HELLBOY

Boy Scout.

Cut to:

Exterior, Countryside—Day. Two gleaming black vans and a truck move through snow-covered Soviet roads.

TITLE

Volokolamsk Fields, Moscow.

Exterior/Interior, Countryside—in the Truck Cab—Day. Myers and Liz struggle with a Moscow map.

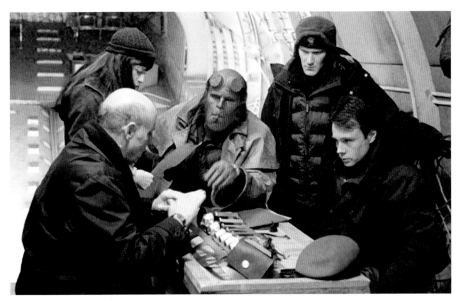

BPRD GRENADE HELLBOY—SEPT. 10, 2002 T.RUBEN ELLINGSON

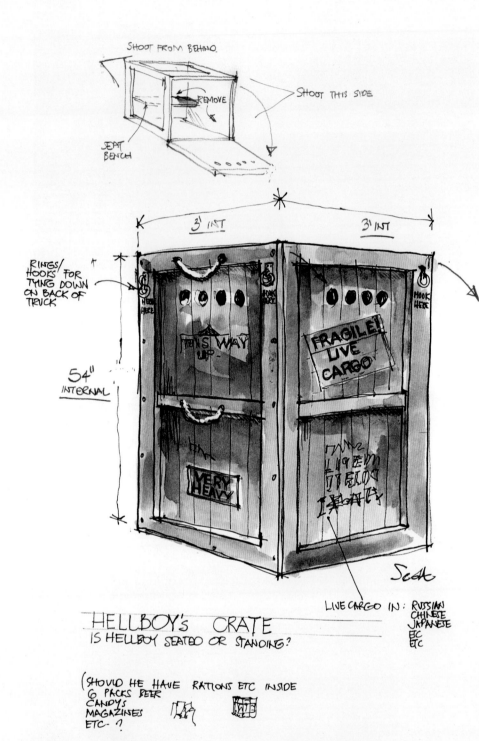

SHOOT FROM BEHIND.

SHOOT THIS SIDE

REMOVE

SEAT BENCH

3' INT   3' INT

RINGS/ HOOKS/ FOR TYING DOWN ON BACK OF TRUCK

HOOK HERE   HOOK HERE   HOOK HERE

THIS WAY UP

FRAGILE! LIVE CARGO

54" INTERNAL

VERY HEAVY

Scott

LIVE CARGO IN: RUSSIAN CHINESE JAPANESE ETC ETC

HELLBOY'S CRATE
IS HELLBOY SEATED OR STANDING?

(SHOULD HE HAVE RATIONS ETC INSIDE
6 PACKS BEER
CANDYS
MAGAZINES
ETC - ?

LIZ (*into a radio*)
Sparky to Big Red …

Popping her head out of the window, Liz looks back at the truck bed.

Exterior, Countryside—the Truck Bed—Day. Fastened to it, the crate labelled: Live Cargo. Small breathing holes have been drilled in the sides.

HELLBOY'S VOICE
Sparky? Who came up with that? Myers?

Exterior/Interior, Countryside—the Truck Cab—Day. Liz snickers.

MYERS
We're almost there.

Interior, Inside the Cargo Box— Day. Hellboy, sitting on the floor, in the dark.

LIZ'S VOICE (*on radio*)
We're leaving the main road, so hang on—

They hit a series of bumps. The box rattles and shakes. Hellboy bangs his head. The vehicle lurches to a halt.

HELLBOY (*on the radio*)
This better be the place or I'll puke.

Motors are turned off. The crate is opened. Liz peeks in.

LIZ
Come out and see.

Exterior, 19th Century Cemetery— Day. Hellboy steps out. Takes a moment to adjust his eyes to the light.

HELLBOY
Sebastian Plackba #16 …

19th Century Cemetery (Matte Shot / Composite). Broken spiked fences succumb to rust and dead vines. Endless rows of crypts and tombstones poke through wild foliage. Our group plus two agents (Lime and Stone) venture into the labyrinthine lanes of the dead. Each carries a backpack, a flashlight and a gun. Dissolve to:

Exterior, Cemetery—Mausoleum Section (Location)—Day. Later. The group gathers in frustration in an area of baroque funerary monuments. Myers—carrying the explosive belts— looks around.

MANNING
Forget it. This is practically a city. And it stinks, and it's muddy. We'll go back, check into a hotel, regroup after breakfast. We'll have to make a grid, go by quadrants. Maybe satellite photography.

Matte painting by Deak Ferrand.

He gestures and all the agents head for the vans.

HELLBOY
Let me ask for directions.

Exterior, Open Grave—Day. The group surrounds a grave. Hellboy raises the broken stone cover and then jumps in—

Exterior, Open Grave (Set)—Day—and lands on a rotten coffin. In it, a mummified Corpse lies in a miserable black suit.

HELLBOY (*whispers*)
Animam edere, animus corpus …

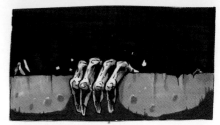

He presses the amulet on the cadaver's forehead. For a moment, nothing, and then—a brutal spasm! The Corpse gasps, breathes … and mutters something in tongueless Russian.

SUBTITLE
What do you want?

Exterior, Moscow Cemetery (Location)—Day. The group gawks as Hellboy climbs out, carrying the Corpse on his back. With an ear-to-ear grin, he approaches the team.

HELLBOY
Sixty feet further, comrades, and three rows in …

The corpse fidgets on Hellboy's back. Its bony hand weakly points, as if in confirmation.

HELLBOY
This here is Ivan Klimentovich— Say "hi," Ivan.

"WHAT DO YOU WANT?"

The corpse mutters again.

SUBTITLE
Go that way, red monkey.

Hellboy. Amulet for
Corpse Sequence Color Study.

*The Amulet was designed by Simeon Wilkins,
whom del Toro nicknamed Sapien during pre-production.*

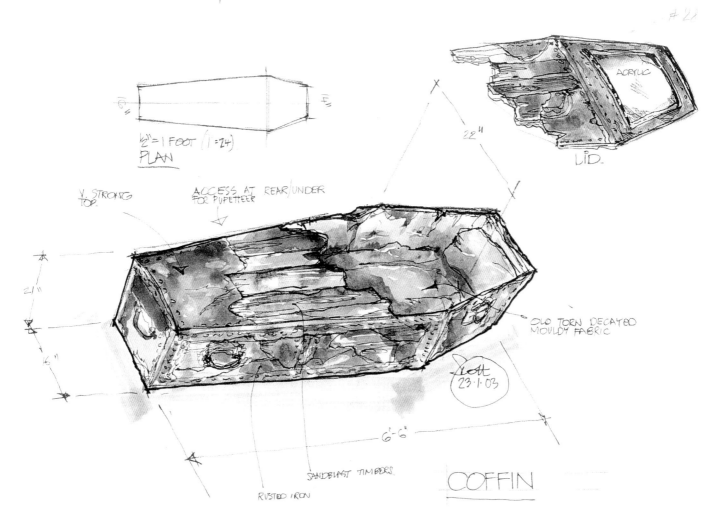

½" = 1 FOOT (1 = 24)
PLAN

AORYLIC

LID.

28"

V. STRONG
TOP.

ACCESS AT REAR/UNDER
FOR PUPETEER

21"

6"

OLD TORN DECAYED
MOULDY FABRIC

23·1·03

6'-6"

SANDBLAST TIMBERS.

RUSTED IRON

COFFIN

OPEN GRAVE STUDY #1

THE CORPSE

One of my favorite drawings—a half corpse with a handy rope for easy carrying. It was del Toro's idea that it would be the corpse of a criminal buried with the noose that hanged him. Nice. The tattered suit coat would eventually be replaced with something more "old Russia."

—MM

HELLBOY
"THE CORPSE"
#2
7/12/02

MIGNOLA

Maquette sculpted by Chad Waters and Matt Rose.

The animatronic puppet created by Spectral Motion.

NO SNOW HERE

EXT MAUSOLEUM
ALL OLD, FADED & PART COVERED IN IVY

Scott
20·1·03.

BEETLES COME OUT OF
EYE SOCKETS

WALL PANEL SLIDES OPEN
IN 2 HALVES

Scott
9·2·0

INT MAUSOLEUM

Exterior, Cemetery—Yefimovich Mausoleum (Location)—Day. A miniature black marble castle. Using a crowbar, Myers pries open the ancient steel door. Hellboy, still carrying the desiccated abomination on his back, walks in.

Interior, Yefimovich Mausoleum Stairs—Later—Day. Two agents stand guard in the mausoleum, while the group descends carefully. The walls are dotted with yellowed skulls.

Interior, Yefimovich Mausoleum—Underground—Staircase. Myers' flashlight flickers. He shakes it back to life.

Interior, Underground—Underground Intersection. They reach the bottom of the staircase: three corridors branch off

in different directions. Hellboy deposits the Corpse atop a pile of coffins.

HELLBOY
We'll be all right … as long as we don't separate—

Interior, Underground Corridor and Intersection—Day. Tchkanggg! large spiked metal plates shoot up from below, blocking both their way out, demolishing the staircase and ramming Stone: he's gone.

Wicked spikes cover the metal surface. Hellboy still bangs on it, but to no avail: it's at least six inches thick. Liz and Myers are on the other side.

HELLBOY (*into his walkie-talkie*)
Okay, someone's expecting us. Turn on your locators—Anyone sees anything …

LIZ
Marco …

HELLBOY
… Polo.

On the other side of the panel, Myers takes the radio from Liz.

MYERS (*into radio*)
Are you sure about this?

HELLBOY
On a scale of one to ten—two. But—(*Beat.*)—she'll take care of you, Myers. She's a tough one.

Liz and Myers move off. Hellboy shines his light down the tunnel on the left. Agent Lime picks up the corpse and follows.

Leo Durañona designed
the hall of blades beneath
the mausoleum.

SPIRAL STAIRCASE TO X CHAMBER

'X' INTERSECTION CHAMBER.

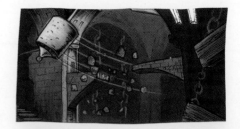

Interior, Tunnel "A"/Chamber—Day.
Hellboy and Manning come into a vast
chamber: Slavic motifs crown the
rugged stone pillars and archways.
Water runs down the walls. Across a
small stone bridge, light pours from a
hexagonal structure. They step onto the
bridge. Klanggg! Two gears release a
steel door from above, forcing them to
forge ahead. Somewhere, a massive
clockwork is ticking.

MANNING
What's that—?

Hellboy motions for silence. The Corpse
mutters.

SUBTITLE
It's something big.

They stare into the darkness.

MANNING
We should go back—you—you could
tear that door apart—

HELLBOY
Don't move. We—

MANNING
—should go back. Now!

HELLBOY
No. Don't—

MANNING
I'm in charge. We go back!

Hellboy yanks Manning just in time.
Bam! A gigantic metal pendulum
swings past and demolishes one third
of the bridge a few feet from their feet.
It takes Lime and the Corpse with it.
Another door on the far end of the
bridge shudders downward.

HELLBOY
Son of a—

Whoosh! The pendulum swings back.
It destroys more of the bridge. Manning

sprints for all he's worth and crawls under the door. Hellboy runs, but chunks of stone disintegrate under his feet. The pendulum swings back taking out the final piece of the bridge just as Hellboy rolls under the door and makes it into the hexagonal building.

Interior, Stone Corridor—Day. Hellboy and Manning find themselves in a very narrow, arched stone corridor. Its walls are lined with endless rows of rusty steel blades. Faint traces of Wagner can be heard. They cautiously proceed …

Interior, Hexagonal Stone Lab—Day. There. In yellow gaslight, Kroenen nods attentively as a phonograph plays the love duet from Tristan und Isolde. *Above him, ropes, hooks and pulleys.*

Interior, Stone Corridor—Day. Manning rests his hand too close to a blade.

MANNING
Ouch!

Interior, Hexagonal Stone Lab—Day. Kroenen comes alert. He scans the room, quietly winds himself up.

Interior, Stone Corridor—Day. Hellboy shoots a dirty look at Manning and then looks back into the chamber— Kroenen is gone.

HELLBOY (*to Manning*)
Crap. This guy moves like a cockroach—

Hellboy readies his gun and then creeps toward the lab.

Interior, Hexagonal Stone Lab—Day. Hellboy's footsteps elicit soft creaks from the wooden floor. Manning moves along behind him. The record finishes playing. Silence—

CLOCK PENDULUM

For this section of the catacombs, del Toro wanted something inspired by the prison etchings of Giovanni Battista Piranesi (1720-1778). When I had finished the first drawing, del Toro came into the office and said that he liked it—and now he wanted to see a giant clock pendulum swinging through and destroying the bridge. That was the first any of us had heard about a pendulum. But that's what it was like—the whole movie kept getting bigger and crazier.

—MM

HELLBOY
TUNNEL "A"/CHAMBER
Bridge leading to Kroenen's Room

MIGNOLA
8/24

HELLBOY
TUNNEL "A"/CHAMBER
leading to Kroenen's Room   Pendulum destroying bridge

MIGNOLA
8/24

HELLBOY
TUNNEL "A"
CHAMBER
Entrance to
Kroenen's
ROOM
#2

BRIDGE

MIGNOLA
8/26

HELLBOY
TUNNEL "A"
CHAMBER

TO Kroenen's
ROOM

MIGNOLA
8/26/02

MIGNOLA
8/26

HELLBOY
TUNNEL "A"
CHAMBER
Entrance to
Kroenen's
Room
#1

FROM BRIDGE

MIGNOLA 8/27

HALL OF CLOCKS

I loved this idea. I thought all of the clock pendulums swinging in unison would be a great effect. This was replaced by the hall of spikes—a visual nod to the hall of razor blades in the film *Tales From The Crypt*.

—MM

KROENEN'S UNIVERSE ROOM (opposite)

This was my crazy first idea for Kroenen's room. Once I drew it, I thought it was just too weird. It looked a little like a set you might have seen in the old *Lost in Space* show. I showed it to del Toro just as a goof. I was amazed when I discovered months later that Production Designer Steven Scott had tried to work elements of this into the final design.

—MM

HELLBOY
Kroenen's CLOCK ROOM
leading toward inner chamber

MIGNOLA 8/27

wooden clock frame

MIGNOLA –

Kroenen's Room
"Lost in Space" Version

KROENEN'S HEX CHAMBER

MODEL
"PIRANESI"
BRIDGES
ETC
BEYOND

WEIGHT

KROENEN'S ROOM

My more sober design for Kroenen's inner chamber. The Nazi Youth poster was meant to show the Nazi ideal Kroenen was aiming for with all of his surgery. The gears would represent his sad reality.

—MM

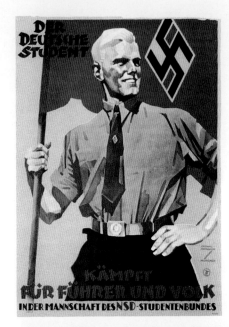

Swish! Kroenen's whirling blades slice the air, ripping into Manning's arm. As Kroenen goes in for the kill, Hellboy thrusts out his stone fist as a shield. Kroenen bears down but Hellboy fends him off with powerful, deliberate blocks. Kroenen hauls out one of his long swords.

HELLBOY
Screw that.

Hellboy yanks it away and bends it like a twig. Bam! He punches Kroenen in the face, crumpling the steel mask, smashing its lenses.

HELLBOY
You killed my father—

Bam! another hit. Kroenen staggers back with each blow. Finally, the mask falls off.

HELLBOY
Give your soul to God—Your ass is mine.

An asthmatic wheeze erupts from his scarred face. Kroenen is laughing.

Interior, Hexagonal Trap Door Pit— Day. Bam! Under his feet, a huge trap-door falls open. He and Manning drop through, along with the phonograph. Hellboy grabs a rope. It spins through a copper pulley, but a large knot jerks him to a stop. Hellboy snatches Manning's hand, but loses his backpack. He looks down. The phonograph hits the ground with a crash.

MANNING (*panting, whispers*)
Well, it's not that big a fall …

Klang! The entire bottom bristles with six-foot, sparkling steel blades.

Interior, Above the Hexagonal Trap Door Pit—Day. Kroenen cautiously leans over the pit. He can't hear a sound. As he peeks—SWISH! A loop of

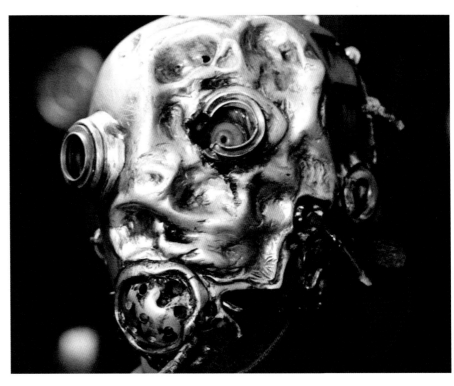

Kroenen after his beating.

the rope wraps around his neck and yanks him forward! Before he goes over, he frantically digs his blades into the floor, anchoring himself.

Interior, Hexagonal Trap Door Pit— Day. Hellboy has used the rope hanging below him as a lasso. Manning clings to his powerful back as he climbs up, hand over hand.

Interior, Above the Hexagonal Trap Door Pit—Day. Kroenen goes to cut the rope.

Interior, Hexagonal Trap Door Pit—Day.

HELLBOY (*reaching the top*)
Oh, no you don't—

Hellboy wraps the rope around his stone fist and, with a brutal stone-fist yank, pulls Kroenen into the pit! With a horrible scream, Kroenen drops head-first past them and onto the spikes. He wriggles like a fish caught on a hook, only making it worse, as he slides further down the blades.

Interior, Above The Hexagonal Trap Door Pit—Day. Hellboy climbs out and sits. Sees Kroenen's blade embedded in the floor. Holding it: the prosthetic hand, still ticking.

Interior, Above the Hexagonal Trap Door Pit—Day. Hellboy peers down. Still alive, Kroenen frees one arm, slicing through his own ropy bicep.

HELLBOY
You like playing possum, you Nazi pinhead? (*Beat.*) Then try playing dead.

Interior, Bottom of Hexagonal Trap Door Pit—Day. Hellboy tips a massive cogwheel over the edge. Kroenen emits a horrid scream as it crushes him.

Interior, Above the Hexagonal Trap Door Pit—Day. Manning sits down, bandaging his injuries. Hellboy kneels down.

HELLBOY
Are you okay?

Manning nods weakly. Hellboy brings out a cigar and fires up his Zippo.

HELLBOY
You'd better stay here. I'll find a way out. We'll come back for you.

MANNING
You call that thing a cigar?

HELLBOY
Yup.

MANNING
You never, ever light a cigar that way.

He digs out one of his fine cigars, cuts it and hands it to Hellboy.

MANNING
Use a wooden match. It preserves the flavor.

He lights it for him. Hellboy grins.

MANNING
Thank you.

HELLBOY (*smiles*)
My job.

Interior, Tunnel "B"—Underground Narrow Tunnel—Day. A narrow tunnel. Liz and Myers advance carefully. Just ahead, a cave-in. Pieces of ceiling, timber, coffins, and corpses form a chaotic barrier. As they squeeze past …

MYERS
So, he thinks that you and I … That's why he's mad at me—

A few bones roll by. Wet earth drops onto their shoulders. They draw their arms close to their bodies, pointing their flashlight beams straight down.

A moment of strange intimacy.

MYERS
But it's not true, is it?

LIZ
What—?

MYERS
That you feel that way about me.

LIZ
You want to know—Now—? Here? Red, white, whatever—Guys are all the same.

Interior, Tunnel "C"—Underground Tunnel—Steep Slope—Day. Hellboy labors up a steep slope, using rocks and roots for handholds. He reaches a dead end and collapses, out of breath. Light filters through a crack in the ground; he can faintly hear Liz and Myers.

UNDERGROUND CAVERN
(MAKE SLIGHTLY WETTER THAN THIS)

Interior, Tunnel "B"—Underground Tunnel—Cavern Area—Day. Liz and Myers reach a wider section of Tunnel "B." They find themselves calf-deep in brown water. Myers lights Liz's path as she steps onto a large stone.

MYERS

Watch out. It's slippery …

His light shorts out. She shines her light past him.

LIZ

Oh, my God …

Myers turns. His flashlight comes back on, revealing a complex natural cavern. An entire wall is covered with translucent eggs.

Sammael is there, gnawing on a dry arm bone, with the hand still attached. When the light hits his face, his milky pupils constrict. A snarl … A second Sammael emerges from the water. It shakes itself off. A third one raise its head.

Myers and Liz try to back away, but a metal wall rises right behind them— Klank! They are trapped! Myers goes to grab a set of explosive belts. Tries to set up the timer. Zip! One Sammael snatches them away. Myers falls to the ground, clothes torn, injured.

LIZ (*into the radio*)

Marco, Marco, Marco … Get your big red butt over here!

Something stomps on the ceiling directly above them. Again and again.

Interior, Tunnel "C"—Underground Tunnel Floor—Day. Hellboy pounds the floor with his rock hand. Furiously.

HELLBOY

Hang on kid, I'm coming for you!

The rocks below him start to crumble.

SAMMAEL EGG GROTTO #2
MIGNOLA
1/17/03

DOOR REVOLVES/ROLLS INTO PLACE

ENTRANCE "DOOR" TO EGG CHAMBER

WATER TERRACE

WATER TERRACES

EGG CAVERN AREA

Exterior, Anthill View Of Underground Tunnels And Pits—Day. In an "Ant Farm" view of the complex, we see Hellboy above, pummeling and—in the cavern below—Liz and Myers.

Interior, Tunnel "B"—Underground Tunnel Cavern Area—Day. Dust and rocks fall from above. The four identical creatures move in on Liz and Myers. Myers shoots one in the head three times. The creature shakes off the hits as if pelted with pebbles.

One of them springs. As it flies through the air, Hellboy crashes through the ceiling. He lands on top of it along with a ton or two of stone. The creature is crushed. Two eggs glow, metamorphosing. Presto—two new Sammaels are born. The first two Sammaels growl, joined by the two new ones. Liz sprints to safety.

HELLBOY
Sorry. Just couldn't leave you two alone.

Hellboy scoops up Myers and deposits him next to Liz. Lit by Myers' flashlight, two of the creatures jump. One clamps onto Hellboy's back, the other onto his leg. Hellboy howls. The third one joins in, like lions dragging down a zebra. This time, though, the zebra fights back.

Hellboy pulls out his gun and fires a round into the chest of a Sammael. Two eggs glow—two new Sammaels are born. They're five. Hellboy's torso is covered in blood. He falls to the ground. A fourth and a fifth creature spring onto him, biting. Hellboy is in trouble. Liz watches and shivers. A ripple of heat shimmers over her body.

LIZ (*at Myers*)
Hit me.

MYERS
What?

Liz is desperate, crying.

RESTRAINT YOKE

Both del Toro and I loved this idea—a nod to Frankenstein chained into the chair in James Whale's classic, brilliant *Bride of Frankenstein.*

—MM

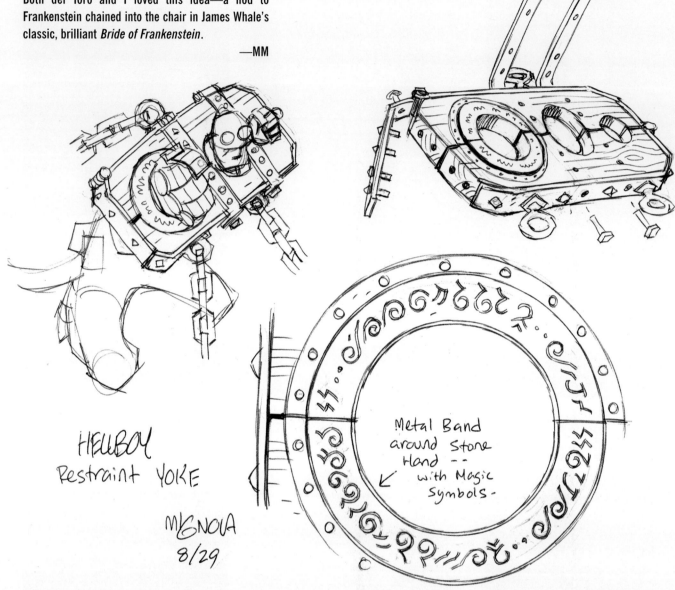

HELLBOY
Restraint YOKE

MIGNOLA
8/29

Metal Band
around Stone
Hand --
with Magic
Symbols-

LIZ
Hit me—(*Beat.*) All of my life I've run away from it … Now I *want* it to happen! Do it.

Hellboy screams. Water explodes under the fighting bodies. Two of the Sammaels turn their attention to Liz and Myers.

MYERS
I can't, I—

Liz slaps him.

LIZ
I know now—I love him. I've always loved him.

A beat of silence, then Myers slaps her across the face, once. Hard. The heat ripple builds. The air vibrates around her. Her pupils kick back light, like an animal's.

LIZ
Go now.

Myers ducks behind a rock as Liz's arms blaze with fire.

The two approaching Sammaels are ready to pounce. On top of Hellboy, one of them turns its head, like a lion hearing the hunter's gunshots. A staggering Hellboy sees Liz's body shake in a surge of white-hot energy.

HELLBOY (*weak*)
Liz …

The water at her feet blows away as a concave shockwave of fire expands. The fire engulfs the creatures. Devours them all.

HELLBOY

GRIGORI

Interior, Tunnel "B"—Underground Tunnel Cavern Area— Day. The screen fades to white and then … Silence, then a pulse. A high ringing tone. A heartbeat.

Hellboy pushes away the half-cooked remains of two Sammaels. The other creatures are little more than blackened bones. He stumbles forward. No water left. Everything is half-buried in a cracked, bone-dry bed of mud. Liz lies on the ground, on her side, unconscious. Myers is alive, but too groggy to even acknowledge it. Weakly, Hellboy turns around: In the eerie silence of his deafness, he sees Grigory—laughing noiselessly, witness to an absurd comedy.

Ilsa approaches. And—in a simple, brutal move—hits him with a hammer—Fade Out / Fade In.

Interior, the Catacombs—Night. Hellboy slowly comes to. He is chained to a massive wooden yoke. He takes notice of his surroundings: a large church-like space, surrounded by funeral niches and statues holding swords. High columns flank huge mechanical gears. A solar system model takes the place of an altar.

Off to one side, Ilsa uses a hammer to destroy the timers on the explosive belts. Next to the main nave, Myers is tied to a stone pillar. Under his feet, a blood channel, leading to the immense stone slab bought from Lapikov.

HELLBOY
CATACOMBS
(under Dome)
Study #3
Myers tied to column

Column Detail

MIGNOLA
8/22/02

CATACOMBS

The bulk of my pre-production art focused on two locations—the abbey ruins at the beginning of the film, and the catacombs under Rasputin's tomb at the end. With the abbey, del Toro was very specific about what he wanted, and I don't think I contributed too many ideas of my own. The catacombs were different. He did have clear ideas about certain things—a certain number of tunnels, the Piranesi-like area with the bridge, the egg chamber, and the big domed room for the final scene. However, unlike with the abbey, he did not give me a lot of detail. The catacomb drawings came near the end of pre-production in L.A., and I think by that time he had a lot of different things on his mind. For whatever reason, I found myself for the first time thinking ahead of him.

The script at that time had the metal walls popping up in the chamber under Rasputin's tomb, but that was the only mechanical thing in all the catacomb scenes. I felt that by itself it just stuck out like a sore thumb, and that if it was going to happen, there had to be more to it. So I went back to Kroenen's crazy clockwork vest. Design-wise it also stuck out all by itself. What if we picked up on that design for the end of the film? The vest had been del Toro's idea, and he loves spinning gears, so I thought he would go for the idea, and he did. I started adding giant gears and counterweights everywhere, but I felt that all of this stuff had to do more than just pop up those walls and open the dome at the end. That's how the Apocalypse Clock came to be.
—MM

HELLBOY
CATACOMBS
(under Dome)
STUDY #1

MIGNOLA -
8/20/02

CATACOMB SET   TUNNEL   9' GEAR WELL

CATACOMB COLOR

From del Toro's memo "Hellboy Visual Notes."
UNDERNEATH MOSCOW: The opposite of BPRD or NEW YORK. Whimsical and full of dreary Rackham-esque forms and buildings. Piranesi times 10, clockwork mechanisms, wooden chambers, black rock, moist earth, pulleys, gears, and rusty spires and domes, etc.

This is a magic land that has been corrupted. A fairy tale gone bad.

In the case of the ICE CAVE and the SAMMAEL CAVE we will go for ALL BLUE sets and light. This will contrast with the eggs and the RED of HELLBOY. We will use Gray/Black rock, Blue light and EVEN blue water. I mean BLUE and Rust in a milky mixture. Once again. This is NOT REAL but is very beautiful and EXPRESSIVE.

—GdT

APOCALYPSE CLOCK

I thought that this would be a great set piece for the final scene. It would be big and smart looking, it would have lots of moving parts, and it would, in some mechanical way, show that the eclipse was coming. And you just can't go wrong with a giant angel. The angel is meant to represent Hellboy's hand being the key to unlocking the door to that other world. As I recall, del Toro never really said much about it, but it went straight into the film so I knew he liked it. For me it felt great to contribute one design idea that was completely my own.

—MM

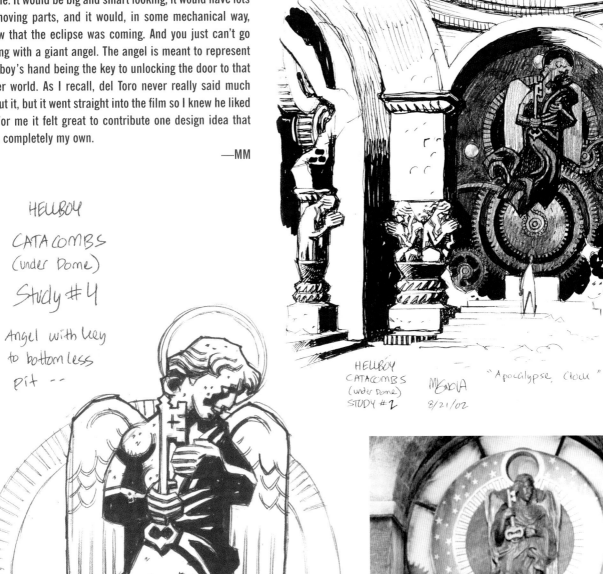

HELLBOY
CATACOMBS
(under Dome)

Study #4

Angel with key
to bottomless
pit --

HELLBOY
CATACOMBS
(under Dome)
STUDY #2

MIGNOLA
8/21/02

"Apocalypse Clock"

center of the
"Apocalypse
Clock"

MIGNOLA
8/22/02

Liz lies at Grigory's feet. He's dressed in a ceremonial robe and holds his leather book open. His back to Hellboy, he faces a mural of the angel Abbadon holding a key.

GRIGORY
"And I looked and beheld an Angel, and in his hand the key to the bottomless pit …"

Hellboy tenses, rage building. The yoke creaks, but doesn't bend.

GRIGORY (*gestures at the stone piece*)
These were the words I heard as a peasant boy in Tobolsk. And now, the door—sent by the Ogdru Jahad so that they might at long last enter our world.

ILSA (*to Hellboy*)
You are the key! The right hand of doom!

Hellboy studies the stone sculpture, its three hand imprints.

ILSA (*triumphant*)
What did you think it was made for? Open the locks.

Hellboy stares at his huge right arm, as if for the first time.

MYERS
Don't do it! Don't do it!

Ilsa kicks Myers in the face.

ILSA
Silence!

The open dome above reveals the moon. An eclipse is beginning. The altar's clockworks monitor its progress.

ILSA
Imagine it—An eden for you and her—

HELLBOY
No.

Grigory turns to Hellboy.

GRIGORY
No? (*Reasonable.*) In exchange for her life then, open the door.

In torment, Hellboy, shakes his head: no.

GRIGORY
As you wish.

He leans over Liz, whispers in her ear: Her body arches, her mouth emits a plume of energy. Grigory greedily inhales it. Then she goes limp.

GRIGORY
She's dead.

HELLBOY
No! No!

He struggles again. One of the cuffs snaps. He swats Ilsa with his free hand. She stumbles backwards. Now Hellboy fights to free his other hand. Indifferent, Grigory watches the eclipse.

GRIGORY
Her soul awaits on the other side. If you want her back … (*Beat.*) Open the door and claim her.

His head and heart racing, Hellboy struggles for an answer. Can't find one … the moon is almost totally eclipsed. He drops his gaze. His voice a hoarse whisper.

HELLBOY
For her.

Grigory moves close to Hellboy. Rips the rosary off his wrist. It lands near Myers.

GRIGORY
Names hold the power and nature of things. Mine for example. Rasputin: "The crossroads." (*Beat.*) And crossroads I have become. (*Beat.*) Your true name—Anung un Rama. Repeat it. Become the key.

HELLBOY (*closing his eyes*)
Anung-un-Rama …

Interior, Catacombs—Night. Hellboy's stone arm glows. Ancient symbols of fire burn the stone. Flames momentarily engulf his body.

A photo-board by Art Lee, indicating special effects over a still.

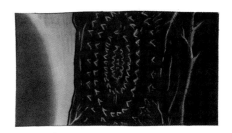

Interior, Catacombs—Night. Hellboy roars as his horns majestically burst forth! Out of his mouth, energy and light boil like condensing breath on a winter's night.

Inebriated with power, the new Prince of Hell smiles with supreme arrogance. His shadow falls on the white marble of the slab and mysteriously spreads over it until the stone turns black as obsidian.

MYERS

No! Don't do it! Listen to me!

Hellboy inserts his enormous paw into the first imprint on the stone slab—Clack! He turns it, like a lock. A beam of crimson light shoots upwards into the sky.

Exterior, View from the City—Night. Visible from all over Moscow, the beam blazes to the moon! The same phenomenon as in the prologue, but this time it's more intense, with ripples and haloes.

Exterior, the Other Side—Night. Again, the infinite, starry space. Again, the Ogdru Jahad. The ruby beam pierces the darkness.

Interior, Catacombs—Night. Hellboy watches as the first imprint disappears. In its place: a burning glyph. Myers struggles with his bindings. The rough hemp cuts his skin, but he manages to free one hand.

Exterior, the Other Side—Night. The Ogdru Jahad shifts, suddenly breaking free. Gelatinous limbs uncurl, expand. Its enormity puzzles the eye, obscuring the frame.

Interior, Catacombs—Night. Hellboy thrusts his hand into the second imprint. Clack! He turns it. Myers spots the broken rosary and reaches for it.

Exterior, the Sky—Night. In the storm clouds, lightning illuminates gargantuan tentacles reaching into the earthly plane.

Del Toro and Mignola worked out a more elaborate sequence with the Block than what appears in the film.

HELLBOY
THE BLOCK
STAGE I

① Symbol in fire appears on the block --

② HB touches symbol and it flickers away -- scatters outward and disappears.

③ HB's shadow remains on the block

④ Shadow spreads to cover the block.

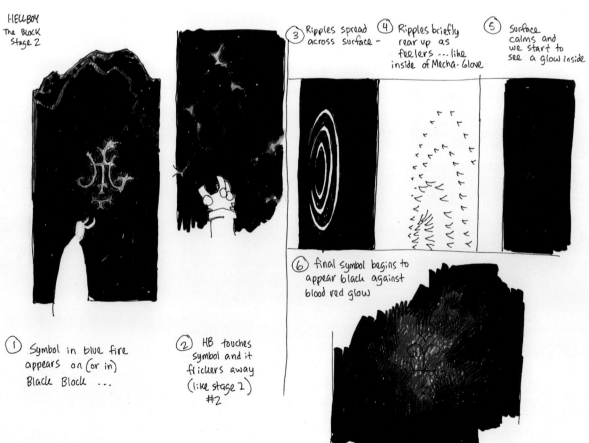

HELLBOY
THE BLOCK
STAGE 2

① Symbol in blue fire appears on (or in) Black Block ...

② HB touches symbol and it flickers away (like stage 2) #2

③ Ripples spread across surface -

④ Ripples briefly rear up as feelers --- like inside of Mecha-Glove

⑤ Surface calms and we start to see a glow inside

⑥ final symbol begins to appear black against blood red glow

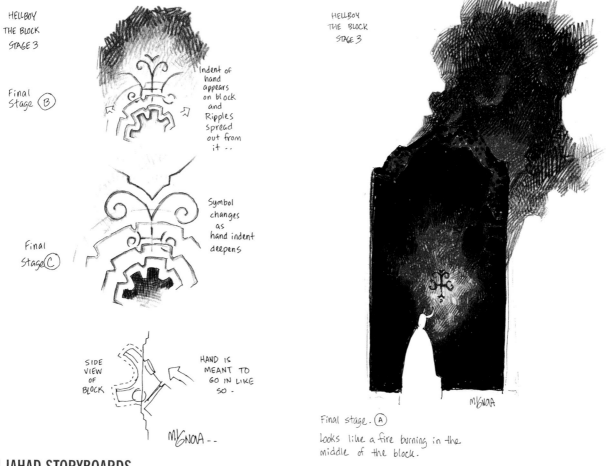

HELLBOY
THE BLOCK
STAGE 3

Final
Stage Ⓑ

Indent of
hand
appears
on block
and
Ripples
spread
out from
it --

Final
Stage Ⓒ

Symbol
changes
as
hand indent
deepens

SIDE
VIEW
OF
BLOCK

HAND IS
MEANT TO
GO IN LIKE
SO -

HELLBOY
THE BLOCK
STAGE 3

Final stage. Ⓐ
Looks like a fire burning in the
middle of the block.

OGDRU JAHAD STORYBOARDS

These are the only storyboards I did for the film. Del Toro and I originally worked this out on a greasy napkin at lunch.

—MM

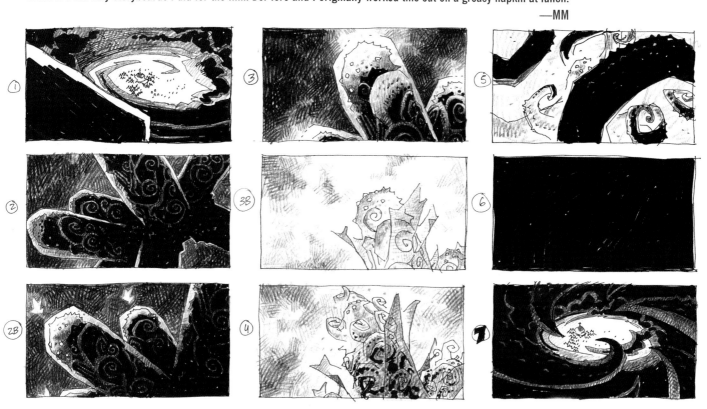

Art from **Hellboy**: Wake the Devil, copyright 1996, Mike Mignola.

Storyboard sequence by Simeon Wilkins mirroring Mignola's version.

Interior, Catacombs—Night. Grigory drinks in the first signs of the arrival and laughs.

GRIGORY
The final seal. Open it!

Hellboy puts his hand inside—Clack! Before he can turn it, Myers reaches the rosary. Ilsa lunges at him. He clobbers her full in the face. She staggers back and down.

MYERS (*to Hellboy*)
Remember who you are!

He throws the rosary at Hellboy. Instinctively, Hellboy catches it. It smokes in his hand. He tosses it away. It lands next to the explosive belts. Hellboy opens his palm, seeing the smoking, charred imprint of the cross and beads. He looks over at Grigory.

With a blood-curdling scream, Hellboy grabs his horns with both hands, brutally snaps them off. Energy spews from the stumps. He stabs Grigory with one of them. Grigory drops to his knees, holding his stomach. Hellboy drops the blood-stained horn.

The final lock disappears into the stone. The light flickers and the connection with the moon is broken. Ilsa, licking her bloody lips, looks up. The sky is silent. The thunderclouds are parting. The eclipse has ended.

Grigory crumples in agony. The burning glyphs in Hellboy's stone hand dim down, his features and body resume their usual shape. All is quiet.

GRIGORY
You will never fulfill your destiny. You will never understand the power inside you.

HELLBOY
I can live with that.

He breaks Myers's chains, helps him up.

Interior, Catacombs—Night. Hellboy painfully takes Liz's limp body in his arms. Myers stands by his side. He kisses her forehead, caresses her hair, then walks down the steps. Myers steps on something. He looks under his foot: A smashed glass eye. Then... out of the silence, a whisper.

GRIGORY
Child …

Hellboy turns. Grigory, on his knees, smiles.

GRIGORY (*dying*)
Look what you've done—

He looks up. In his empty eye socket, fleshy tendrils shift lazily.

GRIGORY
You've killed me—an insignificant man … but you have brought forth a God.

He uncovers his abdomen. Long, fleshy pseudopods spill out of the wound, like intestines. A large entity erupts from Grigory's torso and claws the air.

GRIGORY
Behold, my master, Behemoth. Guardian of thresholds, destroyer of worlds.

Covered in steamy slime, a seven foot, multi-tentacled shape—baby Behemoth—lands on the stone slab. The squirming flesh surges up like greasy pink foam. Growing exponentially by the second.

Ilsa kneels and embraces Grigory's corpse. Kisses him on the mouth. A gargantuan tentacled shadow looms above them.

ILSA
Hell will hold no surprises for us.

A tower of flesh disdainfully crushes them both.

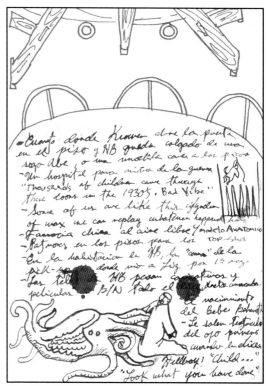

From del Toro's diary.

RASPUTIN'S BELLY

Strangely enough, Rasputin being stabbed in the belly and a creature spilling out was in my original notes for the *Seed of Destruction* comic-book miniseries. I don't remember why I abandoned the idea, and I'm pretty sure I never mentioned it to del Toro. I guess great minds just think alike.

—MM

*Photoshop illustration of Behemoth
by Carlos Huante of Spectral Motion.*

THE SWORD
Toward the end of pre-production in Prague, del Toro suddenly decided Hellboy should use a sword in the final scene.

—MM

Hellboy with a sword? Very Mignola.

—GdT

Interior, Catacombs—Adjacent Tunnel—Night. In a passageway, Hellboy carefully hands Liz's body over to Myers.

HELLBOY
Keep her safe. No matter what. I'll deal with whatever's back there.

MYERS
Alone?

HELLBOY
How big can it be?

As if in response, a massive tentacle fills the tunnel, reaching for him. Oil lamps hanging from the ceiling smash onto Hellboy's head as he is pulled back at breakneck speed, finally confronting—

Interior, the Catacombs—Night. Behemoth! The size of a house.

Hellboy—head smoking—writhes in the grip of the tentacle. It suddenly throws him toward the ceiling. As he arcs back down—Bam!—he cracks the floor wide open. Next to him: the rosary and the explosive belts. He tries to grab them. The tentacle slams down, blocking his way. The vibration sends the belts down into the crack. They bounce off a small ledge and land further down. Far below, grinding cogwheels and gears.

Hellboy manages to pull a steel sword from the closest marble statue. Hellboy stands up and swings the sword for all he's worth. Fwap! He cuts clean through the tentacle. The tip hits the floor, rolling into the crack.

From out of Behemoth's stump … a mass of wriggling tentacles replaces the cut-off section! They squirm around Hellboy's face as he slashes, again and again, fighting his way forward. He leans into the crack, stretches his arm, struggling to grab the belts. A few inches short. He jumps into the crevice, onto the first ledge. It crumbles! The gears below grind a few falling bricks. The belts slide away.

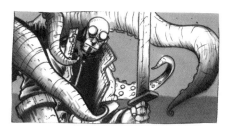

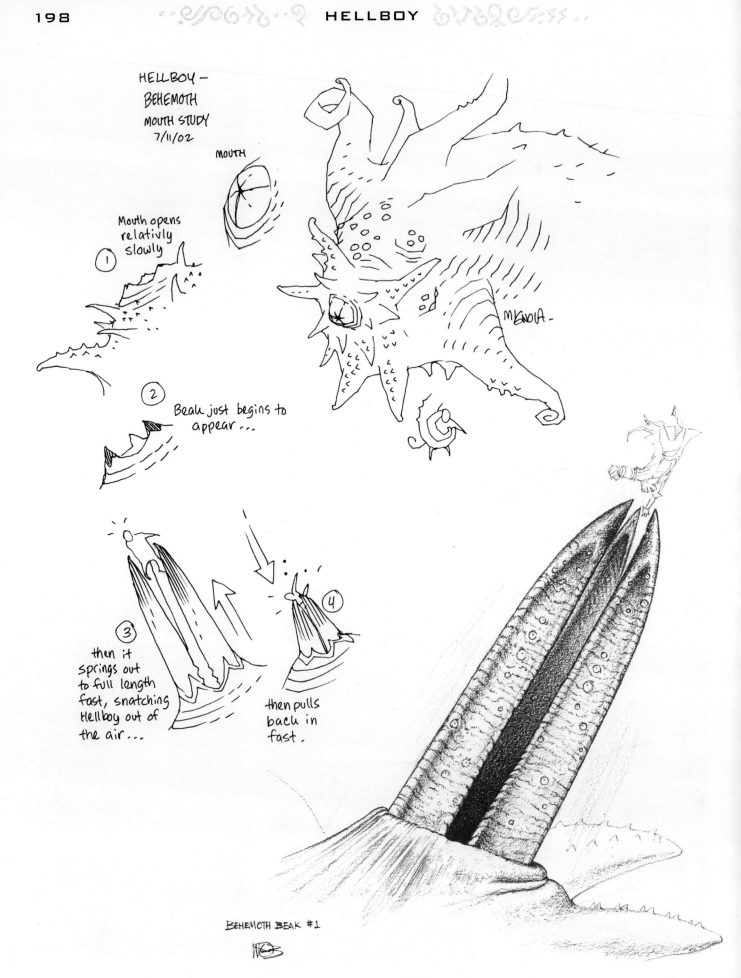

HELLBOY —
BEHEMOTH
MOUTH STUDY
7/11/02

MOUTH

Mouth opens
relativly
slowly

①

② Beak just begins to
appear...

③ then it
springs out
to full length
fast, snatching
Hellboy out of
the air...

④ then pulls
back in
fast.

MIGNOLA-

BEHEMOTH BEAK #1

A tentacle captures Hellboy, pulls him up. At the last second, he grabs the belts with his tail. The beast raises Hellboy high. A multi-layered mouth opens in the body of Behemoth. The most horrible proboscis ever seen.

Hellboy's tail passes him the belts. The timers on them are crushed. A spark spurts: Useless.

HELLBOY
They never work—

He wraps them around his stone arm.

HELLBOY
Ugh—Now, this is gonna hurt—

He pulls the pin on all the explosives. Behemoth drops him into a squid-like beak and gulps him down. After a moment, a weird gurgle emanates from the creature's innards. Then a surge of light roils within the thing, outlining the pulpy organs. The creature starts to burn. A chain reaction yields a cacophony of explosions as Behemoth is enveloped in a cloud of fire, goo and soft flesh. Hellboy lands with a sickening, bone-crunching Thud!

With a bellow, Behemoth goes down, the limp tentacles missing Hellboy as they vanish in a blaze of energy and light. Finally, just a few cinders of flesh float in the air.

Hellboy stands, covered in goo. Two final shockwaves of light ripple over the ground.

HELLBOY
Ouch—it did hurt.

Interior, Adjacent Tunnel. Hellboy lurches into the passageway and spots Myers. Painfully drags himself over. Liz's body is on the floor.

Manning limps in from an adjacent room. Hellboy cradles Liz's head in his huge hand. Holds her against his powerful chest and whispers in her ear. A beat or two, then a moan.

LIZ
In the dark—I heard your voice—What—did you say—?

He looks at her, lovingly caressing her hair.

HELLBOY
"You, on the other side—let her go. Because for her, for her—I'll die. I'll cross over." (*Beat.*) "And you'll be sorry I did."

Myers smiles. Liz looks at Hellboy for the first time as what he is: the man she loves. A warm, gentle fire rims her body. Manning watches. Agent Myers smiles a sad smile, illuminated by the flames. Hellboy and Liz kiss. The fire haloes them and builds.

Fade Out.

Prague, CZR, 06-14-03 03: 50 A.M.

MEN-AT-ARMS SERIES

EDITOR: MARTIN WINDROW

U.S. Army Combat Equipments 1910-1988

Text by GORDON L. ROTTMAN

Colour plates by RON VOLSTAD

OSPREY PUBLISHING LONDON

Published in 1989 by
Osprey Publishing Ltd
59 Grosvenor Street, London, W1X 9DA
© Copyright 1989 Osprey Publishing Ltd

British Library Cataloguing in Publication Data

Rottman, Gordon L.
  U.S. Army Combat equipments, 1910–1988.—
  (Men-at-arms series; 205).
  1. United States, Army. Infantry. Army equipment,
  1910–1988
  I. Title   II. Series
  356′.186′0973

  ISBN 0-85045-842-0

Filmset in Great Britain
Printed through Bookbuilders Ltd, Hong Kong

Artist's Note

Readers may care to note that the original paintings
from which the colour plates in this book were
prepared are available for private sale. All
reproduction copyright whatsoever is retained by the
publisher. All enquiries should be addressed to:

Ronald B. Volstad
P.O. Box 2730
Canmore, Alberta,
Canada TOL OMO

The publishers regret that they can enter into no
correspondence upon this matter.

Acknowledgements

Information does not exactly abound on the subject of
web gear, especially in regard to its development, this
information being lost in Quartermaster reports and
studies, many of which are retained for only a few
years. It is because of this that collectors of these
'smelly old' treasures are of particular value. A
number of collectors willingly made their collections
available for study and shared information. I wish to
record my special appreciation to the 36th Infantry
Division Association Ceremonial and Demonstration
Auxiliary, a Texas-based World War II re-enactment
organisation, and in particular to Marvin F.
Schroeder, President, for sharing his collection of
equipment from the first half of this century. Paul
Lemmer deserves special thanks for sharing his World
War I and earlier period collection and reference
library. Shelby Stanton generously provided many
photographs from his vast collection, some of which
appeared in his excellent *Order of Battle U.S. Army
World War II*, (Presidio Press). Thanks too to the
Public Affairs Office, US Army Infantry School for
providing the latest equipment information. I wish
also to thank my wife, Enriqueta, for her support.
And last, but not least, a very special thanks to Ron
Volstad whose artistic efforts have added so much to
this and my previous books.

U.S. Army Combat Equipments 1910-1988

Introduction

Whether referred to as web gear, TE-21, TA50, LBE or LCE, the American soldier's individual combat equipment was seldom praised—except by its developers. Nevertheless, it has always been, and will continue to be an essential part of the fighting man's burden. To say that a soldier's web gear (the most common soldier's term for it from World War I to the present) is close to him is an understatement. It has long been a precept that while he is in the field, if a soldier is not actually wearing his gear, it had better be within arm's reach. A combat soldier withdrawn to the rear can feel quite naked without his gear—his attitude now is very different from his reaction during the first days in basic training, when staring down at a confusing tangle of belts, straps, pouches, and unknown objects, while the drill sergeant announced, 'I'm gonna show ya all how to put this junk together . . . it's gonna be part of ya!'

Correct **terminology** has long been a military obsession, but in the field of combat equipment it has never been quite standardised. A magazine pocket, ammunition pouch, magazine carrier, ammo bag, and small arms case all do the same thing—carry bullets. It is not uncommon for the terms pouch, pocket, and case to be used interchangeably for the same items, even in different official publications. In this book I will attempt to use the correct terms, but there has always been a degree of variance. I will avoid the unintelligible quartermaster's reversed nomenclature, e.g.,'Pack, field, combat, medium, nylon, olive green', in favour of a more coherent jargon.

Equipment **colours** have changed little over the years. Original M1910 and most earlier gear was 'olive drab shade no. 9', actually khaki, a sand colour which varied from a mustard shade to almost white. It was standard until late 1943 when 'olive drab shade no. 7' (OD) was introduced. This was a dark brownish green, the green much more pronounced. Olive green (OG) was adopted in 1956, and is a dark green colour. With the introduction of nylon equipment OG became even darker, though some has a distinctly brownish tint. A black 'U.S.' is printed on virtually all items.

The realities of the soldier's load remain the same to this day . . . what is perceived to be needed, as opposed to what is actually required. (From *Corporal Si Klegg and His 'Pard'* by Wilbur F. Hinman, published by N. A. Hamilton and Co., Cleveland, Ohio, 1888)

How Si Started In   A Serious Miscalculation   The Shrinkage Begins   How Si Came Out

With regard to equipment **issue and replacement**, it has generally been the year following its adoption before it was actually fielded, and it could be several years before it was fully issued. Current contracts were usually completed and existing stocks exhausted before new gear was issued.

The development of US combat equipments has been evolutionary since the introduction of the first 'modern' system after the turn of the century. A number of factors have a direct influence on its development. Materials have a great deal to do with it. For centuries, leather was used for the soldier's equipment. While suitable, it had many drawbacks. The industrial revolution saw enormous advances in the textiles industry, leading to the development of durable cotton canvas and webbing suitable for combat equipments. The demand for even more durable materials, per-

mitting lighter weight construction, led to the adoption of nylon. The heavier the soldier's equipment, the fewer combat-essential items he can carry. Lighter weight gear also permits a more efficient soldier by allowing more freedom of movement.

The physiological, or 'comfort', factor is just as important as the more obvious considerations of material and weight. The ability of the soldier to maintain an erect posture and a balanced centre of gravity are critical. The equipment must not interfere with respiration, perspiration, or circulation. Chaffing and cutting must be prevented, accomplished by the use of padding or softer materials.

A critical factor is the trade-off between light weight and durability. If the materials are too light, they simply will not stand up to the rigours of combat abuse. The gear must also be 'soldier proof'. While a recreational backpacker may get years of service from an ultra-lightweight pack, he paid a considerable sum for it and will take great care of it. The soldier, on the other hand, had his 'given' to him—and 'there's always another to replace it'!

Regardless of developments in new materials, the search for the elusive 'light load', and improved designs allowing greater agility and comfort, most major changes in combat equipments have in fact been caused by the adoption of new weapons and the need to transport their ammunition. But weight is the key factor governing the design of combat equipment, and the overriding factor in most writings and studies of the soldier's load:

'The Infantryman of nearly every army today groans under the pack that is required to be carried in campaign. To reduce that burden is a matter that should be a prime consideration of the designers and approving authorities of many arms and equipment and certainly should be foremost in the minds of those who prescribe the articles to be carried on the person of the soldier.'

'(The) risk analysis approach for lightening the soldier's load must now address a mission load item that almost triples the load on a foot soldier. Those of us who, in the past, have humped and jumped the old loads can only marvel at what the Army has done in its "attempts" to take care of the troops.'

The first statement was written by the editors of *Infantry Journal* in the July 1926 issue; the second by

A rifleman, (left) equipped with the bedroll, M1907 suspenders, M1907 cartridge belt, M1905 bayonet, M1908 haversack, M1907 canteen, M1909 shovel carrier, and M1907 first aid pouch (not visible); contrasted with (right) the M1910 equipment. (US Army)

a retired officer in a letter to the editors of *Infantry Magazine* in the July–August 1987 issue.

A cavalryman with the M1912/14 cavalry equipment, with the M1903 rifle carried in the belt ring. (US Army)

Predecessors of the M1910 Equipment

Leather dominated combat equipments for most of the 19th century. It was expensive, heavy, stiff, easily cracked, prone to damage when wet, and required constant work to keep it clean and serviceable. It also caused brass cartridges to corrode after prolonged contact. In 1880 the Army adopted the Mills cartridge belt of dark blue machine woven web, with loops for 40 × .45–70

Springfield cartridges. Wider use of canvas and webbing came with the M1885 equipment, which added a khaki canvas haversack and a round, stamped metal, cloth-covered canteen[1] to the belt; both being carried by leather shoulder slings. A blanket, poncho and shelter-half (half of a small button-together two-man tent) were rolled into a blanket roll and worn over the left shoulder in a fashion reminiscent of the American Civil War. A

[1] A water-bottle, in British parlance.

khaki double-loop cartridge belt for 90 × .30–40 Krag rifle rounds was adopted in 1896.

This gear saw the Army through the 1898 Spanish-American War, which nevertheless demonstrated its defects. It was not until after the turn of the century that replacements were adopted, and not as a collective system, but piecemeal. The first item was the M1903 cartridge belt, the first to have pockets for loading clips, later replaced by the M1907, similar, but with small metal eyelets along the top and bottom edges, or selvage—the former for attaching M1907 'X'-back suspenders, and the latter for equipment items. This was to be a characteristic of all subsequent belts. The M1907 round, stamped, metal canteen and M1907 first aid pouch followed. The M1908 haversack was an improvement over the M1885. Following European practice, an M1909 shovel and carrier were added. The slightly modified M1909 suspenders replaced the M1907. Each of these items was attached to the belt by a double hook which matched pairs of lower selvage eyelets. A two-pocket (12 rounds each) revolver belt for officers, and an M1903 seven-pocket (six rounds each), were also introduced.

Though the individual items were improvements over the M1885 gear, the overall system had a number of disadvantages, the principal being that the blanket roll exerted pressure on the chest, interfering with breathing. Most of its weight was borne on the left shoulder, and this, plus the haversack carried on the left hip, caused an unbalanced load. The haversack, shovel, and canteen also had a severe 'bounce' effect. While lighter than many foreign infantrymen's loads, at 56 lbs it was still judged too heavy.

The adoption of canvas duck and webbing can be traced to Capt. (later Brig. Gen.) Anson Mills. While campaigning against the Indians he found the leather gear then in use had many disadvantages. In 1877 he developed a web cartridge belt; and in conjunction with weaver Charles Gilbert, he established the Mills Woven Cartridge Belt Company in Worcester, Mass. in 1880. It was through the efforts of this firm that the M1885 gear was adopted. The company developed cotton canvas duck[1] and cotton webbing specifically for

A cavalryman with the M1914 cavalry equipment configured for dismounted use. Note the ration bags strapped together to form a knapsack. (US Army)

[1]A heavy tightly woven cotton fabric with water repellent qualities, hence the name 'duck'.

use in military equipments, along with metal fittings. The firm was responsible for developing most of the web gear used by all US armed forces, and manufactured most of it until America's entry into World War I. Many of the design styles and methods of manufacture developed by the Mills Company are still in use today.

The M1910 Infantry Equipment

Historical

Around the turn of the century the British, German, and French armies began to study the soldier's load and how he carried it. They each came to the same conclusion: the soldier should carry no more than one-third of his own weight. Earlier tests had found that the soldier burned 5,000–6,000 calories a day. Just over 3,000 calories were needed to 'fuel' basic life and movement; the remainder was available for marching, working, and fighting. To expend more energy resulted in a rapid loss of efficiency, followed by exhaustion. These studies led not only to the realisation that the soldier's load must be kept as light as possible, but to recognition of the importance of sufficient rations. The physiological effects of combat stress and its subsequent energy drain also began to be appreciated.

A scientific analysis of the soldier's load, coupled with dissatisfaction with the blanket roll and haversack, led the US Army to re-evaluate its equipments. The Mills Company worked closely with the Infantry Board to develop a new system specifically designed to meet the soldier's physical requirements. This early 'human engineering' effort set a maximum weight of 50 lbs, on the soldier's load. The total weight of a rifleman's M1910 gear came to 48 lbs.

Although well designed for its time, the system did have shortcomings. The principal one was the design of the haversack and pack carrier, together carried as a backpack. It was designed solely to transport a prescribed and restricted load, due to the specified weight limitations. This prevented even a few additional items—including cold weather clothing and shelter, extra mission-essential equipment, or even extra rations—from being carried. The length of the securing straps and

the size of the flaps were cut to accommodate solely the prescribed load, which looked great on the parade ground, but was a monster for a tired soldier to pack in a muddy field with wet, numbed fingers at 0400 hours.

Another problem was that the haversack could not be worn without the cartridge belt as it was not equipped with shoulder straps, but with integral suspenders that attached to the belt. Likewise, if the haversack was removed, the belt's support suspenders went with it. A few units issued M1909 suspenders for this purpose; but the idea was for the haversack, with essential items, to be retained by the soldier at all times.

The M1910 equipment, though often modified,

The original version of the M1910 haversack and pack carrier with the components identified. (US Army)

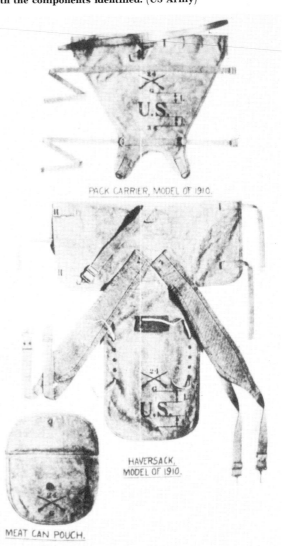

PACK CARRIER, MODEL OF 1910.

HAVERSACK, MODEL OF 1910.

MEAT CAN POUCH.

was to provide the basic concept of equipment used by the Army until 1956, and even then its influence was not to disappear.

Description

This gear was made almost entirely of khaki webbing and canvas duck; the few leather components were russet brown. The metal fittings were of bronze or brass of a dull dark bronze colour, the same as prescribed for uniform buttons. The snap fasteners bore in relief the US coat of arms, again the same as on uniform buttons. All items, unless otherwise noted, were designated M1910.

The dismounted cartridge belt was a three-part assembly: right and left pocket sections and an

M1918 Browning automatic rifle (BAR) equipment: (*top to bottom*) BAR cover, assistant automatic rifleman's belt, automatic rifleman's belt, and left and right automatic rifle ammunition bearer's bandoleers. (US Army)

adjusting strap. On each end of the adjusting strap was a metal tab with two hooks. The strap was passed through the adjustment buckles on the back ends of the pocket sections. The hooks matched two rows of round eyelets set in the backs of the pocket sections, allowing an easy and balanced adjustment of the belt's waist size from the back centre, rather than from the front ends as on the M1903 and M1907 belts. The five cartridge pockets on each section 'puckered' at the bottom, each held two five-round .30 cal. loading clips for the M1903 Springfield. A small retaining strap was fitted inside each. One clip, bullet points up, was inserted in front of the strap, and the strap snapped to a fastener on the pocket front. The second clip, points down, was inserted behind the strap and first clip, and was to be used first. The pocket flap was then snapped to its own fastener below that of the retaining strap. Washer-reinforced round eyelets

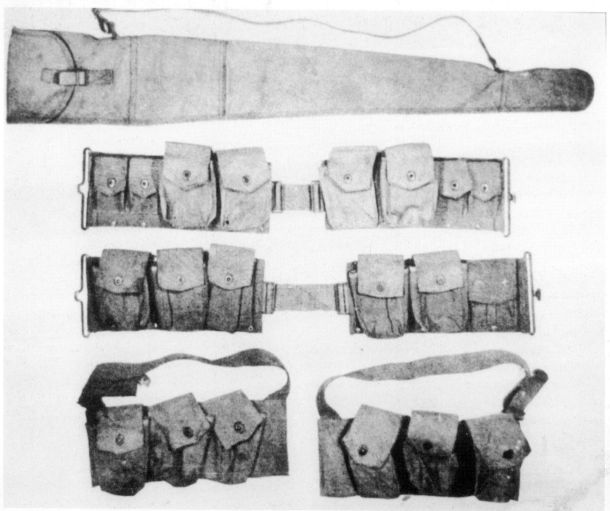

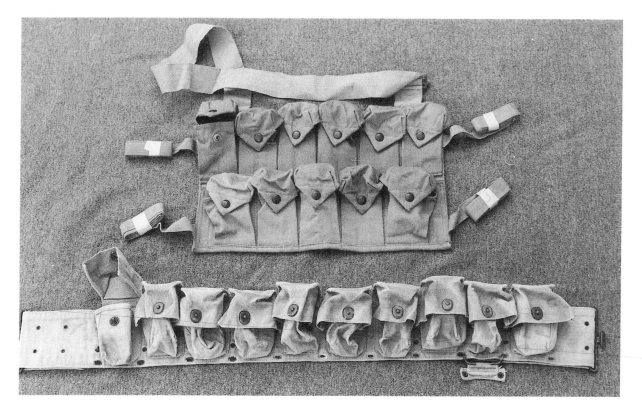

were placed on the belt's top selvage between each pocket and to the rear of the last at the back to attach suspenders. Elliptical (oval) eyelets were fitted in corresponding positions on the bottom selvage, to attach equipment items. The belt was buckled with a male 'T'-fastener on the right end and a female 'U'-fastener on the left, as were all subsequent belts.

The mounted cartridge belt (not all infantrymen walked) was of the same design, but without a left front pocket. In its place was a web extension of the pocket section backing. A two-cell magazine pocket for the .45 cal. M1911 Colt pistol's seven-round magazines was designed to be slipped on to the belt over the buckle fastener. On its back was a web loop of the same width as the pocket; it was a tight fit to hold it in place. The web pockets were puckered at the bottoms, and closed by a two-snap flap.

A mounted cartridge belt for revolvers was also developed, with four rifle cartridge pockets on each side along with two revolver cartridge pockets, each holding six .38 cal. M1892 or five .45 cal. M1909 Colt revolver cartridges.

Additional ammunition was carried in cotton M1903 bandoleers with six pockets each for two clips. In combat a rifleman was to carry two, slung over his left and right shoulders and crossed on his front.

The first aid pouch was a horizontal web packet closed by a two-snap flap. It was attached by means of a double hook; where on the belt it was carried depended on the period or unit.

The dismounted canteen cover was lined with $\frac{1}{4}$ in.-thick grey felt; serving to insulate the canteen and, when wet, to keep it cool. Two snap-secured flaps retained the canteen; initial issue covers had 'square'-end flaps secured by tab fasteners on the cover that fitted through metal eyelet slots in the flaps and rotated 90°. The quart-capacity flask-shaped canteen, with a flat bottom and slightly concave on the side next to the body, was of aluminium. An aluminium pint-capacity canteen cup with a folding metal handle fitted over the canteen's bottom. Canteens and cups have retained this basic design to this day.

The mounted canteen cover was of the same design as the dismounted, but did not have a double hook; instead it was attached to the saddle by an inch-wide web loop strap with a snap hook on the end.

For individuals armed only with a handgun, two belts were adopted. The M1910 revolver belt had four pockets on the left front and side, each holding six .38-cal. or five .45-cal. rounds. It was adjusted by doubling back the belt's right end and securing it with a single hook to eyelets in a row down the centre. A sliding keeper was provided at the 'male' end. Round eyelets were fitted on the top and bottom selvages. The M1912 pistol belt was a plain belt without fixed cartridge pockets. The same .45 cal. pistol magazine pocket as used on the M1910 dismounted belt was slipped on to it and usually worn on the left front. Two models were issued, with and without a sabre ring—a small brass trapezoid ring $10\frac{1}{8}$ in. from the belt's left end, issued to officers, staff NCOs, and first sergeants.

Five models of garrison belts were also issued. They had no selvage or visible adjustment eyelets set in the belt. They were adjusted by doubling back both ends, on which were tabs with two hooks, which hooked into eyelets set in loops woven in the back of the belt. There were sliding keepers on both ends. The male buckle fastener of enlisted men's models was a round disc with a raised red 'U.S.'. Officers' models bore the eagle coat of arms. The female end was a round ring, the officers' model having a raised oak leaf wreath design around it, all others being plain. Double sabre carrier straps were

The M1918 Pedersen device enabled the M1903 Mk. I rifle's specially modified bolt to be removed and the device inserted in its place; this permitted full-automatic fire, using a pistol-type .30 cal. cartridge. Never used in combat, almost all of the 65,000 devices were destroyed after the war. (*Top*) Pedersen device combination tool and a three-pocket bandoleer for 200-round cartons. (*Bottom*) The M1910 cartridge belt; canteen and first aid pouch have added, (*L to R*) an M1903 Mk. I rifle bolt carrier; M1918 Pedersen device in its black metal carrier; and Pedersen device magazine pouch for five 40-round magazines. (Paul Lemmer)

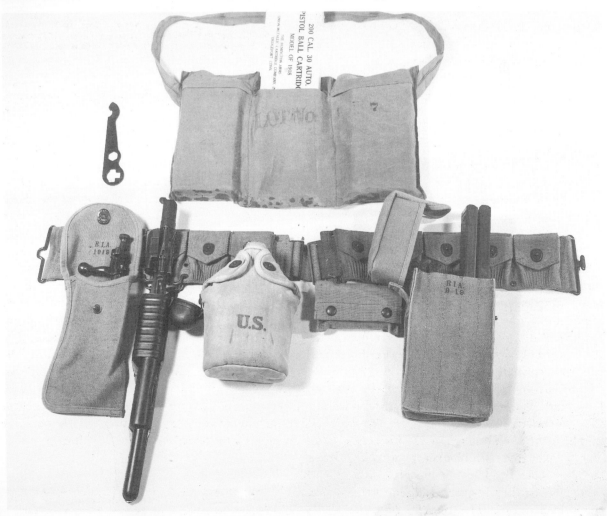

Co. E, 31st Inf. Regt. marches down a street in Vladivostok, Russia during the Allied 1918 occupation. Some of the men in the front ranks wear the M1918 BAR ammunition bearer's bandoleer. (US Army)

fitted to the left side of the officers', staff NCOs', and first sergeants' models, which had no other fittings. Enlisted men's had two sliding rifle cartridge pockets each for one loading clip, one near each end, and a web bayonet carrier slide. The orderlies', scouts' and machine gunners' model had the cartridge pockets, but no bayonet slide. The bandsmen's and musicians' model had no attached items. These fell out of use after World War I.

The haversack and pack carrier were an almost nightmarish assembly of canvas and webbing far too space-consuming to fully describe here—see Plate A. The system's concept envisaged the haversack being worn at all times so that critical items remained with the soldier. Its integral suspenders had two straps each on the front, two being attached to the front and one to each side of the belt. A single rear strap attached back centre of the belt. Rations and toilet articles were carried in the haversack; the mess kit (then called a 'meat can') was carried in a detachable outer pouch; the M1905 bayonet was carried on the left side by a web loop, and the shovel carrier attached under the meat can pouch. The overcoat, if carried, was rolled in a horseshoe and fastened to the haversack's top. The blanket roll, with blanket, poncho, and extra clothing rolled inside a shelter half, was strapped vertically into the pack carrier, and protruded over the soldier's hips. The pack portion could be detached and left in a unit position or carried on transport.

Several different tools were available to the soldier and distributed within his squad. Most men carried a shovel[1] in a canvas carrier hooked to an attachment tab above the meat can pouch, which was secured to the haversack only at its sides, allowing the carrier to be placed under it. A hand axe was also issued with its own carrier. The pick-mattock broke down into a handle and head, and its unusual carrier permitted it to be carried in this manner. The Army's Philippine experience led to the adoption of the bolo, a short, heavy-bladed tool useful for clearing brush. It used a wood scabbard, wrapped in rawhide, and covered with duck. The M1909 bolo, still in use, had a longer blade. The wire cutter had insulated handles to protect against 5,000 volts. All of these tools' carriers and scabbards were fitted with a double hook to permit attachment to belts or the haversack. The engineer compass was carried in a leather belt case.

[1]Initially called a shovel, it was soon officially redesignated the intrenching tool. English also accepts spelling it entrenching . . . it was not long before the soldier coined the common acronym 'E-tool'.

The M1912/14 Cavalry Equipment

Historical

The cavalry had long used equipment designed specifically for its needs. Leather gear was retained by some units after the introduction of the M1885 web equipment, specifically the Dwyer and McKeever cartridge boxes, belts and suspenders. The cavalry did use the M1903 and M1907 cartridge belts, M1907 canteen and first aid pouch, and M1907 and M1909 suspenders. Some units initially used the M1910 mounted cartridge belt. Personal and horse equipment were carried on their mount in M1904 leather ration bags, pommel pockets and saddle bags.

The Cavalry Board developed two sets of equipment: the M1912 gear, first issued in 1913, consisted principally of items carried on the saddle, while the M1914 gear was the trooper's counterpart to the M1910. A few M1910 items were incorporated with the M1912/14.

The most disliked items were the ration bags, designed to fit together forming a knapsack when dismounted: they proved to be a poor backpack and only marginal as ration bags. The principal complaint was that the canvas bags failed to keep dust out, nor were they sufficiently water-repellent; the old leather ones were sorely missed.

The various tools based on the picket pin were eventually dropped from use, as is often the case when something is designed to do too many things. It proved to be a good shoeing iron and picket pin (for tethering horses), but made a poor entrenching tool, pick, or hatchet handle.

Another item dropped from use was the cartridge belt's folding rifle ring, itself replacing the M1904 leather rifle scabbard. The rifle's forearm, protected by a leather sleeve, was placed through the ring while the butt was inserted in a leather rifle carrier boot attached to the left rear of the saddle. A leather rifle strap secured to the ring's mounting bracket was snap-hooked to the triggerguard. To use the rifle the trooper had to remove the butt from the boot, unsnap the triggerguard hook and, keeping the weapon vertical, lower it toward the ground before he could bring it to his shoulder. This system could cause injuries to rider and horse during a fall. It was eventually decided simply to sling the rifle across the back.

With the decline of the cavalry in World War I, followed by the adoption of the principle of moving mounted and fighting dismounted, and subsequent mechanisation, the need for special cavalry equipments began to diminish; the M1914 items were gradually replaced by dismounted gear. One point to remember is that all cavalrymen, besides being armed with an M1903 rifle, also carried an M1911 pistol.

Description

The M1914 cavalry cartridge belt was made in one section. Adjustment was accomplished by doubling the ends back through the buckle fasteners. Metal end tabs with two hooks fastened into two rows of eyelets running down the belt's centre. Round suspender eyelets were fitted between the cartridge pockets on the top selvage and elliptical ones in corresponding positions on the bottom. The nine pockets were the same as on the M1910. A riveted leather tool frog was affixed between the first and second pockets on the left side, but later deleted. The rifle ring was attached under the third pocket on the left. The same pistol magazine pocket as used with the M1910 mounted and M1912 pistol belts

A cavalryman, demonstrating the folding of a saddle blanket, wears the M1923 mounted cartridge belt, M1909 suspenders, M1912 magazine pocket, and M1916 holster (with M1911 pistol): early 1920s. (US Army)

was slipped on the left end. The M1909 suspenders were sometimes used to support the belt.

The M1910 dismounted canteen cover was attached on the left hip, the M1910 mounted cover to the saddle's right rear. Troopers armed with only the pistol used the M1912 pistol belt and magazine pocket.

Additional ammunition was carried in the M1914 cavalry bandoleer with 12 pockets (one rifle clip each) and three pistol cartridge pockets (seven .45 cal. rounds each). The bandoleer was made in a curved form so that it would lie close to the body. A web adjusting strap fastened to a buckle on the other end. This strap was worn over the left shoulder so that the pistol cartridge pockets were at

the wearer's right waist. The M1905 bayonet, with a slip-on cloth scabbard cover, was carried behind the left shoulder by attaching it to the adjusting strap.

The M1912 ration bags consisted of two large duck pouches with strap-closed flaps. A long web strap was attached at the top back of each by a 'D' ring. A short strap was buckled to another sewn to the bags' bottom rear. The long strap of the opposite bag was snapped to the back of the other and secured to the back of the saddle, allowing one bag to hang on either side. When dismounted the cavalryman needed a backpack; he unsnapped the two long straps and laced the bags together side-by-side with a lacing strap, forming a two-

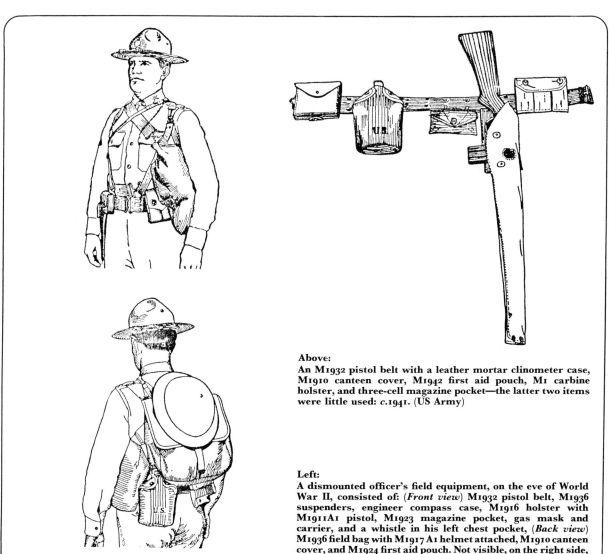

Above:
An M1932 pistol belt with a leather mortar clinometer case, M1910 canteen cover, M1942 first aid pouch, M1 carbine holster, and three-cell magazine pocket—the latter two items were little used: *c*.1941. (US Army)

Left:
A dismounted officer's field equipment, on the eve of World War II, consisted of: (*Front view*) M1932 pistol belt, M1936 suspenders, engineer compass case, M1916 holster with M1911A1 pistol, M1923 magazine pocket, gas mask and carrier, and a whistle in his left chest pocket, (*Back view*) M1936 field bag with M1917A1 helmet attached, M1910 canteen cover, and M1924 first aid pouch. Not visible, on the right side, is a leather binocular case. (US Army)

compartment knapsack. The two short straps were unbuckled from the bottom straps and rebuckled to similar straps on the long straps. The long straps were now snapped to rings on the bags' bottom, forming shoulder straps; and the short straps, now on the front of the shoulder straps, were snapped to the front of the cartridge belt. The meat can was carried in the left bag, toilet articles in the right, and rations in both.

The M1912 picket pin, a 13¾-in. steel spike, had a small claw-hammer head for nailing and pulling horseshoe nails. It was carried in a leather case; on its back was an 'O' ring to attach it to the saddle. A 15-ft khaki lariat was supplied, with an 'O' ring on one end through which the pin was slipped before being driven into the ground, and a hook on the other to attach to the horse's bridle.

The pin had another purpose, as a handle for one of three tools. As an entrenching tool, a shovel blade was fitted to the pin's pointed end. A cotter pin on a small chain, attached to the blade, was placed in a hole in the picket pin's shaft to retain the blade. The other tools were the hatchet and pick, which slid on to the picket pin towards the hammer head, and were held in place by giving the hammer head a sharp rap on a solid object. Duck covers were provided for both, but they had no carrying attachments. A leather E-tool carrier was issued to all troopers, in which was carried the E-tool blade, hatchet, or pick head. Horseshoes were also carried, along with nails (in a small leather bag, secured to the inside by a short thong). Its flap was secured by a leather billet (strip) threaded through two staples. These tools were unpopular due to the abuse inflicted on hands by a grooved steel handle. When mounted, the E-tool carrier was attached beside the sabre carrier on the saddle's right rear. When dismounted, the entrenching tool was assembled and attached to the cartridge belt's tool frog with the blade's concave side towards the body and the handle hanging beside the leg. All cavalrymen below the rank of major were issued the M1910 wire cutter as a shoeing tool, but no carrier was provided as it was carried in the M1912 service pommel pockets (double leather bags for tools, brushes, combs, etc., carried across the saddle front).

The cavalry's affection for leather caused it to retain leather garrison belts with all-leather attachments. An enlisted man's M1912 belt is depicted in Plate A. The officer's was similar, but had fitted only the leather magazine pocket, sabre frog and strap, and two slides, for the M1910 first aid pouch and M1912 holster.

The M1917/18 Equipment

Historical

While all armies involved in the Great War were ill-prepared for the conflict, the US Army was even less ready than most to fight a European war; it was still a frontier army trained and deployed to defend the nation and its overseas possessions. Not only was it not trained and organised for such a conflict, but its rapid expansion in late 1917 meant that a completely new, and vastly larger army had to be re-armed and equipped. The further evolution of the soldier's combat equipment was governed by these same circumstances: new organisations and units, new weapons and tactics, and the need to manufacture the gear quickly.

The first formations deployed overseas were outfitted with standard M1910 gear. It was not long before existing stocks were depleted, even with the Mills Company and the newer Russell Manufacturing Company of Middletown, Conn., working at full capacity. Before long another dozen textile companies were producing web gear; some of them had previously made cotton belts, fire hoses, and asbestos brake linings. To speed manufacture, many of the woven items were redesigned to be sewn and stitched, which could be accomplished on industrial sewing machines instead of the special weaving looms possessed by Mills and Russell.

The robust 'lift-the-dot' (LTD) fastener, a large egg-shaped 'doughnut' snap that fastened to a metal stud and was less prone to jamming by mud, replaced the smaller snap fastener on most items manufactured after March 1917, but not redesignated.

Conservation of leather was critical; a Hide and Leather Control Board was even established. While many items had to be made of leather, as many as possible were now replaced by web and canvas equivalents. One obsolete item, the M1908 haversack, was resurrected and issued to aviators as

a map/document bag. The profusion of new weapons demanded the development of new means of carrying ammunition. The inability to produce sufficient qualities of standard weapons also required that new items be developed for their substitutes. No complete new system of web gear was fielded, but rather a hotch-potch of easily manufactured, substitute and new items.

Description

Most M1910 items were modified to some degree to speed manufacture. The cartridge belts' lower selvage elliptical eyelets were replaced by round ones, as along the top. The M1910 haversack and pack carrier were also modified to speed manufacture, but no improvements were made to ease the soldier's difficulties with the infamous 'long pack'.

To further speed the manufacture of cartridge belts, the M1918 dismounted and mounted belts were adopted, although the M1910 models were still manufactured by the companies possessing the required looms. The M1918 had a canvas backing rather than the M1910's heavy woven back, and lacked the pocket 'puckers'. The M1918 cavalry cartridge belt and M1918 bandoleer likewise had sewn pockets rather than the M1914's woven pockets. There was also a limited-issue M1917 bandoleer made straight rather than curved as the M1914 and M1918. Due to shortages of M1903 rifles the M1917 Enfield was also adopted, a .30 cal. version of the .303 P-14 rifle made in the US for Britain; the M1910 and M1918 belts carried its clips as well.

(*Left*) Experimental jungle packs in the South-West Pacific, 1942; these are the small models which proved uncomfortable and made it difficult to reach the bayonet. (*Centre*) The M1943 field pack, formerly the improved jungle pack, was issued only in limited numbers. (*Right*) The top compartment of the M1943 jungle/field pack could be detached and used as a combat pack, similar to the new field pack adopted in 1987. (*Infantry Journal*)

A little-used 20-round extension magazine was adopted for the M1903 rifle. It was fitted into the magazine well with the floorplate removed and reloaded with five-round clips while in the rifle. Consequently, only one magazine was issued per man. When not in use it was carried in a pouch attached to the cartridge belt by a double hook on a $5\frac{1}{2}$ in. web strap, the pouch resting on the wearer's thigh and secured by leg tie-cords.

The M1910 mounted canteen cover's web carrying strap had proved to be prone to wear. Even though there were restrictions on the use of leather, the web strap was replaced by a leather one on the M1917 canteen cover.

A severe shortage of M1911 pistols soon developed. Colt and Smith & Wesson modified their existing 'New Service' and 'N'-frame 'Hand Ejector' model revolvers, respectively, to handle the M1911 pistol's rimless .45 cal. cartridge, accomplished by the use of three-round 'half-moon' clips. These weapons were almost identical, and were both designated M1917. The M1917 revolver cartridge pouch had three pockets with two half-moon clips carried in each two-cell pocket. The back of the top pocket was fitted with a canvas loop (same width as the pocket) which slipped on to the pistol or mounted cartridge belt. The Army quickly adopted the Winchester Models 1897 and 1910 and Remington Model 11 trench guns—short 12-gauge pump shotguns. The M1917 shotshell pouch had 28 internal shell loops and was carried by a web shoulder sling. A new two-cell pistol magazine pocket was adopted; the M1918 was of the slip-on type like the M1912, but had a rounded flap, rather than 'V'-shaped, with two LTD fasteners, and without 'puckers'. The M1912 pocket, still in use, had its small snaps replaced by LTD fasteners.

The massive use of hand grenades required some means to transport them. This resulted in the 11-pocket grenade carrier and ten-pocket grenade belt, both seeing limited use. A shoulder strap was provided, along with corner tie-tapes permitting it to be worn square on the chest. The M1918 grenade belt was of almost identical design to the M1918 cavalry cartridge belt, but with ten grenade pockets.

The adoption of the M1918 Browning automatic rifle (BAR) saw the introduction of several magazine carriers, all designated M1918. The automatic rifleman's belt was made in three sections like the M1910 cartridge belt, but the cartridge pockets were replaced by three BAR magazine pockets on the left section and two BAR pockets and

an integral two-cell pistol magazine pocket on the right. Each BAR pocket held two 20-round magazines. A later version had the second pocket on the right side replaced by a metal butt holder on a leather base. The assistant automatic rifleman's belt was of the same design, but both front end pockets were replaced by two rifle cartridge pockets. One other squad member carried BAR magazines in mirrored left and right side bandoleers with three magazine pockets, carried on shoulder slings.

The M1910 wire cutter was not capable of cutting German manganese barbed wire. The issue French two-hand cutter, capable of resisting 10,000 volts, was adopted as the M1918 and issued with a leather carrier. The M1917 bolo was the same as the M1910, but lacked a locking device on the guard and scabbard. Some were issued with stamped sheet metal OD-painted scabbards.

Early World War II
Improved M1910 Equipment

Historical

The end of the 'war to end all wars' found the Army with vast amounts of equipment, with many contracts being continued after the cessation of hostilities, as a large Army of Occupation remained in Europe until 1919. The demobilisation of the Army was accomplished swiftly, to almost pre-war

(*Left*) **The M1944 field combat pack with blanket roll and the M1943 E-tool carrier, worn without the cargo pack. (*Centre*) The M1944 combat pack with the cargo pack, blanket roll, and a poncho under the E-tool carrier. (*Right*) The M1944 combat pack, with an M1910 E-tool, was sometimes carried by artillerymen using an M1936 carrying strap. It permitted ease of carriage since they transported it in vehicles and could not be encumbered while manning the guns. (*Infantry Journal*)**

levels; but the USA now found itself in a new position, with more troops deployed overseas. It was hoped that the gear available would suffice the Army for some time as its peacetime budget was rather lean.

The first new items were the M1923 dismounted and mounted rifle cartridge belts, and a pistol magazine pocket for the mounted belt. The M1912/14 cavalry equipment was replaced by M1910 items and the M1923 mounted belt. The haversack and pack carrier were modified and issued as the M1928, but still with the same limitations as the M1910; it was to see the Army through most of World War II.

Several equipment items were adopted in 1936 specifically for officers: the M1936 pistol or revolver belt[1], suspenders, and canvas field bag. Issued in lieu of the haversack, the latter was modelled on the French musette bag, coveted by many Doughboys, and was almost universally referred to by that name. The pistol belt was also issued to enlisted men armed with handguns, sub-machine guns, and carbines. The suspenders, improved over the still-in-use M1909, were likewise issued to some enlisted personnel.

[1]Officially designated the 'pistol or revolver belt', it was commonly referred to as the 'pistol belt', and this phrase will be used in this book.

A wide assortment of gear is carried by these 29th Inf. Div. troops near Brest, France, 1944. (US Army via Shelby Stanton)

The M1937 automatic rifleman's belt had only BAR magazine pockets and none for the pistol or rifle; it was adopted to replace both the M1918 automatic rifleman's and the assistant's. Assistants now carried the BAR bandoleers and normal rifle cartridge belts.

The M1 rifle was adopted in 1937, and while its eight-round *en bloc* clips could be accommodated by the M1923 belts, the new clips required less space. The dismounted and mounted M1938 cartridge belts were developed; these were almost identical to the M1923, but the dismounted had 12 pockets rather than ten, and the mounted 11, plus space for an M1923 pistol magazine pocket. Few of the belts were actually issued; in fact manufacture ceased in the early 1940s, and the M1923 continued as standard.

In 1941 the Army began to develop a vast assortment of clothing and equipment for specialised units such as mountain and ski troops. Alaska was becoming a major area of concern, and it was found that few existing items were suited for this harsh environment—especially the M1928 haversack, which could not carry the necessary loads. A pack was required that permitted the

Troops of the 96th Inf. Div. advance on Leyte Island, 1944. The kneeling man wears the M1928 haversack, jungle first aid kit, and two canteens as authorised for Pacific Theatre troops. (US Army via Shelby Stanton)

unrestricted movement needed by skiers. The Norwegian Bergen-type *Norse Pac* was used as a model for a new mountain rucksack.

It was with this gear—Table of Equipment 21, or TE-21—that the American soldier entered World War II.

Description

The M1923 cartridge belts were similar to their M1918 counterparts, but simplified and of slightly lighter weight. A female snap was fitted to the mounted belt's pistol magazine web backing to better secure the magazine pocket, itself fitted with a matching male snap. The M1923 magazine pocket reverted to a 'V'-shaped flap secured by one LTD fastener, but retained the pocket-wide web loop on the back. The M1938 rifle cartridge belts were the same, but with two more pockets and no clip retaining straps.

The M1924 first aid pouch was a larger version of the M1910, so that a larger field dressing could be accommodated. The M1928 haversack was simplified for manufacture and slightly modified.

The M1936 pistol belt was identical to the M1912, most being modified to M1936 standards by the addition of a female snap to secure the M1923 magazine pocket. The M1936 musette bag was a simple pouch-like bag with two internal compartments. There was a small pocket on the left side and a thin one on the back. Two short straps were fixed to the top back with snap hooks on their ends for attachment to 'D' rings on the shoulders of the M1936 belt suspenders or shoulder carrying strap. The suspenders were of the 'X'-back type, similar to the M1909. Officers carried their mess kit, rations, raincoat, toilet articles, and some extra clothing in the musette bag.

The M1937 automatic rifleman's belt, besides having six pockets, differed from the M1918 by the use of rifle cartridge belt-size buckle fasteners rather than the earlier full belt-width ones. M1918 belts modified to M1937 standards had the smaller buckles installed and the pistol and rifle pockets and butt holder replaced by BAR pockets at depots. The limited issue BAR suspenders were a very simple lightweight 'H'-style; M1909 and M1936 suspenders were also used. The Thompson sub-machine gun 20-round magazine pocket had five cells, carried on the pistol belt by means of two wide web loops.

The mountain rucksack was a large canvas bag closed by a drawstring and a flap secured by two web straps. On the sides were two large leather strap-secured cargo pockets. Equipment attachment tabs and securing straps were also fitted to the sides. The rucksack was mounted on a thin tubular steel frame, two of which could be lashed to a pair of skis and used as a litter. A large leather bracket secured the frame's top and protected the shoulders; a web band rested the rucksack on the hips, and sway was reduced by a web waist strap. A snow-camouflage cover was issued with it. There were some problems with its design, and several minor modifications were made during the course of the war.

The M1941 mounted canteen cover was

basically an M1910 with two horizontal securing straps on its back, a strap with a snap hook on its upper end and a web carrier on its bottom for the cover's double hook to fasten to. The strap could be removed and the hooks attached to the belt in the normal manner, a requirement long demanded by the cavalry.

Late World War II M1910 Equipment

Historical

Climatic extremes as well as new weapons led to the introduction of further equipment items at a rapid pace. But other factors affected the design of equipment, principally material shortages and the use of substitutes. Brass fittings were replaced by enamelled steel and zinc hardware. Canvas and webbing began to be treated to prevent mildew. New weapons meant new means of carrying their ammunition and a wide range of pockets, pouches, and bags were introduced accordingly. Some equipment items were produced under contract in Britain and Australia.

(*Left*) **M1944 cargo-and-combat field packs.** (*Right*) **M1945 cargo-and-combat field packs. The cargo packs are detached in order to display them better. (Schroeder collection)**

In late 1943 it was directed that 'OD shade no. 7' replace the 'OD no. 9', the khaki shade. The brownish green OD shade had several advantages over khaki: it blended in better with European forests and Pacific jungles. Crude camouflage patterns were occasionally applied with green or brown paint to some khaki items, especially in the Pacific. Though OD items were soon put into production, existing stocks of khaki gear were still issued and remained in use for years. It is not unusual for items to be found made of both colour materials, e.g. a cartridge belt with khaki backing, adjusting strap, and flaps, but with OD pocket bodies; or a khaki wire cutter carrier with OD edge binding. Some items were repaired using contrasting old or new colour materials.

There were problems caused by conflicts between the different agencies tasked with equipment

development, either developing items suited to their needs alone, or disputing which items were standardised. One of the principal battles in the logistics war was fought over the adoption of a new combat pack. As the war progressed it became more apparent that the M1928 haversack was ill-suited to the soldier's needs, especially in the tropics where the dry, level, ground needed to lay out and roll the gear was a rarity. Development of a jungle pack began in Panama in early 1942. Test models were issued in New Guinea, and certain problems identified: inability of the wearer to reach his bayonet, cargo compartment too small, and the shoulder straps uncomfortable. Improved test models were issued in early 1943, but there were still some problems.

In the spring of 1943 contracts for the M1928 haversack were being completed, and it was deemed that a replacement was needed. Army Ground Forces (AGF) desired that the jungle pack be adopted to replace the haversack and musette

Heavily armed 42nd Inf. Div. troops in Germany, 1945. The bazooka man carries a general purpose ammunition bag. (US Army via Shelby Stanton)

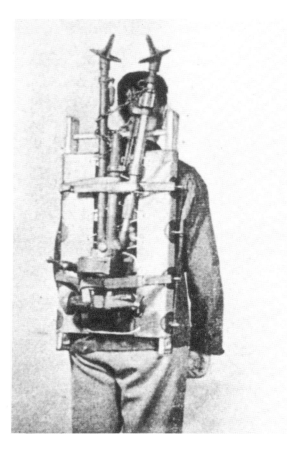

(*Left*) A Yukon pack board, consisting of a wood frame with a laced canvas backing, loaded with an 81mm M1 mortar bipod. There were a wide variety of cargo attachments, with every test agency inventing its own, leading to confusion in proper use of the board. (*Right*) The plywood pack board loaded with a 60mm M2 mortar. It replaced the Yukon model in 1944, though old-timers preferred the former. To prevent confusion, only three accessories were authorised: cargo attachment, quick-release strap, and lashing rope. Later versions had metal pins on the top and sides allowing a rifle to be hung. It was used into the 1970s. (*Infantry Journal*)

bag. The Quartermaster Corps Technical Committee redesignated the jungle pack the M1943 field pack in late 1943, but only as limited standard due to continuing problems.

That same year also saw the AGF test the Marine Corps' M1941 pack. This was a two-piece assembly consisting of a backpack and a detachable cargo pack strapped under it, permitting essential items to be carried by the soldier in the backpack while the cargo pack, with extra clothing and non-essential items, could be dropped in the rear areas. In April 1944 the AGF reversed its request that the jungle pack be made standard and the Marine pack be adopted without further testing—an action opposed by Office of the Quartermaster General (OQMG), which recommended that a new pack incorporating the two-piece feature be developed.

This was begun, and the M1944 cargo-and-combat field pack was standardised in July 1944.

Numerous improvements were recommended by the Infantry Board and incorporated into production packs. These and further improvements were included in the new M1945. AGF wanted the new items issued to the troops as they became available; OQMG, on the other hand, wished to exhaust existing stocks of haversacks and musette bags because of the 1944–45 canvas and webbing shortage. The M1945 was made standard in April 1945, and the M1944 made limited standard. Regardless, most troops finished the war with the M1928 haversack.

The M1936 musette bag was dropped from TE-21 with the adoption of the M1945 pack, but it remained in use until the end of the war. Besides issue to officers, it was issued to mountain troops (to supplement the rucksack) and all motorised units (tank, armoured infantry, artillery, cavalry reconnaissance, etc.) in lieu of the haversack.

The equipment adopted prior to and during the war served the American soldier through the Korean War (1950–53) and into the late 1950s.

Description

The M1923 rifle cartridge belt remained standard, but the clip retaining straps were deleted in about 1943, though British-made belts retained them. The M1942 first aid pouch with a 'V'-shaped flap, influenced by a British-made pouch for US forces, replaced the M1924, which remained in use, however.

The M1 Thompson sub-machine gun was adopted in the spring of 1942 and the M3 'grease gun' at the end of the year. With the M1 came the 30-round magazine, which also fitted the M1928A1. A three-cell magazine pocket with a wide web belt attachment loop, was adopted for both. A shotshell pouch with 12 internal loops for 12-gauge shells was also introduced, attached to the pistol belt by two web loops.

The M1 carbine was adopted in late 1941 to provide a more substantial alternative to the pistol. A very limited issue was made of a three-cell pocket closed by a two-LTD-fastener flap for its 15-round magazines. It was soon replaced by a web two-cell pocket with a canvas loop fitted with a male snap fastener to secure it to the pistol belt. By removing the carbine's stock, a pocket could be slipped on from the forearm end, resting on the right side of the butt after re-assembly. In 1942 a more versatile pocket was introduced; made of canvas, the cells were slightly larger to accommodate an M1 rifle clip. A pair of eyelets were fitted to the bottom edge permitting attachment of other items. Belt attachment was by two web loops; no snap was provided. The selective fire M2 carbine was adopted in September 1944 and with it the 30-round 'banana' magazine. The first 30-round pocket consisted of two cells attached to the belt by two web loops. This was followed by a single compartment pocket; inside were two cells sewn to the backing for one magazine each, and two more magazines were carried in the main compartment.

Two- and three-pocket hand grenade carriers were issued on a limited basis; each pocket held two grenades. Attached to the belt by a double hook, they were further secured by leg tie-tapes. A

(*Top*) **A former M1918 automatic rifleman's belt converted to an M1937. Note the difference between the right and left side pocket flaps, indicating that it was assembled from components; note the special BAR suspenders introduced between the wars.** (*Bottom*) **An M1937 BAR belt. (Schroeder collection)**

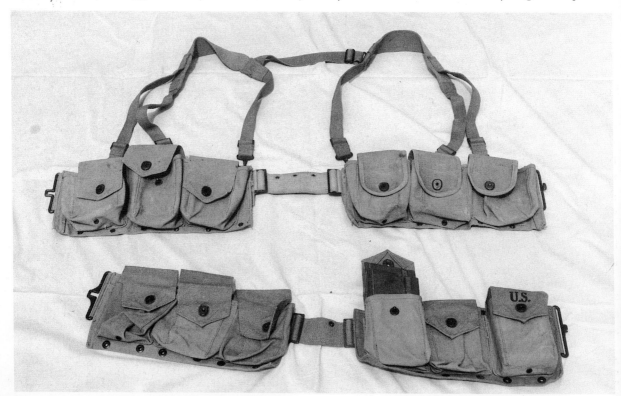

general-purpose ammunition bag, designed for 19 different types of ammunition and grenades, was adopted in the spring of 1943. Often used by paratroopers to carry extra ammo, this was a large pouch with a strap-closed flap. 'D'-ring-fitted straps were sewn to the sides for attachment of the musette bag's carrying strap. The M1936 musette bag was made slightly larger, and an equipment attachment tab added on the flap, in 1943.

The jungle M1943 field pack was basically a canvas bag, made in either OD or camouflage pattern, with integral shoulder straps. The top flap was secured by two web straps; extra long to permit loading additional gear, these were sewn to the pack's back, ran through retaining loops on the bottom, and thence to the flap's buckles. The main compartment was also secured by a drawstring. Two horizontal straps allowed tightening if a full load was not carried. On the flap was a separate zippered compartment; on the later models it could be removed and worn as a small combat pack. Equipment attachment tabs were fitted on both sides of the pack and the top flap. A waterproof clothing bag was issued with it as a liner.

The M1943 folding entrenching tool was copied from a similar German design, and a carrier developed for it was attached to the pack or belt by a double hook.

The M1944 cargo-and-combat field pack consisted of a small backpack attached to 'X'-shaped suspenders. The inside was divided by canvas partitions, themselves designed to accommodate ration cans. On the right side was a small pocket, and equipment attachment tabs were fitted on the flap and left side for the E-tool and bayonet respectively. On either side and the top were three straps to secure the horseshoe bedroll. The cargo pack was a separate single-compartment bag attached under the combat pack by three quick-release straps. Both packs' mouths had rubberised fabric collars which helped protect the contents from rain.

The M1945 cargo-and-combat field pack was similar, but the combat pack was slightly larger, a simplified cargo pack attachment system was used, and the suspenders were more comfortable.

A 36th Inf. Div. Ceremonial & Demonstration Auxiliary member displays the twin medical packs and their special yoke-type harness. (Schroeder collection)

The M1956 Load Carrying Equipment

Historical

The Army began to take a fresh look at its gear in 1950. The Quartermaster Research and Engineering Laboratories conducted tests to appraise the soldier's load under realistic combat conditions, studying what was carried and how, and the gear's physiological and bio-mechanical aspects. This led to a new authorised load weight of 45 lbs in 1952: a combat load of 20 lbs, and an existence load of 25 lbs. The former consisted of weapons and battlefield survival gear carried on the cartridge belt and in the M1945 combat pack. The latter was made up of

additional shelter items and extra clothing carried in the cargo pack and bedroll. Table of Allowance 21 was still much the same as the World War II TE-21 gear.

Development of new equipment began in 1954, coinciding with the search for an M1 rifle replacement. The new concept foresaw the elimination of the cartridge belt, replacing its clip pockets with magazine pouches. Another aspect was a new means of attaching items to the belt in order to eliminate the double hook's 'bounce' effect. A vertical sliding bar attachment—the slide keeper—was developed to secure items against the belt rather than hanging them.

The M1956 load carrying equipment (LCE) was introduced along with the new M14 rifle in 1957 under TA-50. It included several innovative features: pouches that could carry most types of ammunition, slide keepers for attachment, a small combat pack attached to the belt and not carried behind the shoulders, and a sleeping bag carrier. The M1956 LCE was to serve the soldier fairly well in Vietnam, though a suitable combat pack was needed to carry more than just a day's rations and two canteens. Like the M1910 gear, the M1956 was to influence all future equipments.

Members of the 25th Inf. Div. receive decorations in Korea, 1951. Gear includes M1945 suspenders, M1932 pistol belts, M1942 first aid pouches, M1918 pistol magazine pocket, and compass cases. (US Army via Shelby Stanton)

Description

The M1956 LCE was made of olive green (OG) cotton canvas and webbing; hardware was of black painted steel alloy. The pistol belt was similar to the M1936, but was adjustable at both ends. The male buckle fastener had a small round end rather than the earlier 'T'-shaped one. In 1966 a large 'quick-release' buckle was adopted, which sometimes came unfastened at the wrong times. The suspenders were a lightly padded 'H'-harness; the front straps were attached to the belt and the rear to the pack—or the belt if the pack was not carried—by simple hooks. It was found that the rear hooks often came unfastened, and these were replaced by snap hooks.

Two universal small arms ammunition cases (pouches) were attached to the belt's front. There was some criticism that they might invite groin area injuries; though this seldom happened, a semi-rigid plastic panel in the back of the case helped to prevent this. Two slide keepers attached it to the belt and a small strap fixed to the top back was attached to a square ring on the front of the suspenders to help bear the load. It was 'universal' to the maximum extent and could carry: two M14 rifle 20-round magazines, four M2 carbine 30-round magazines, four M16 rifle 20-round magazines[1], six M1 rifle 8-round clips, 24 × 12-gauge shotshells, three 40mm M79 grenade launcher rounds, or two hand grenades internally; two more grenades could be attached to the case's sides by web loops and snap straps. In 1968 a shorter case, otherwise identical to the universal model, was adopted for M16A1 rifle 20-round magazines.

The canteen cover was similar to the M1910, but fitted with slide keepers and snaps and lined with acrylic pile ('fake fur'). An OG plastic canteen was adopted in the mid-1960s. The entrenching tool carrier was attached by two slide keepers. An M8A1 bayonet scabbard[2] attachment tab was sewn to a leather base on the carrier along with a snap strap. The first aid pouch was of a vertical design and was also intended to carry the lensatic compass; it could be attached to the belt, the side of an ammo case, or the suspenders.

The combat field pack, more commonly referred

[1]The case was too deep for these so many troops put an extra field dressing in the bottom to raise them.

[2]The M8A1 scabbard carried the M4 (M1/M2 carbine), M5 (M1 rifle), M6 (M14 rifle), M7 (M16 rifle), XM8 (M16) bayonets.

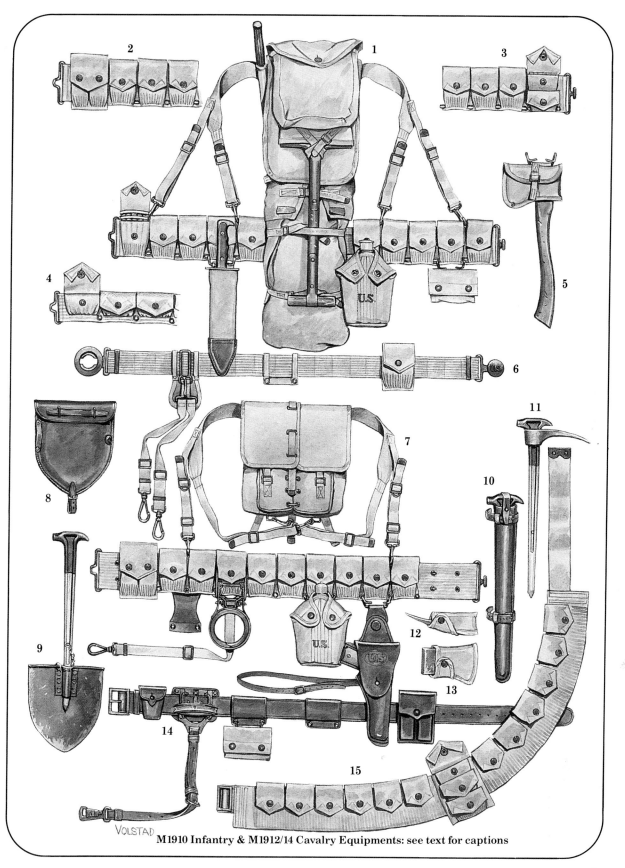

M1910 Infantry & M1912/14 Cavalry Equipments: see text for captions

A

World War I M1917/18 Equipment: see text for captions

B

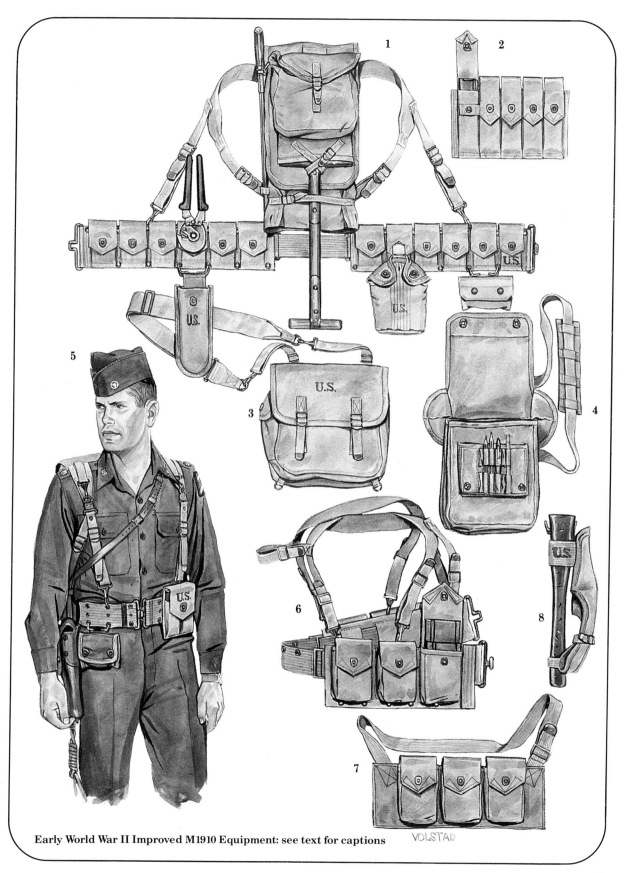

Early World War II Improved M1910 Equipment: see text for captions

VOLSTAD

C

Late World War II Improved M1910 Equipment: see text for captions

D

M1956 Load Carrying Equipment: see text for captions

M1967 Modernized Load Carrying Equipment: see text for captions

F

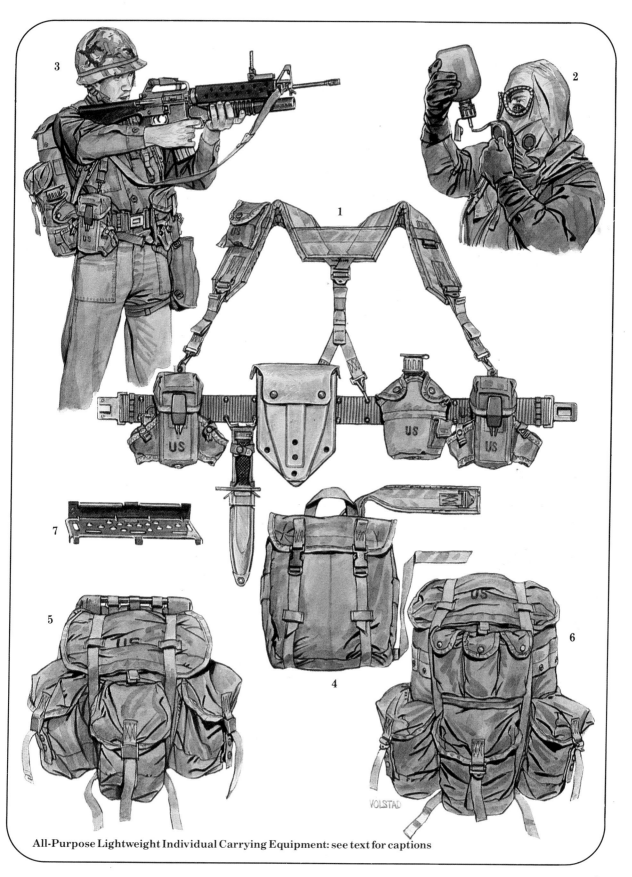

All-Purpose Lightweight Individual Carrying Equipment: see text for captions

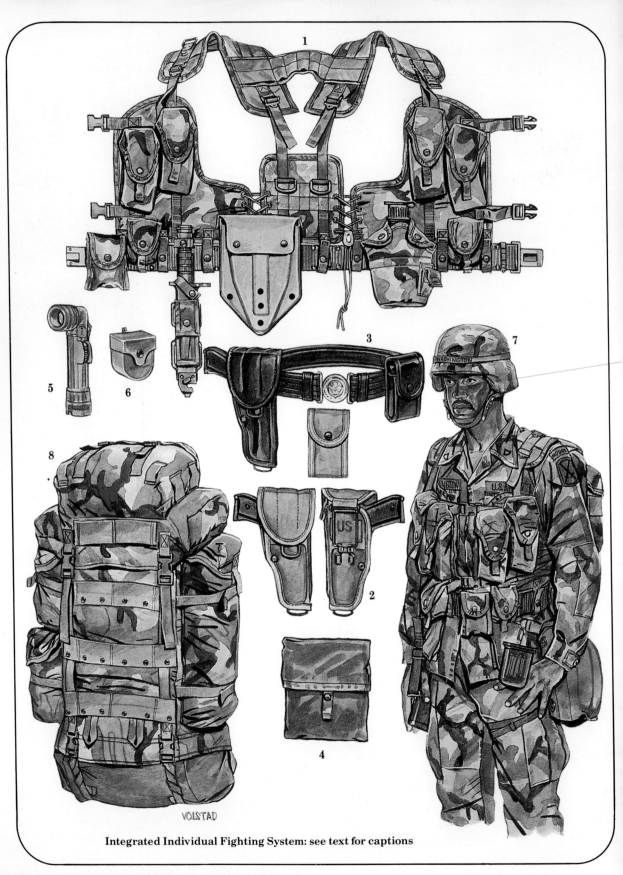

VOLSTAD

Integrated Individual Fighting System: see text for captions

to as the 'butt' or 'ass' pack, was attached to the belt's back by two slide keepers, and the suspenders hooked to tabs on the back top. On the sides were loops to attach other equipment, and a rolled poncho was strapped underneath. It had room for only one or two C-ration boxes, a change of underwear and socks, and toilet articles—hardly sufficient for the extended operations in Vietnam. A slightly improved model, the M1961 pack, was developed, but the M1956 remained the more common. The slightly larger M1961 had a flap which covered the pack's opening better, a rubberised fabric collar around the opening, and longer poncho straps.

Much of the existence load was borne by the sleeping bag carrier, a double 'H'-strap affair in which the sleeping bag and inflatable pad (air mattress) were rolled. This was secured to the suspenders by running straps through web loops on its front. This arrangement proved to be an awkward burden, far too heavy to be carried in such a manner, especially since some units required shelter-halfs and extra clothing in the 'bedroll'. There was a great deal of side sway and pressure on the shoulders, and it often caused the belt and ammo pouches to be pulled up under the ribs.

Two-quart bladder canteens were developed in the mid-1960s, consisting of a plastic bladder contained in a nylon cover; both square and rectangular shaped examples were issued.

In the early 1960s another tangle of straps was introduced as the 'pack adaptor strap assembly', permitting the pack to be worn on the shoulders when the bedroll was not needed, but it was seldom used. Space to carry additional rations, water, and other items was critical in Vietnam where troops were often 'out' for several days between helicopter resupply runs. A few units adopted the field expedient of using both the M1956 and M1945 packs.

One of the few Korean War era items adopted was the M1951 mountain rucksack, essentially an improved 1941 model. It incorporated a better designed tubular steel frame, had three cargo pockets rather than two, and used leather flap securing straps. The lightweight rucksack was introduced in 1961 to replace the M1951, though the latter remained in use with some Special Forces units well into the 1960s. It consisted of an OG 106

nylon combat pack with three cargo pockets and equipment loops on the sides and back, and a flap storage compartment. The pack was attached to a tubular aluminium frame, usually on the bottom, but it could be fitted to the top part. Normally the bedroll was strapped above the pack. Web waist and upper back straps were provided along with a rifle carrier strap and pocket that fitted to the frame's right side. The padded shoulder straps were attached to the frame, the left having a quick-release device. A cargo support shelf could be fitted to the frame, after removal of the pack, so that it could be used as a packboard. Both this and the

Components of the M1956 load carrying equipment: (1) pistol belt, (2) suspenders, (3) first aid or compass pouch, (4) universal small arms ammunition case, (5) E-tool carrier, (6) combat field pack, (7) canteen cover, (8) sleeping bag carrier. (US Army)

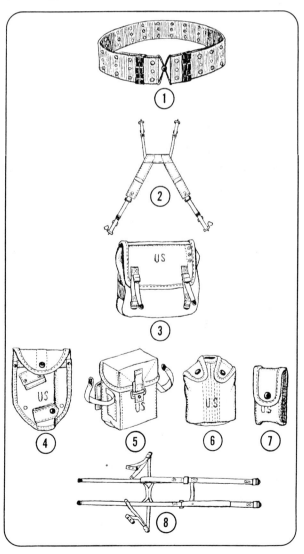

M1951 were issued with snow-camouflage covers, since they were principally intended for arctic use.

The lightweight rucksack was also intended for jungle use, but as the frame rested on the back of the pistol belt, items could only be attached to the front and sides. Consequently, the lightweight rucksack was little used in Vietnam, but was much used by troops in Alaska, by Special Forces, LRRPs and Pathfinder units elsewhere.

Troops who did use it in Vietnam usually carried all their canteens on the rucksack. Some took this to the extreme and used no web gear; everything except ammo was attached to the rucksack. M16 magazines were carried in the seven-pocket cotton bandoleers in which 5.56mm ammo was issued in ten-round loading clips (two clips or one magazine per pocket). Magazines, grenades, and 40mm rounds were also carried in M18A1 Claymore mine bags and canteen covers—especially 30-round magazines, first issued in the late 1960s, since a standard pouch for them was not adopted until 1974.

(*Left*) **Experimental 1954 MG belt carrier with prototype slide keepers.** (*Right*) **ALICE E-tool carrier displaying the standard slide keepers adopted with the M1956 gear. (Lemmer collection)**

The M1967 Modernized Load Carrying Equipment

Historical

As with just about everything else used in Vietnam, from boots to field dressings to ammunition packaging, the design of LCE was also changed in an effort to provide light-weight gear that could better withstand the rigours of a tropical environment. Cotton duck and webbing, even when treated to prevent mildew, is still affected by it, along with dry rot due to constant wetting and drying. Cotton gear also absorbs a great deal of water (40%), adding to its weight, and is slow drying; it also withstands abrasion poorly.

Nylon had already proven itself in the light-weight rucksack. It is lightweight, unaffected by mildew, fast-drying as it absorbs little water (only 8%), and resists abrasion well. It does have limitations; it is shiny when new; being somewhat stiff, it makes a rustling noise against vegetation; and it melts when exposed to high heat ($482°F$—but cotton deteriorates at $300°F$).

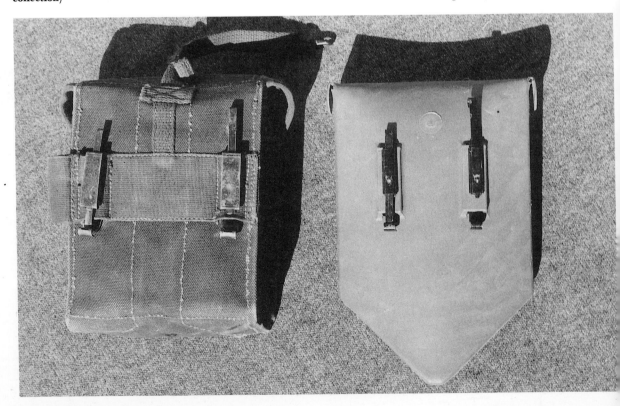

The M1967 modernized load carrying equipment (MLCE), or lightweight LCE, was developed specifically for use in Vietnam, its issue beginning in 1968. Even so, issue was limited, and the M1956 LCE remained in general use; some was issued in other areas. M1967 MLCE consisted essentially of the same items of a similar design as the M1956, but substituted nylon for cotton, and aluminium and plastic for steel and brass hardware where possible.

A suitable combat pack was desperately needed in Vietnam, leading to the appearance of the nylon tropical rucksack in 1967. (A cotton canvas version saw very limited issue in the USA.) Its design was influenced by the indigenous rucksack used by the Special Forces-advised Civilian Irregular Defense Group (CIDG). Usually referred to as 'cidge' or 'indig' rucksacks, they were procured through the Special Forces' Counter-insurgency Support Office (CISO) on Okinawa. A captured North Vietnamese Army rucksack was sent to the CISO as a model in the early 1960s. Soon issued to the CIDG, they were often used by US LRRP and Ranger units. The indigenous rucksack was very simply made, with crude fittings and devoid of any amenities. Three cargo pockets were fitted on the sides and back. Most were made of a stiff waterproof-treated grey-green canvas, but some were of untreated OD canvas.

Description

The M1967 equipment belt, suspenders, small arms ammunition case, canteen cover, and first aid pouch were essentially the same as their M1956 counterparts. The combat pack was similar to the M1961. The belt was issued with both standard and quick-release buckles. The suspenders had snap hooks fitted to the shoulders permitting the pack to be worn in this position, though, again, this was seldom done. Only an M16 magazine-sized ammo case was issued, closed by a plastic clip fastener. M1956 cases were used when the M14 rifle was issued. The canteen cover had a small Velcro®-secured water purification tablet bottle pocket. The sleeping bag carrier consisted of a nylon panel with two web straps. The E-tool carrier was designed for the new all-metal collapsible E-tool; the M1956 carrier was used when the old E-tool was issued, but the new model would fit in it.

The collapsible two-quart canteen was made of

The M1956 combat field pack attached to the suspenders by means of the field pack adaptor assembly. The adaptor assembly and M1956 suspenders are pictured below. The 'cute' rolled pack straps may have looked great at service schools, but had no place in the field. (US Army)

OG plastic. Its cover was nylon, lined with acrylic pile, the flap secured by a plastic clip fastener. It was either carried by a web shoulder sling or could be attached to a rucksack by two slide fasteners; it is still standard. The five-quart flotation bladder canteen was a clear vinyl bladder carried in a nylon cover. It had retaining loops and tie-cords at each corner so that it could be secured to a rucksack. Both were fitted with water purification tablet bottle pockets. The one-quart arctic canteen was made of insulated aluminium with a pop-off plastic cap. Its acrylic pile-lined nylon cover was fitted with two slide keepers.

The tropical rucksack had three large cargo pockets and equipment loops on the sides and back. The pockets were sewn to the rucksack only at their sides, forming a tunnel to permit a machete to be attached to a loop and passed under the pocket. The flap, secured by two straps, contained a thin rubberised fabric-lined pocket. The rucksack's opening was also secured by a drawstring. A flat metal riveted frame supported the rucksack; some tended to bow outward, rubbing against the wearer's back. The detachable shoulder straps were padded, the left having a quick-release device. Rubberised fabric waterproof liners (drawstring bags) were issued with it, three small ones for the pockets and a large one for the main compartment.

The All-Purpose Lightweight Individual Carrying Equipment

Historical
Nylon's light weight and durable qualities led the Army to consider the M1967 MLCE for Army-wide adoption. A study was undertaken in the early 1970s to identify any shortcomings and to propose improvements for a new LCE system to replace the

M1956 and M1967. The new system was developed by the US Army Material Command and extensively tested at the Infantry School.

The result was the All-Purpose Lightweight Individual Carrying Equipment or ALICE system (the use of year models ceased). This was adopted in 1974, and issue began the following year, though the ammunition cases were released in late 1974 since no other 30-round magazine pouches were available. The fighting and existence loads concept was retained, with the former items carried on the belt and suspenders and the latter in the combat field pack. The designation LC-1 or -2 (load carrying) was used to additionally identify some items.

The Army learned many lessons from Vietnam, and one was the need for a rucksack capable of carrying complete mission loads. Included in the system were medium and large combat field packs, provided with a common frame, and both derived from the tropical rucksack. Though officially termed 'pack', most troops call them rucksacks, or simply 'rucks'. The medium combat pack was very similar to the tropical rucksack and could be used with or without the frame. It was issued to all

Typical individual equipment display: 91st Engr. Bn., Ft. Belvoir, Va, c.1962. Note that only a single late carbine magazine pocket, capable of carrying two M1 rifle clips, was issued along with World War II gear. (Shelby Stanton)

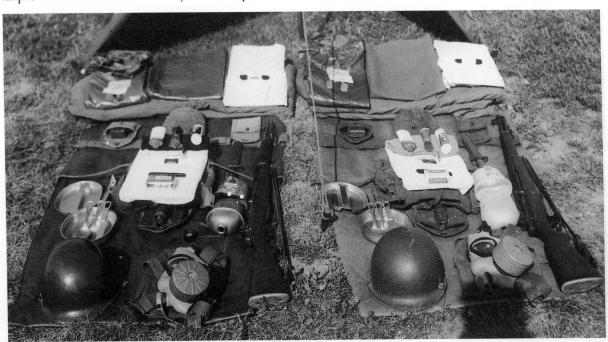

Two Special Forces troopers display early tropical gear at Ft. Bragg, NC, c.1964. (Top, L to R) Tropical uniform (jungle fatigues), rainsuit, long range patrol rations, M1942 machete, lightweight nylon rucksack and frame. (Bottom) Tropical boots, tropical sleeping shirt, multipurpose net, poncho liner (early camouflage pattern), early 2-quart bladder canteen and cover, tropical survival kit, lensatic compass, and snake bite kit (US Army)

combat troops; support troops often used M1961 or M1956 butt packs. Later, they too were often issued the medium pack, without a frame, which was generally issued only to airborne units and those in extremely cold regions. Butt packs were also used in basic and advanced individual training units. The large pack replaced the lightweight rucksack issued to Special Forces, Ranger, LRRP and Pathfinder units as well as troops in arctic regions and, from 1985 to the new light infantry battalions. It had to be used with the frame due to the weight of the loads carried.

ALICE, M1967 and M1956 equipments were interchangeable. It was, and is, not uncommon to see them mixed, especially in Army National Guard and Army Reserve units where equipment wear-out is not as rapid as in the Active Army. As in the past, existing stocks of equipment were depleted before new items were issued.

Description

All ALICE items were of OG nylon, with the exception of the E-tool carrier, and made of light green plastic.

The equipment belt and first aid pouch were identical to the M1967, the former initially being fitted with the standard buckle, replaced in the mid-1980s by an OG plastic type. The suspenders were of the 'Y' type with a single back strap; an inverted web 'V' at its lower end had two snap hooks for belt attachment. The LC-2 canteen cover was similar to the M1967.

The small arms ammo case was secured by a plastic clip fastener and attached to the belt by two slide keepers. A strap fitted to the top back secured it to the suspenders. A pocket and retaining strap were fitted to either side for 'baseball'-shaped grenades. The interior was divided into three magazine cells by straps, for 30-round M16A1 magazines only. The flexible moulded plastic E-tool carrier, fitted for the collapsible E-tool, was secured by two snaps and attached to the belt by two slide keepers.

At the development stage the medium combat field pack was to have three detachable cargo pockets, attached to web loops on the pack by slide keepers. It was envisaged that they could be removed and attached to the belt, or carried by shoulder slings as utility or ammo bags for short duration missions. Just before contract production began it was decided to attach them permanently to the pack, as it was thought that if they were detachable some troops would neglect and lose them.

The medium pack was of the same basic design as the tropical rucksack, but was slightly larger and a little more stoutly built; it had a thick shoulder pad under which the pack frame was slipped, and a strap secured a pocket sewn to the inside for an AN/PRC-25 or -77 radio (or other gear). Initial issue packs had spring-loaded buckles on the pocket and flap straps; these proved easily damaged and were replaced by conventional ones. All three cargo

A radio-telephone operator (RTO) and rifle platoon leader of the 9th Inf. Div., Vietnam, 1968. The RTO has an AN/PRC-25 radio, Claymore mine bag, and radio accessory bag attached to a lightweight rucksack frame. The officer carries the frame with the rucksack. His M16A1 magazines are carried in the bandoleer. (US Army via Shelby Stanton)

pockets were tunnelled. One large and three small waterproof liners were issued with the pack, but these were dropped in 1976 as they were seldom turned in when a soldier left a unit. The padded shoulder straps, each with a quick release device, could be attached directly to the pack or removed and attached to the frame. A sleeping bag could be secured under the pack by either cargo tiedown straps or the ALICE sleeping bag carrier.

The large pack was simply a deeper and slightly wider version. Its centre back cargo pocket was larger, and there were three small pockets above it. A snow-camouflage cover could be used on both packs.

The ground combat troops pack frame consisted of a tubular aluminium frame reinforced by vertical and horizontal stamped braces. A wide web waist band and waist strap were fitted. The frame bottom was narrower than the lightweight rucksack's 'wrap around' version, but use of the frame still limited the items carried on the belt. A metal cargo support shelf could be attached to the frame's bottom or middle brace, allowing it to be used as a packboard; cargo tiedown straps were issued with it. The early LC-1 frame was black anodised; the LC-2, introduced in the early 1980s, was dark OG anodised, and had other minor improvements.

Troops of the 198th Inf. Bde. (Light), Vietnam, 1969. The man on the left has an M1951 rucksack, and the RTO to the right a lightweight rucksack festooned with smoke grenades and canteens. (US Army via Shelby Stanton)

The Integrated Individual Fighting System

Historical

The Army has occasionally used vest-type load-bearing systems for special purposes: the British-developed battle jerkin[1], aviator's survival vests (used by some recon units in Vietnam), 40mm grenade carrier vest and police-type assault vests (used by selected Ranger battalion elements). In Vietnam a Special Forces NCO developed a combat vest in the early 1960s; it was studied, but turned down. Three versions were designed: rifleman's, machine gunner's and medic's.

A vest's advantages include: more items can be carried, as they are not only secured to the belt, but distributed over the torso; the load's weight is more equally distributed with the soldier actually 'wearing' it rather than having it hung on him; and it permits more flexibility in mission load configuration. Its principal disadvantage is that body heat is trapped and causes more perspiration.

Development of the Integrated Individual Fighting System (IIFS) began in 1984 at the Army's Natick Research and Development Center, Massachusetts. Further development was approved in early 1985. It is compatible with the Personal Armor System for Ground Troops (PASGT), adopted in 1978[2]. It consists of the Individual Tactical Load Bearing Vest (ITLBV) designed to replace ALICE gear in all infantry units, though the latter will continue in use in most others. The second IIFS component is the Field Pack, Large, Internal Frame (FPLIF) which will replace the large ALICE pack in units that presently use it. Mechanised infantry units will retain the medium ALICE pack. The IIFS was presented for type classification in April 1987, but not approved for adoption due to minor deficiencies. It was finally adopted in October 1987; fielding will begin in mid-1988. Test units were the 7th Inf. Div. (Light), 10th Mountain Div. (Lt. Inf.), and Special Forces elements.

[1]Issued as the 'assault pack' to the 16th and 18th Inf. Regts., 1st Inf. Div and 116th Inf. Regt., 29th Inf. Div. for the Normandy landing; most were discarded in the first few days. See MAA 108, *British Infantry Equipments 1908–80*

[2]See MAA 157, *Flak Jackets*.

Description

The ITLBV is made of woodlands-pattern camouflage Kevlar® ballistic fabric (offering only very limited fragmentation protection) and OG and woodlands pattern nylon. It consists of wide foam-padded shoulder straps and a harness system fitted with Kevlar® chest panels, secured by two plastic quick-release buckles. On each are an upper two magazine and a lower one magazine pocket for M16-series rifle 30-round magazines and a grenade utility pocket, all secured by Velcro® and snap tabs. Across the shoulders is a web yoke on which the patrol pack fits. The small of the back has a Kevlar® panel laced to the chest panels by parachute cords permitting full adjustment; two plastic equipment 'D' rings are fitted to it. The back panel has two and the chest panels four snap loops for attaching the ALICE belt. Empty, the ITLBV weighs only 1.8 lbs. Woodlands-pattern first aid pouch and canteen covers of the same design as the ALICE versions, are attached to the belt as is the ALICE plastic E-tool carrier. A carrier for the M249E1 squad

This is not southern Germany, 1945, but Camp Drum, NY, 1970. This 42nd Inf. Div., NY National Guard BAR man was still equipped with World War II gear. (US Army via Shelby Stanton)

automatic weapon's 200-round magazine can also be attached to the belt.

The FPLIF is made of woodlands-pattern Cordura® nylon and has a larger capacity than any previously standard pack. Two aluminium internal frame bars can be bent to conform to the soldier's back contour and can be used as splints. The padded shoulder straps have a quick-release system. Two horizontal compression straps permit tightening the load. It has four deep side pockets. On the bottom is a zippered sleeping bag compartment. The top flap is detachable, and is actually a two-compartment patrol pack that can be attached to the ITLBV's shoulders by slide keepers for short-duration missions; it is also provided with separate straps for use without the ITLBV. Both the large pack and the patrol pack are closed by two straps, and the former additionally by a drawstring.

The grenade carrier vest, constructed of nylon fabric front panels and nylon mesh back and shoulders, had pockets for 20 HE and four pyrotechnic 40mm rounds for the M79, XM148, and M203 grenade launchers. The longer pyro rounds (flare and smoke) were carried in the two upper pockets on each side. (US Army)

The Plates

(*Note*: When identifying items attached to belts, the order of description is: the pack, suspenders, and the items attached to the belt from the reader's left to right.)

A: M1910 Infantry and M1912/14 Cavalry Equipments
(*1*) A rifleman's M1910 infantry equipment included the haversack and pack carrier with the long pack roll, on which are attached the shovel carrier and M1905 bayonet. The dismounted cartridge belt carries the bolo, original style dismounted canteen cover and first aid pouch.
(*2*) Left end of the M1910 mounted pistol cartridge belt with the two-cell magazine pocket.
(*3*) Right end of the M1910 mounted revolver cartridge belt, with two pockets on both ends.
(*4*) Left end of M1910 four-pocket revolver cartridge belt.
(*5*) M1910 hand axe and carrier.
(*6*) A composite M1910 garrison belt (not an actual

configuration). Only the officers' and staff NCOs' belts were fitted with the sabre sling. The bayonet sliding frog was worn only on enlisted men's belts. Two cartridge pockets were fitted near both ends of the enlisted men's and the mounted orderlies', scouts' and machine gunners' belts. The band and musicians' belt had no fittings.

(7) Cavalryman's M1912/14 equipment (configured for dismounted use) included the left and right side M1912 ration bags assembled as a knapsack, M1914 cavalry belt with M1912 magazine pocket, tool frog, rifle belt ring (lowered)

Below:
Components of the experimental model of the nylon MLCE: (1) equipment belt (with quick release buckle), (2) suspenders, (3) M14 magazine pouch (never issued, M16A1 model used instead), (4) first aid pouch, (5) E-tool carrier (with bayonet attachments, not on issue model), (6) combat field pack, (7) canteen cover, (8) sleeping bag carrier. (US Army)

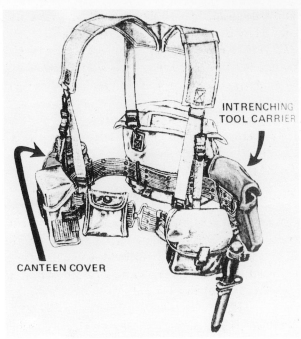

Above:
A diagram of the issue model M1967 MLCE gear assembled in a standard configuration. (US Army)

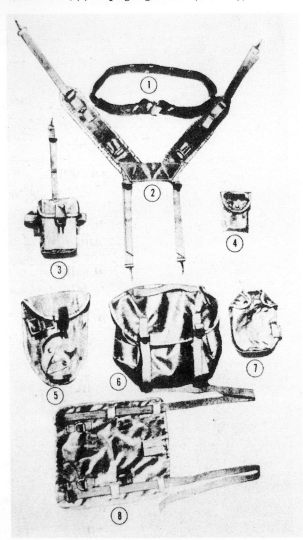

and rifle strap, M1910 dismounted canteen cover, and M1912 holster with an M1911 pistol.

(8) M1912 E-tool carrier, also used to carry a pick or hatchet head, and horse shoes and nails.

(9) M1912 E-tool assembled with a picket pin handle.

(10) M1912 picket pin and carrier.

(11) M1912 pick assembled with a picket pin handle.

(12) M1912 pick head in its cover.

(13) M1912 hatchet head in its cover.

(14) Cavalryman's M1912 garrison belt with a rifle cartridge pocket (five loose rounds), rifle belt ring (raised) and rifle strap, two sliding frogs for the M1910 first aid pouch and the M1912 holster (not pictured), and the M1912 leather magazine pocket.

(15) M1914 cavalry bandoleer.

B: World War I M1917/18 Equipment

(1) M1918 dismounted cartridge belt with a 20-round extension magazine carrier, M1917 trench knife, M1910 canteen cover, and first aid pouch.

This depicts the belt back made of duck rather than the M1910's woven webbing.

(2) Mk. I trench knife, sometimes incorrectly referred to as the M1918.

(3) M1917 mounted canteen cover. The M1910 mounted cover was similar, but had a web strap.

(4) M1912 pistol belt with an M1917 revolver cartridge pouch, and M1917 revolver holster with a S&W or Colt M1917 revolver.

(5) M1918 pistol magazine pocket on an M1912 pistol belt.

(6) This 1918 rifleman is outfitted with the M1910 wire cutter and carrier and armed with an M1917 Enfield rifle and M1917 bayonet.

(7) The M1918 shotshell pouch carried 28 × 12-gauge shells for trench guns (Model 1897 pictured).

(8) This 1918 automatic rifleman has the M1918 automatic rifleman's belt and is armed with the

Special Forces-advised Civilian Irregular Defense Group (CIDG) Strikers wear a mix of World War II and M1956 gear. The men to the left carry the indigenous rucksack. Vietnam, c.1968. (US Army)

M1918 BAR, and M1911 pistol in an M1916 holster. His modified M1910 haversack is without the carrier and long pack roll.

(9) Both sides of the M1918 assistant automatic rifleman's belt had two each BAR magazine and rifle cartridge pockets.

C: Early World War II Improved M1910 Equipment
(1) By the beginning of World War II, little of the rifleman's 'M1910' equipment was actually M1910. The M1928 haversack, with a short pack roll, has an M1910 E-tool and carrier and M1942 bayonet (M1903 series and M1 rifles) attached.

Experimental nylon three-pocket carriers for six 30-round M16A1 magazines were tested by the Infantry School in 1975. Each version utilised different pocket closures and straps, which could be worn over the shoulder or around the waist. The system was rejected due to circulation restriction caused by the leg straps, and the fact that the carrier bounced, even with tight tie-straps. (US Army)

The M1938 12-pocket dismounted cartridge belt is fitted with the M1938 wire cutter and carrier, M1910 canteen cover, and M1924 first aid pouch.

(2) Thompson M1928A1 sub-machine gun magazine pocket holding five 20-round magazines.

(3) M1936 field, or musette, bag fitted with the carrying strap used on many other bags.

(4) M1938 dispatch bag, often called a map case.

(5) This 1942 infantry officer is outfitted with typical dismounted officer's field gear: M1936 field bag attached to M1936 suspenders, M1936 pistol belt, engineer compass case, M1923 magazine pocket, M1 (formerly M1916) holster with M1911A1 pistol, and (not visible) M1924 first aid pouch, M1910 canteen cover, and M17 binoculars case.

(6) M1937 automatic rifleman's belt with its special suspenders.

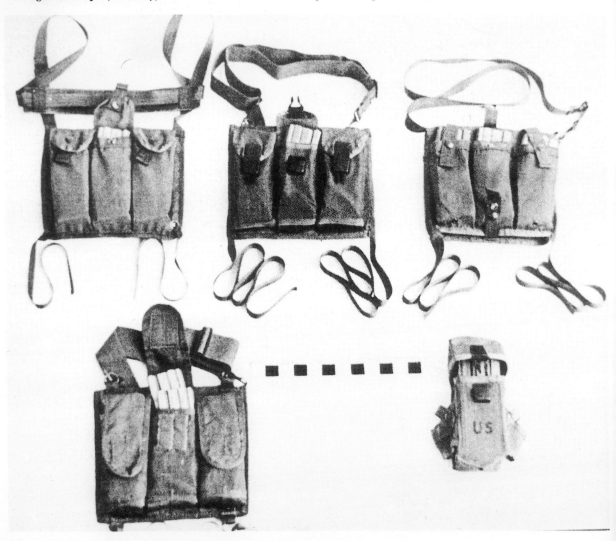

(7) M1918 right-side automatic rifle ammunition bearer's bandoleer.

(8) M1910 pick-mattock rigged in its carrier.

D: Late World War II Improved M1910 Equipment

(1) The rifleman's 'M1910' equipment had evolved even further by 1945. The M1945 combat field pack has its cargo pack attached below. The M1 bayonet (M1 rifle) and M1943 E-tool and carrier are attached to the pack. The M1923 dismounted cartridge belt is fitted with the M1910 canteen cover (with a black enamelled canteen issued only in 1942), and British-made first aid pouch. A Mk.IIA1 fragmentation grenade is attached to the suspenders.

(2) M1941 mounted canteen cover.

(3) Sub-machine gun magazine pocket for three 30-round M1928A1, M1-series (Thompson), and M3-series ('grease gun') magazines.

(4) An individual armed with an M1 carbine might be equipped with an M1936 pistol belt, two or more 15-round carbine magazine pockets (the left pocket is the early web version and the right is the later

A 1st Cavalry Div. trooper attending the Northern Warfare Training Center, Ft. Greely, Alaska, wears the ALICE large combat field pack and frame with the arctic 1-quart canteen, early 1980s. (US Army)

duck model), three-pocket grenade carrier (the two-pocket was similar), M4 bayonet (not issued until very late in the war), jungle first aid bag issued in the Pacific, and M1942 first aid pouch.

(5) A 15-round carbine pocket converted for 30-round magazines by adding a flap extension; 30-round pocket production did not keep pace with M2 carbine production.

(6) Early pocket for two 30-round carbine magazines.

(7) Late pocket for four 30-round carbine magazines.

(8) Shotshell ammunition case for 12 × 12-gauge shells.

(9) General-purpose ammunition bag with M1936 carrying strap.

(10) The jungle pack, later redesignated the M1943 combat pack, was also issued in an OD version.

E: M1956 Load Carrying Equipment

(1) A rifleman's M1956 equipment consisted of a combat field pack with a poncho secured under it, suspenders, pistol belt, two universal small arms ammo pouches, E-tool carrier with the M1943 or combination E-tool, and M6 bayonet (M14 rifle),

A diagram of the ALICE gear assembled in a typical configuration. (US Army)

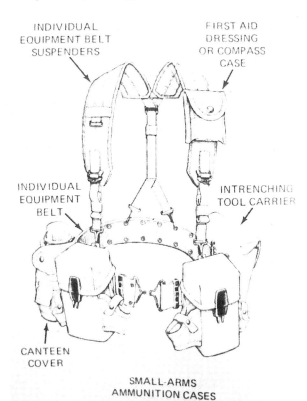

INDIVIDUAL EQUIPMENT BELT SUSPENDERS

FIRST AID DRESSING OR COMPASS CASE

INDIVIDUAL EQUIPMENT BELT

INTRENCHING TOOL CARRIER

CANTEEN COVER

SMALL-ARMS AMMUNITION CASES

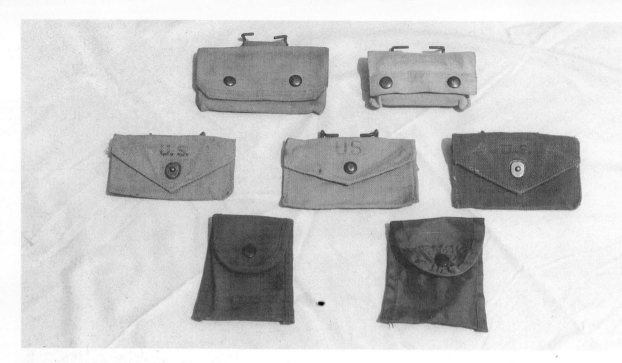

First aid pouches: (*Top, L to R*) **M1924 and M1910.** (*Centre*) **M1942 khaki, British-made *c.*1941, and M1942 OD.** (*Bottom*) **M1956 and M1967 MLCE/ALICE.** (Schroeder collection)

canteen cover (metal ones remained in use well into the 1960s) and first aid pouch. An M26 fragmentation grenade is secured to an ammo pouch.

(2) The early two-quart plastic bladder canteen and cover.

(3) The quick-release pistol belt buckle, with an M16A1 pouch attached.

Entrenching tool carriers: (*Top, L to R*) **M1909, M1910 and M1943.** (*Bottom*) **M1956, M1967, and ALICE.** (Lemmer collection)

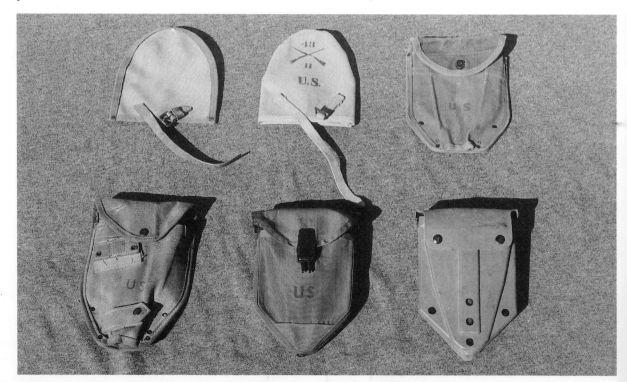

(4) The small arms accessory case was made of synthetic rubber-coated nylon.

(5) The M16A1 rifle XM3 bipod carrying case also accommodated cleaning items and rod.

(6) This 1965 automatic rifleman, armed with an M14E2 AR, is outfitted with standard M1956 gear, but with the M1961 combat pack. His canteen is attached to eyelets on the right side of the pack flap. He is carrying the unpopular M1956 sleeping bag carrier with an M1949 mountain sleeping bag.

(7) A combination E-tool.

(8) The M1951 mountain rucksack replaced the 1941 model and was itself replaced by E9.

(9) The lightweight rucksack with frame. Since the E-tool was seldom used by Special Forces, this was a common method of carrying it.

F: M1967 Modernized Load Carrying Equipment (MLCE)

(1) A rifleman's M1967 MLCE gear consisted of basically the same items as the M1956 gear, but made of nylon. The combat field pack, with the lightweight poncho secured, is attached to the shoulders rather than the belt. Two M16A1 ammo cases, M7 bayonet (M16-series rifles), E-tool carrier, plastic canteen and cover, and first aid pouch complete the equipment. An M68 impact-detonated fragmentation grenade is secured to an ammo pouch.

(2) The still-standard two-quart plastic collapsible canteen and cover.

(3) The five-quart flotation bladder canteen and cover.

(4) The one-quart arctic canteen and cover.

(5) The M18A1 Claymore anti-personnel mine bandoleer, or simply the 'Claymore bag', was often used in Vietnam to carry magazines, grenades, and other items in its two compartments.

(6) This 1968 fire team leader carries typical Vietnam M1967 MLCE. The pack, with a poncho and poncho liner, and an M1956 E-tool carrier attached, is fastened to the belt. Additional M16A1 magazines are carried in seven-pocket bandoleers. M18 coloured and AN-M8 HC white smoke grenades are attached to the gear.

(7) A partly folded collapsible E-tool; test models were OG.

(8) The nylon tropical rucksack, with an 18-in. M1942 machete in a plastic sheath.

The individual tactical load bearing vest (ITLBV) worn over the PASGT armour vest with the Kevlar® 'Fritz' helmet, 1987 (US Army)

(9) The indigenous rucksack was used by the Civilian Irregular Defense Group (CIDG) and some US LRRP and Ranger units, since a comparable US-made model was not available until F8 was introduced.

G: All-Purpose Lightweight Individual Carrying Equipment (ALICE)

(1) A rifleman's ALICE gear consisted of suspenders, equipment belt, two small arms ammo cases, M7 bayonet, plastic E-tool carrier (with collapsible tool), LC-2 canteen cover (with the plastic canteen and an M1 NBC drinking cap), and first aid pouch. An M67 fragmentation grenade is secured to an ammo case.

(2) Outfitted in a chemical protective suit, this soldier demonstrates the use of the M1 NBC drinking cap with the M17A1 protective mask and M6A2 hood.

(3) This 1976 grenadier is outfitted with normal

The complete integrated individual fighting system (IIFS): field pack, large, internal frame (FPLIF) worn with the ITLBV, 1987. (US Army)

ALICE gear. He has the ALICE medium combat pack, without a pack frame, and an M17A1 protective mask carrier. He is armed with an M16A1 rifle with a 40mm M203 grenade launcher attached.

(4) This simple two-compartment combat field pack was developed for use by the Contras in the early 1980s and subsequently adopted by the Army for limited issue.

(5) Medium combat field pack with the early LC-1 frame.

(6) Large combat field pack with the later LC-2 frame.

(7) Pack frame cargo support shelf, here the black LC-1; the LC-2 is the same, but OG.

H: Integrated Individual Fighting System (IIFS)

(1) This rifleman's IIFS gear is made up of the ALICE belt attached to the individual tactical load-bearing vest (ITLBV). On the belt are the first aid pouch, M9 multipurpose bayonet (M16-series rifles), plastic ALICE E-tool carrier, and canteen cover.

(2) Front and backside views of the 'ambidextrous' Kevlar® M12 holster for the M9 pistol (Beretta 92SB-F 9mm) and magazine pouch.

(3) The general officer's leather version of the M12 holster with a leather magazine pouch, attached to the leather general officer's belt.

(4) Carrier for the M249E1 squad automatic weapon's belted 200-round magazine.

(5) MX-991/U flashlight used since the late 1950s.

(6) M2 compass moulded plastic case used by artillerymen, mortarmen, and forward observers.

(7) This 1988 light infantryman is outfitted with IIFS gear and armed with an M16A2 rifle. He wears the patrol pack (detached from the large field pack) and an M17A2 protective mask carrier, on which is attached an M258 individual decontamination kit.

(8) The field pack, large, with internal frame (FPLIF).
